Carmen
From Silent Film to MTV

Critical Studies

Vol. 24

Amsterdam - New York, NY 2005

Carmen
From Silent Film to MTV

Edited by

Chris Perriam
and
Ann Davies

Cover design: Pier Post

Cover photo: '*Carmen*' (1926), directed by Jacques Feyder, starring
Raquel Meller as Carmen.
Cover photo: provided by the British Film Institute Stills Archive

The paper on which this book is printed meets the requirements of "ISO
9706:1994, Information and documentation - Paper for documents -
Requirements for permanence".

ISBN: 90-420-1964-6
©Editions Rodopi B.V., Amsterdam - New York, NY 2005
Printed in the Netherlands

Acknowledgements

The editors would like to thank all those who participated at the Carmen Conference, University of Newcastle, March 2002; and in particular our colleagues Professors Phil Powrie and Bruce Babington. This volume and the conference form part of the University of Newcastle's Carmen Project, which was funded by the Arts and Humanities Research Board.

Contents

Introduction

Ann Davies

Commentators sometimes refer to Carmen as myth, implying (intentionally or not) the timelessness of her story, an idea that implies that somehow Carmen has always been with us in Western culture. And Carmen's story taps into age-old concerns about sexual and ethnic otherness. The specific origins of Carmen have been much more recent, however. The original Carmen narrative appeared as a short story by the French writer Prosper Mérimée, published in 1845 and revised in 1847 to include a general ethnographic concluding chapter on Gypsy customs. This novella offers us Carmen's story at third hand: it is told by an imprisoned don José to an unidentified traveller, who in turn recounts it to us the readers. The narrator had earlier assisted the bandit José to escape from the forces of the law, and José has since returned the favour by rescuing the narrator from Carmen's seductive clutches. Finally awaiting execution for Carmen's murder, José bemoans to the narrator the perfidies of women that have brought him so low. The narrator, in listening to and recording the story in order to pass it on, connives to join José in a narrative conspiracy against independent women such as Carmen. The refusal of patriarchy to allow Carmen to speak for herself is of a piece with the misogynistic tone struck from the very beginning with the story's preceding epigraph, which informs us that women are as bitter as gall and only offer any pleasure when they are either in bed or in the grave. Nonetheless, the story simultaneously celebrates the illicit desirability of the woman who wishes to free herself from patriarchal constraints; and thus ever since Mérimée first offered us Carmen, subsequent attempts to tell Carmen's tale trace the struggle between her efforts to tell her own story and those of others to tell it for her.

The first version of Carmen, however, is not the most familiar. Most people do not come to Carmen through the Mérimée novella at all, but through the vastly better known operatic adaptation of 1875 by Georges Bizet with his librettists Meilhac and Halévy. Bizet's opera overshadows most if not all subsequent attempts to adapt Carmen's story in various media, and his imprint is to be found in many of the film versions made throughout the last century, and indeed in the discussions of many of the contributors to the present volume. Filmmakers had perforce to acknowledge, at least implicitly, the authority of the opera over the story in legal terms at least. Although

Bizet died only months after the first performance of his *Carmen*—a
death sometimes attributed to his chagrin at the opera's initially
savage reception—his librettists were longer lived, and thus the opera
did not come out of copyright until 1981. Directors and scriptwriters
laid claim to Mérimée rather than Bizet as their source to get round
this problem, even though many versions display more than a passing
awareness of the latter. But despite the opera's initially poor reception
it rapidly gained a permanent hold in the repertoires of opera houses
worldwide as one of the most popular operatic works ever written.
And thus it consistently provokes an anxiety of influence in
subsequent film versions. Directors such as Peter Brook and
Francesco Rosi attempt to embrace what they see as the authoritative
Bizet (and come to very different cinematic conclusions as to what
that is), while others such as Cecil B. DeMille and Otto Preminger
invoke Bizet as a form of high cultural gloss. Yet other directors such
as Carlos Saura, Jean-Luc Godard and Vicente Aranda explicitly
reject Bizet as arbiter over the Carmen narrative, although the success
of the attempt to elude his influence varies.

Mérimée's novella allowed Carmen to be confined to the
libraries of educated gentlemen. Bizet's opera facilitated her move to a
more general and more popular domain. The opera's accessible tunes,
capacity for colourful spectacle, and use of spoken dialogue rather
than recitative (depending on which version of the opera is used), in
themselves indicate a move away from the sense of opera as
essentially a highbrow art form. Early performances in Spain, for
example, were mounted first in the comedy theatres of Madrid and
Barcelona before reaching the opera house. Cinema would perpetuate
this straddling of high and low culture: it has always attempted to lay
claim to the artistic high ground (and the silent filming of operas such
as *Carmen* were often exercises in this endeavour), but it has never
been able to escape a popular and populist taint. The papers in this
volume will frequently touch on the constant tension between high
and low culture that arises within the Carmen story (the encounter of
the bohemian Carmen with the bourgeois don José) and within efforts
to marry elite opera with popular cinema.

The encounter between two opposite poles of culture that
occurs within the opera embodies the thematic dialectic between self
and other that is perpetuated not only by Bizet and Mérimée but by
many of the film adaptations since: a dialectic that plays itself out in
terms of gender, ethnicity, and class and social sphere. The novella
and the opera allow bourgeois readers and audiences to indulge

vicariously in low-life pleasures while simultaneously retaining the moral high ground through an anticipated pleasure in Carmen's death. Bizet attempted to soften the rawness of the encounter with bohemian life and sexual mores by introducing the character of Micaela, the respectable woman from José's own town, the girl he *ought* to marry. But this may simply serve to heighten the perverse attraction of Carmen, indicating that part of the desirability of Carmen lies in the desire to transgress bourgeois norms. The constant return to Carmen in the cinema reinforces what the popularity of the opera already facilitates, a sort of reverse *fort-da* movement in which we can draw towards us the potential fulfilment of illicit desires, only to push them away again and thus regain security in our sense of self.

All the above might suggest that cinema versions of Carmen merely offer faint echoes of Bizet and Mérimée, serving ultimately and simply to confirm the resonance of these. It might imply that Carmen films can have nothing new or independent to say. In offering the present volume for consideration we are, of course, arguing the contrary. The sheer number of films involved tells us that the figure of Carmen cannot simply be contained within her nineteenth-century constructions: instead, the Carmen narrative demonstrates that, like Carmen herself, it does not know its place and has broken free of its high cultural constraints. Although many of the earlier Carmen films now appear to be lost, reviews and news items allow us to assert that these, together with those films still extant, amount to an approximate figure of eighty films.[1] And the number continues to increase. Confusion surrounds the question of who directed the very first Carmen film (it may have been the pioneer French director Alice Guy), while the most recent (at the time of writing) came out in 2003 (a Spanish version, Vicente Aranda's *Carmen*). The most recent film dealt with in this collection came out only two years before that: the MTV *Carmen: a Hip-Hopera*. Carmen films over the last century have also assumed a variety of film genres: while the Carmen narrative as filmed opera comes as no surprise, it has also been a vehicle for parody (such as Charlie Chaplin's *Burlesque on Carmen* of 1916), animation (Lotte Reiniger's *Carmen* of 1933), arthouse (Jean-Luc Godard's *Prénom Carmen*), the Hollywood star vehicle (*The Loves of Carmen*, 1948), and even the Western (*L'uomo, l'orgoglio, la vendetta*, 1968). The cinema Carmen also refuses to be confined to her own territories of France and Spain. While these countries function as the default setting for the narrative, other films transplant Carmen to the USA, Latin America, Africa and the Far East. The study of these films can never completely avoid the looming figures of Mérimée and Bizet, and the essays here will refer to them time and again. It is, however, time to allow the films to emerge from the shadow of their forebears and be critiqued in their own right, rather than as mere adjuncts to the ur-narratives of the nineteenth century.

The comparative neglect of such a large body of films inspired the Centre for Research into Film and Media at the University of Newcastle upon Tyne to undertake a major research project on the cinema Carmen, with funding from the Arts and Humanities Research Board. The present collection is a part of that initiative. Its impetus was the Carmen Conference, held in Newcastle in March 2002, where scholars from a variety of disciplines—including musicology, film studies and modern languages—came together to talk about different Carmen films. Some of the essays included here also featured at that conference. Others have been specially commissioned for the volume. This collection of essays gathers together a body of scholarly critique focused on the Carmen narrative in film that will allow new insights into the Carmen phenomenon from a number of aspects: cultural studies, gender studies, studies in race and representation, musicology, film history, and the history of performance.

The essays are arranged more or less chronologically by the date of the film or films discussed, thus taking us from the days of silent film to twenty-first century hip-hop style. One thing that this chronological sweep demonstrates overall is that, despite social and cultural transformations—particularly in terms of gender, sexuality and race—that have occurred since Mérimée and Bizet's nineteenth century, remarkably little has changed in terms of basic human desires and anxieties. The social changes tracked by over a hundred years of cinema do not appear to have altered the conception of Carmen's independent sexuality as a source of danger both to men (and occasionally women) and to respectable society. Nor has sexual and ethnic otherness lost its appeal. On the other hand, the corpus of Carmen films is more than a simple recycling of stereotypes. As the essays in this collection demonstrate, the Carmen narrative also allows film to take up and negotiate social and cultural issues resonant to the time in which they were made. These include increasing economic and political freedom for women, the integration of African-Americans, the rise of various forms of fascism and the cultural nuances of international relations.

Nicholas Till's opening essay deals with the very first Carmen film still extant, the Film d'Art version of 1910, and in doing so he introduces us to the complex negotiations involved in the transfer of the narrative from one medium to another. The notion of filmed opera in the silent era deprives Carmen once more of the opportunity to speak/sing in her own voice that Bizet had restored to her; but it also raises the possibility of women's increasing—and increasingly unfettered—access to public spaces. Till draws on the use made by silent film of theatrical staging traditions to explore issues of spatialization within the Carmen narrative and within this particular film, concluding that Carmen's eventual death allows for a masculinized control of space as a sphere of action rather than a feminised space of inertia, thus pointing towards the 'institutional mode of representation that ensures the reproduction of traditional— institutionalized—gender functions.

Gillian Anderson continues the exploration of Carmen on the silent screen in her study of Cecil B. DeMille's 1915 *Carmen*. Anderson draws on her familiarity with the film and its original music score, having prepared the score and recorded the music to accompany the film's recent revival and release for DVD and video, which she recounts in her essay here. She also discusses matters of performance and reception on the film's release, emphasizing the negotiation of what was perceived at the time as Carmen's overt physicality and sexuality. In addition she considers the transfer from opera to film in terms of the star—Geraldine Farrar, a noted American opera singer (with her own cohort of fans) who, in taking the leading role in DeMille's film, attempted the crossover between opera and film stardom.

With Jacques Feyder's *Carmen* of 1926, Winifred Woodhull develops still further an exploration of the tensions between the elite culture implied by opera and the commercial considerations indicated by film, as she explores the tensions and alignments between Feyder's aspirations towards artistic expression and the more commercial resonances of French cinema at the time. Her essay proceeds to focus on the visual techniques used by Feyder to express the struggle between Carmen and José over subjectivity. Woodhull also probes how the film reflects the way in which French culture—from which the Carmen narrative emerged—has attempted to come to terms with its southern neighbour, Spain, as well as its own internal tensions and contradictions.

The Carmen narrative is familiar as a narrative that acquires almost tragic overtones with Carmen's death at the end; but the tragic and bloody ending is not inevitable. Lotte Reiniger, an animator currently being rediscovered, rewrites Carmen's story to provide a light-hearted film where Carmen bests both José and Escamillo and survives to ride in triumph from the bullring with Escamillo and the bull too. Harriet Margolis heralds the film as an attempt to wrest the Carmen narrative from its patriarchal grooves, making men rather than women the object of the gaze and the woman confirmed as the subject of her own desire—and her own story. Reiniger's silhouette animation gently parodies both the Carmen narrative *per se* and the pretensions of José and Escamillo to exert masculine control. Margolis thus warns us against dismissing the film too readily as escapist pastiche: despite Reiniger's own lack of pretensions to political filmmaking she has nonetheless offered us one of the earliest surviving films to challenge the misogyny at the core of the Bizet and Mérimée versions.

While Woodhull's essay on Feyder studies how French culture negotiated cultural tensions with Spain as other, the next two essays (as well as the later essay by Lema-Hincapié) take as their starting point the ways in which Spanish culture attempts to come to terms with images of itself. Carmen generically has come to function as a form of shorthand for a notion of Spain as a hot land of primitive passion, an idea that goes back to the nineteenth-century travel writings of French authors such as Théophile Gautier. This sense of Spain as other has continued to pervade cinema adaptations of the Carmen narrative throughout the twentieth century. Hilaria Loyo teases out the references to Carmen as Spanish other in the Marlene Dietrich vehicle, *The Devil is a Woman*, and uses the similarities and contrasts between Dietrich and the Carmen figure to consider the reception of Spanish otherness in both the USA and Spain itself.[2] The negative reaction of the Spanish government indicates the problematic negotiation of Carmen undertaken by Spanish film. This subject forms the basis of José Colmeiro's essay, which considers the ways in which Spanish culture and Spanish cinema attempts to come to terms with a stereotype that has essentially been forced upon it. Focusing on three films that span nearly fifty years, Colmeiro argues that, whether they wished it or not, Spanish cinema participated in the commodification of Carmen—and indeed, of Spanishness—through reproducing her image and her story. But he also points to the fact that the contestation of the clichés of Spanishness within Spain offered an opportunity to work through key issues of cultural national identity at crucial points in Spain's history.

The recycling of Spanish and Gypsy stereotypes recurs with Rita Hayworth in *The Loves of Carmen* (1948): Peter Evans offers a star study of Hayworth that details the absorption of a Gypsy identity within Hollywood values, a move that brings to mind orientalist and postcolonial theories. Hayworth becomes a site of American colonization. Evans posits her as a form of Homi Bhabha's mimicry, a Hayworth/Carmen who is almost American but not quite; but also of the masquerade of femininity proposed by Joan Riviere. Nelly Furman's discussion of *Carmen Jones* (1954) reveals the extent to which the Carmen narrative can speak not only of timeless anxieties to do with gender, sexuality and ethnicity, but also speak to the social concerns of the day. *Carmen Jones* offers a negotiation of the possibilities for African Americans to be upwardly mobile in the USA of the fifties. Carmen Jones dies not so much because she is unfaithful, but because she aspires to a middle-class, urban lifestyle.

Amy Herzog's essay on Godard's *Prénom Carmen* posits the continued revisiting of the Carmen story as a form of refrain, not simply in terms of Bizet's music but also of themes common to both Bizet and Mérimée and other adaptations since. Godard seems deliberately to erase the more familiar refrains and motifs of Carmen, but in fact he reintroduces them precisely by drawing attention to their absence. Godard nonetheless neglects motifs of ethnicity in favour of an emphasis on gendered difference, which is in turn incorporated into a greater differentiation between music and representation. Herzog coincides to some extent with Till in perceiving this move between sound and image in terms of (de)territorialization, for Carmen's refrains lay bare the constraints of the narrative and thus the potential to elude them.

Andrés Lema-Hincapié explores the notion of Carmen as hybrid through Carlos Saura's flamenco adaptation of the tale and his piece dovetails well with Colmeiro's readings of stereotype. Lema-Hincapié perceives Saura's film as an effort to challenge the power of cliché within what has by now become an over-familiar narrative. Even within this particular version, cliché still tends to 'petrify' Carmen and thus constrain the director and his choreographer Antonio Gades. Nonetheless, Saura's struggle to defy the opera's authority results in an exercise of intertextuality in the intercutting of opera score and flamenco, and the ghost of Andalusia haunting the setting of twentieth-century Madrid.

There then follows two different takes on Francesco Rosi's attempt to reassert Bizet's authority over the Carmen narrative with his adaptation of the opera. Jeremy Tambling considers the function of the gaze in both Rosi's film and the contemporary adaptation

Mongkok Carmen, arguing in both cases that the seductiveness of the woman as object of the gaze is not sufficient to counteract the destructive violence of the male. Don José must destroy both Carmen and himself, so that Carmen rather than don José is betrayed. Mary Wood approaches Rosi's film as a component part of the director's political *oeuvre*, as well as of his visual style. She thus provides a discussion of the Carmen narrative in terms of auteurial vision, and sites the attempt to re-create an authoritative Bizet within the context of the intersection of the drive of an individual auteur style with the demands of the film industry, itself divided between the desire to produce quality films and the imperatives of mass entertainment.

If, after a hundred fifty years of existence, Carmen tends towards cliché, Susan McClary reminds us that even in the twenty-first century Carmen still retains the capacity to shock and scandalize. She touches on earlier film versions by Preminger and Godard before taking us into a new century of Carmens with one of the most recent versions at the time of writing, the MTV *Carmen: a Hip-hopera*. McClary suggests that those films that use music as a form of outrage remain truer to Bizet than attempts at authenticity such as Rosi's film, since they celebrate the ambivalence of an opera that straddles high and low cultural styles.

Notes
1. See Carmen filmography at:
http://appserver.pads.arts.gla.ac.uk/cgi-bin/WebObjects/Carmen
2. See also on this film Kathleen Vernon, 'Remaking Spain: Transnational Mythologies and Cultural Fetishism in *The Devil is a Woman* (Sternberg, 1935) and *Cet obscur objet du désir* (Buñuel, 1977)' in *Journal of Romance Studies* 4/1, 13-27.

Editorial note

The contributions cover an exciting range of takes on the Carmen story and we have also attempted to offer the reader a variety in modes of presentation. We are especially pleased, for example, that Gillian Anderson's piece is able to give readers such a strong sense of the experience of Carmen for the practitioner; similarly, a feel for the effects of performance has been cleverly and appropriately woven into the fabric—or, rather, the imagined sound—of Susan McClary's piece.

Ann Davies and Chris Perriam

Space, Time and Gender in the
Film d'Art *Carmen* of 1910

Nicholas Till

The Film d'Art *Carmen* of 1910 was one of a number of films in which the Film d'Art company sought to give cultural status to the new medium of film through the high-art connotations of opera, effecting a natural transference of the melodramatic stage-style of opera to the newly evolving dramatic language of silent film. As in most Film d'Art productions, the company employed already acknowledged stage performers, including a well-known contemporary performer of the role of Carmen from the Opéra Comique, and sets copied from the original 1875 staging of Bizet's opera. The essential paradox of silent-movie opera is here rendered especially pointed by the fact that Carmen is figured as 'singer' in Bizet's opera. However, as popular singer Carmen represents cultural energies that must be suppressed. The silent movie assures these ends, depriving Carmen even of her voice. Her muteness is compensated by an extreme physicality that fights to assert itself against the tightly constrained stage-set spaces of the film. This paper will offer a reading of the Film d'Art *Carmen*'s physicality as a transgression of accepted gender roles that thematizes social concerns about the challenge to conventional ideas of masculine and feminine space in early modernity. The paper will also offer an analysis of the narrative construction and *mise en scène* of the Film d'Art *Carmen* in the context of the deployment of space and time in related pre-1910 films, examining this issue in relation to the gendering of space and time in traditional art forms. The paper will argue that the character of Carmen in the Film d'Art film figures the problematic spatialization (and hence feminization) of narrative action in early film, suggesting that the destruction of Carmen prefigures the eventual triumph of the 'masculine' principle of narrative action over 'feminine' spatial inertia in what film historians describe as the 'institutional mode of representation'.

Film d'Art: *Carmen*
Filmic space
Gender and space
Institutional Mode of Representation
Primitive Mode of Representation
Silent Film

This essay was first presented as an accompaniment to a showing of the sixteen-minute Film d'Art *Carmen* of 1910. Silent movies were, of course, never silent, and in delivering the paper in this fashion, which allowed the audience to see for themselves the points I was making as the film unfolded, I made appeal to the practice of the silent movie lecturer, whose ubiquity is much disputed, but whose employment was certainly encouraged by a critic in 1911: 'If you have seen a picture ten times you can be of great help to the man who sees it for the first time. You can explain and point out things that at first exhibition of the release even a man of average intelligence and good education might very easily miss' (Burch 1990: 133).

Although for copyright reasons the opening title declares that the film is based upon Mérimée's novella, the narrative presentation of the Film d'Art version of *Carmen* in fact relies upon the dramatic structure of Bizet's opera, except that the dramatically redundant character of Micaela is excised. Indeed, the film's general intention to refer to the opera rather than the novel is clear: the film sets are derived from stage productions of the opera (Susan McClary identifies the sets for the final scene as being copied from the original 1870 stage production),[1] and the performer of the role of Carmen is identified as 'Mlle Regine Badet of the Opéra Comique', a seasoned performer of the role of Carmen.

These references to the opera are an important indicator of the aspirations of the Film d'Art *Carmen*. The first context for the showing of films had been the variety halls, peep-show arcades and fairs associated with working class leisure: by 1905, the art historian Erwin Panofsky recalled, there were in Berlin still only 'a few small and dingy cinemas mostly frequented by the "lower classes"' (Panofsky 1985: 216). But film historians note that around the years 1909 and 1910, after the economic recession of 1907, the emergent film industries in Europe and the USA began to pitch for more affluent, middle-class audiences. In the USA the Biograph company, with Griffiths as its star director, started to produce moralizing films with increasingly sophisticated narrative structures. In France the Film d'Art company, whose name itself indicates its pretensions, was set up in 1908 as a subsidiary of Pathé to make films based on classical theatre and opera, advertising them quite shamelessly as being for 'the higher class of audience' (Abel 1994: 261). One of their first, and best-known, efforts was *L'assassinat du duc de Guise* (1908), noted for its score by France's most eminent composer Saint-Saens. The *Carmen* of 1910 was one of a number of opera films, which included *Tosca* (1909), another drama about a female singer.

This turn to opera came about primarily as a result of opera's high art connotations: *Carmen*, dressed up with recitatives, had by now migrated securely from its ambiguous status as *opéra comique* to that of full-blown grand opera. But it was perhaps also because opera relied upon a broadly melodramatic performance style that could be transferred with relative ease to the emergent dramatic language of silent film. Indeed, Noël Burch suggests that silent film should be seen as a form of 'lyric theatre […] wherein the voice figures as gestus and the word as graphy. These displacements, moreover, call to mind those peculiar to opera, where the word dissolves into song, silence becomes orchestral sound and plot is read […] in the programme notes' (Burch 1990: 241). In this essay I want to suggest that these displacements from opera to silent film must be examined in relation to the way in which they map onto the Carmen narrative. For these displacements obviously arise in the first place due to the essential paradox of silent movie opera, which is here rendered especially pointed by the fact that the character of Carmen herself is figured as 'singer' in Bizet's opera; indeed, this is one of the meanings of her name. The operatic narrative of Carmen can be said to effect a drastic resolution to some of the problematic social and cultural issues of nineteenth-century France arising from the need to establish the hegemony of class, race, gender and 'high' art. In the opera, as Susan McClary has demonstrated, the character of Carmen figures the Other as an independent and sexual woman, Gypsy, quasi-oriental, and thence, by a sequence of metononymic musical associations, these features of otherness are attached to popular music, exoticism and chromaticism. Both the dramatic and the musical narratives of the opera effect a removal of these alien and subversive elements; the restoration of masculine normalcy, represented formally through the masculine forms of symphonic (Germanic) music, and diatonic harmony (McClary, 1992: 29-61). The translation of the opera to the medium of silent movie effects additional closures; a closure upon the problematics of female vocality in its very medium, and upon female physicality in its representation of the narrative

Whilst she is alive the operatic Carmen is in general permitted to 'speak' only in the borrowed voices of popular song. Unlike the character of Micaela, introduced into the opera to provide a respectable ideological counterweight to the protagonist, Carmen lacks interiority. The silent movie ensures an even more complete control over the character, depriving Carmen of her voice altogether. Carmen's muteness is compensated in the film by an extreme physicality that struggles against the constraints of the filmic spaces, which are, save for two *plein-air* scenes, confined to a series of tight theatrical stage sets. It is this physicality that now becomes the problem, for in this displacement of vocality into gestus, the film *Carmen* adds a number of new transgressions to those of her operatic forebear. These point specifically to what were increasingly perceived to be the problematic freedoms—freedoms of a bodily rather than

vocal nature—being made available to women in the modern city. In
dealing with this particular issue the Carmen narrative is exemplary,
since I can think of no other dramatic work of the nineteenth century,
or even the early twentieth century, that shows women in possession
of such freedom to roam and to occupy public spaces so boldly (this is
true not only of Carmen, but also of the surprisingly intrepid Micaela).

These were, of course, freedoms that the film industry itself was
willing to take advantage of, and indeed to promote in its efforts to
reach wider audiences, since the development of the cinema as a
commercial proposition depended in part upon a specific appeal to the
economic potential of women as consumers of entertainment. An
outcome of this was that particular concern was evinced by
conservative social theorists that the appeal to women inevitably
entailed the congregation of women of different social classes, often
on their own, to enjoy private pleasures in public spaces. 'The cinema,
as an institution', suggests film historian Miriam Hansen, 'threatened
to blur not only the boundaries maintaining hierarchic distinctions of
class but also the boundaries between public and private' (Hansen
1990: 238). A further outcome of this appeal to women was the
supposed feminization of film as a medium, which inevitably led male
critics to condemn film for its irrationalism and seductive and
contagious powers. Hansen notes the often made association of film
with prostitution. We may also note that the terms of this critique were
very similar to those that writers in the seventeenth and eighteenth
centuries had used to condemn opera, which was also condemned as
an effeminate and irrational art form (Oliver 1947: 6). Indeed, if film
wanted to accrue cultural value through its association with high art
then opera was surely the most problematic genre for this function,
since opera has always been the art form that exposes high art to the
popular and the feminized. To Hansen's list of the boundaries blurred
by the emergent culture of film I would add the boundaries of high
and low art, the boundaries of gender distinction, and, what I want to
concentrate on for the rest of this essay, the boundaries of space and
time. Poor Carmen, she has a lot to take the rap for.

My thesis is that the Film d'Art presentation of the Carmen
narrative figures the problematic relationship between space and
narrative in early film, problems that would be resolved by the
emergence and eventual dominance of what film theorists have
described as the Institutional Mode of Representation, or IMR. It was
the achievement of the IMR to find a relationship between space and
time in film that, in effect, subordinated filmic space to temporal

S p a c e + t i m e

development and narrative action, depriving space of its coherence
and continuity so that it could be cut up into pieces to serve the
demands of narrative presentation. This outcome is conventionally
described in teleological terms as an effect of increased formal and
technical sophistication allied with the inevitable market triumph of
fictional narrative as the predominant genre of film. But the
fragmentation of filmic space that takes place as result of this
development is no less an attribute of Soviet-style montage, which
also destroys spatial continuity to serve its dialectical (and hence
essentially temporal) ends. The similarity of means to serve such
different ends in American and Soviet film points to a broader
ideological imperative behind the formal devices that emerged in the
development of film. I want to suggest that this imperative is the
priority accorded to time over space in modernity.

The policing of acceptable lines between space and time also
has important gender implications, which may be traced back as far as
the eighteenth century. 'Time & Space are Real Beings, a Male & a
Female,' said William Blake, 'Time is a Man, Space a Woman, & her
Masculine Portion is Death' (Blake 1966: 614). W. J. T. Mitchell has
demonstrated how clearly gendered in these terms is Lessing's famous
effort to hold the line between the spatial and the temporal arts in
Laocoön. According to Lessing, the spatial arts of painting and
sculpture, assumed to be predominantly French, are seen as essentially
feminized, carrying bodily attributes, being limited in their sphere of
action and silent. By comparison, the literary arts, Germanic and
masculine, are of the mind, have infinite range and are eloquent
(Mitchell 1986: 95-115). In the terms established by these discourses,
space is represented as passive and static, a receptacle or container for,
and sometimes a hindrance to, the male principle of temporality and
action, as in H. L. Mencken's infamous characterisation of Dreiser's
representation of women in his novel *The 'Genius'* of 1915: 'Women
are the conservative and conservators, the enemies of hazard and
innovation, the compromisers and the temporizers. The very capacity
of mothering which is their supreme gift is the greatest of all foes to
masculine enterprise' (cited in Bowlby 1985: 124). The silent-movie
version on the Carmen story challenges and transgresses the
spatialization of the feminine in a number of ways, and in effect her
destruction prefigures the imminent triumph of time over space in
both the IMR and Soviet montage, a triumph that itself conforms to
the privileging of temporality over space in modernity in general.

The Film d'Art *Carmen* conforms to one of the main modes of what film historians have come to describe as the 'primitive mode of representation' in that it largely employs the spatio-temporal conventions of nineteenth-century theatre (which themselves derive from the unities of space, time and action of classical theatre). The action for the main part takes place within a series of stage sets, and the narrative is divided up into dramatic scenes that are each filmed in continuous real time. This was, by 1910, a matter of deliberate artistic choice rather than mere lack of filmic sophistication: montage editing, cross-cutting of parallel narrative actions, and the shot-reverse-shot formula had all been developed by this date. The appeal to the conventions of bourgeois theatre is in part self-explanatory, given the declared intentions of the Film d'Art company. We may also note that the use of theatre sets allows the film to re-deploy the long-established gender hierarchies of theatrical space, going back to Greek theatre, in the fundamental discourses of inside/outside, private and public space. For instance, the Film d'Art *Carmen* chooses to take us inside the tobacco factory to witness the fight between Carmen and a fellow worker, clearly representing an interior space occupied exclusively by women as hysterical.[2] But the most obvious effect of the predominantly theatrical sets of the 1910 *Carmen*, along with the fixed mid-distance camera position, and the single-take shots, is to present filmic space as the container of dramatic action. The box stage sets, with their implied proscenium, double the authority of the film frame, re-enforcing the pictorial conventions of centred perspectival space that were relied upon for legibility in early film. It has often been noted that, as opposed to the contemporary American development of shallow staging and fast cutting, the Film d'Art directors invariably employed a notably deep staging combined with slow cutting (Brewster 1990: 49). The stage sets in the Film d'Art *Carmen* are certainly deep, and this depth is taken full advantage of in the *plein-air* scenes, as for instance in Scene 10, in which the smugglers are ambushed by soldiers, where the possibilities of depth are exploited fully in a shot in which Carmen enters from the rear of the space and exits out of the bottom of the frame. This use of *plein-air* locations may be seen as an opportunity to naturalize the spatial conventions of the film, suggesting that they are derived from perception of the real world rather than from the conventions of theatre (or, to put it another way round, as a means of naturalizing the conventions of theatrical space itself).

This effect of spatial 'anchorage [...] stability [...] persistence', as film historian Andre Gaudreault describes it, re-enforces the containment of narrative by space (Elsaesser 1990: 24). The result of this in films with more complex or extended narratives such as the Film d'Art *Carmen*—narrative forms that were still only really possible at this early date if they were based on existing stories that were already known to the audience—is to constrain and compress the narrative action, restricting dramatic action to spatial intervention and ensuring that the narrative is only legible in spatial terms. The over-emphatic gesturing of the silent-movie Carmen is a clear symptom of this problem. In the opening scene of the film Carmen enters the space and immediately picks an apparently unmotivated fight with another woman, an action that is clearly necessitated by the need to make something 'happen' visually. In effect, narrative development in films like this is restricted by space, to the point where it is in fact often difficult or impossible to follow what is actually happening in the narrative. Watching the 1910 film, the viewer quickly sympathizes with a critic of the period who complained about the 'over-rapid, over-feverish, sometimes over-crowded, over-compact pictures' (Burch 1990: 59). In films of this period the construction tends to alternate between this kind of kinetic de-composition, close to the de-centered pictorial de-composition of, say, Impressionist paintings or the kind of pictorial representation of movement sought by the contemporaneous Futurist painters, and tableau-like compositions based on the conventions of classical pictorial composition, freeze-frame tableaux of this kind being necessary to provide some sort of visual point of repose, dramatic punctuation and narrative legibility.

On occasion the tableau format overrides narrative development altogether, as in Scene 5 of the film, where the filmmakers insert a scene showing the smugglers unloading their contraband in the courtyard of the inn. This scene clearly belongs to an earlier film genre, the autonomous tableau of what Richard Abel calls 'the cinema of attractions'. Redundant in dramatic or narrative term, this scene conforms to Abel's observation that a number of films of this period employed a technique of what he describes as 'bricolage': 'a combination of narrative and spectacular elements'. In the spectacular tableau of this kind the actors serve simply as 'performers of physical action' (Abel 1994: 105). Indeed, this may be identified as one of the major distinctions between the primitive mode and the institutional mode of representation. In the former its ability to capture movement—Panofsky's 'movement for movement's sake'—is

predominant (Panofsky 1999: 279). Thus the essential subject-matter
of early films is things in motion: animals (numerous dog and horse
chase sequences—the most famous and influential example being
Rescued by Rover (Hepworth, 1905), but also events such as bullfights
or horse races); machines (industrial machinery was popular—e.g.
Visit to Peak Freans (Cricks and Martin, 1906), but also cars,
steamboats and trains (the classic example is Lumière's *Arrivée d'un
train*, of course); and natural phenomena such as the effect of wind in
trees, or water (*Barque sortant du port, Niagara*, both by Lumière
(1895/1897), *Rough Sea at Dover* (Acres, 1895)). Equally popular
were modes of human activity which took place on one spot, such as
repetitive forms of labour, of which the Carmen tableau under
discussion is a typical example (*Démolition d'un mur* (Lumière,
1896), *Pompiers à Lyon* (Lumière, c1896), *Day in the Life of a
Coalminer* (Kineto, 1910)), or fights and dances, both of which also
play an important part in the Carmen narrative (for instance, *Batailles
de Boules de Neige* (Lumière, 1896)). It is noteworthy that Siegfried
Kracauer considered dance, along with chases, to be 'specifically
cinematic' (Kracauer 1999: 294).

What links all of these kinds of subject matter is that the motion
portrayed is in general either that of essentially inanimate objects that
are somehow animated to create motion (e.g. natural phenomena or
machinery, but sometimes, as in Edison's *Dream of a Rarebit Fiend*
of 1906, or the fantasies of Méliès, immovable furniture or scenery
that are animated by trick photography), or animals, whose actions
lack longer-term goal orientation or the possibility of historical
development. If the action is human it is often unmotivated, recurrent
or repetitive (dance or chase sequences), or divorced from sensible
motivation (such as drunken sequences, as in Edison's *Dream of a
Rarebit Fiend*). In each case the possibility of goal-orientated action,
and hence of progressive narrative development, is somehow limited
or constrained by spatial anchorage and temporal repetition. This
distinction between pure movement and action—also noted by
Deleuze in his distinction between the perceptual 'movement image'
of pre-classic film and the 'action image' of what he identifies as
classic film (Deleuze 1992: 64-65)—is a crucial difference between
the primitive and the institutional modes of film. We may note that in
the contraband scene in the Film d'Art *Carmen*, Carmen herself, who
otherwise always serves to initiate dramatic action throughout the
film, is of necessity relegated to the background of the tableau as a
secondary figure. But we may in addition observe that even though

Carmen initiates dramatic action, her actions are often apparently unmotivated (as in the fight she picks with another woman in the first scene of the film). By implication, as a woman who is not safely confined to the home, Carmen is equated with children and animals as a being who is physically restless but lacking in goal-orientated moral purpose (which is, of course, the essential criterion for dramatic action in Aristotelian theory).

This subservience of temporal and narrative development to space in early film cannot, of course, be countenanced. Modernity demands constant change and renewal, and as geographer David Harvey suggests, citing Marx's famous formulation, 'Progress entails the conquest of space, the tearing down of all spatial barriers, and the ultimate annihilation of space through time' (Harvey 1989: 205). In Goethe's *Faust*, the founding allegory of modernity, the final event of Faust's life represents precisely this image of spatial conquest: the clearing of land for development, and the eviction of the aged peasant couple Philemon and Baucis from their cottage:

> *Faust*
> Yon aged couple ought to yield,
> The linden still I have to gain,
> The clustering trees above the weald
> Mock and destroy my wide domain (Act 5, Scene 3: line 258).

As the emblem of modernity's restlessness Faust himself is forbidden one thing on pain of damnation: that he should express the desire that any moment should be suspended to last for ever. The imperative of temporality and progress is no less urgent in narratives of emancipation than in those of capitalist development. Marx considered the spatial preoccupations of geography, with its stress upon the environmental determinants upon human behaviour, to be an obstacle to the consideration of the possibilities of historical progress, and he also considered the localism of geography to be a hindrance to the internationalism demanded of class allegiance. But even someone as anti-historicist as Foucault, who once questioned why space was invariably 'treated as the dead, the fixed, the undialectical, the immobile' (Foucault 1991: 70), offered a reading of spatial formations as sites of social control, containers which constrain the forces of desire and becoming. We find this privileging of temporality in many strains of early modernist art. In both Cubism and Futurism, which are exactly contemporaneous with the developments in film that we are discussing here, we recognize a desire to challenge the spatial solidity and fixity of the pictorial image, and there is a clear strand in modernist thinking about music—primarily deriving from the Schoenberg/Darmstadt axis—that stresses the importance of temporal development over quasi-spatial repetition. Adorno dismissed dance music, whether classical or popular, for its circularity and lack of development, and this was one of the atavistic aspects of Stravinsky's music that he considered to be ideologically so pernicious (Adorno 1980: 196). In the more recent postwar period Iannis Xenakis similarly expressed a typically modernist exasperation with classical musical form: 'Why do Bach and Beethoven repeat themselves all the time? I'm sick and tired of music that doesn't move' (Hamilton, 2002: 68). Insofar as Stravinsky is representative of the strand of modernism that privileges quasi-spatial forms over temporal development, Adorno's critique is supported by literary critics such as Kermode or Jameson who attack this mode of modernism in literature for its mythologizing tendencies, pointing to the frequent association of writers such as Yeats or Pound with regressive ideologies such as nationalism and fascism (Mitchell 1986: 97). Closer to film, the theatre of Meyerhold, and subsequently Piscator and Brecht, challenged the fixity of conventional theatrical space, insisting that theatrical space must be represented as subject to human alteration.

Deleuze talks about the evolution of film in terms of its 'conquest of its own essence' through the progressive 'emancipation' of space in the development of film (Deleuze 1992: 3). But I would suggest that if filmic space is emancipated it is in similar fashion to the way in which the feudal serf or slave must be 'emancipated' to be free to sell his or her labour on the market. For the narrative mode of the IMR in fact renders filmic space clearly subservient to the dominant discourse of narrative in precisely the same way that capitalism, in Harvey's term, 'annihilates' space through time (Harvey 1989: 232). Space is deprived of its power to anchor and contain narrative by being cut up and re-assembled according to the primary requirement of narrative development, just as capitalist modernity replaces the specificity of place and locality with the universal abstraction of space as commodity. This homogeneity of space is achieved through its total 'pulverization', in Harvey's words, and its 'fragmentation into freely alienable parcels of private property' (Harvey 1989: 254). The obverse of this, if we seek a spatial equivalent to the practices of Russian montage, is the way in which the modernization project of Soviet communism abstracts space not by parcelling but by collectivizing it, removing the farmer from his close relationship with an individual plot of land to work as part of a collective.

Having fragmented space, of course, capitalism has to put in place that which will counterbalance its own destructiveness: rootless global capitalism requires political nation-states to provide the security of law and the means of ideological reproduction. The rapacious businessman returns home at night to the cosy and stable nest maintained by his wife. Like the woman, space is represented as either abstract commodity, to be penetrated and owned at will (we may recall here Benjamin's description of the classical filmic relation to space as being comparable to the probing and penetration of the surgeon (Benjamin 1973: 235), or guarantor of private security and stability. Carmen, of course, is neither of these, and for this she must pay the price.

The problematic subservience of narrative to space in early film is clearly figured in the narrative of the Film d'Art *Carmen*, in which anxieties about the feminized power of space to capture and contain the masculine principle of narrative action are mapped onto the already over-determined discourses of the Carmen story. Put simply, the film Carmen effects a disruption of filmic space that, by embodying what should be the masculine prerogative of narrative action, exemplifies the unacceptable feminization of action by the all-containing passivity of pre-modern filmic space. In the opening scene of the film the arrival of the group of solders to replace the guard may be seen as an assertion of masculine order. The straight lines of the file of solders serves to impose a spatial and visual order, but this imposition of order must be seen as a reassertion of a previous state of affairs (the guard is changed in this way every day); as a cyclical event that ensures continuity rather than as a narrative departure. And as Julia Kristeva makes clear, it is supposed to be women's time, not masculine time, that is based on 'repetition and eternity', the 'cyclical or monumental' (Kristeva 1986: 191-192). The possibility of narrative departure only occurs with the disruptive arrival of Carmen herself. In contrast to the hyperactive activities of Carmen, José remains seated and passive throughout this first scene. The problematic here, and throughout the film, is that the spatial feminine has exceeded her boundaries to emasculate time and narrative ('her masculine portion is death', we may recall from William Blake), and thence to assume their function. The problem can only be resolved in narrative terms through the killing of Carmen by don José. The problem will be resolved in filmic terms when the IMR learns how to transform spatialized motion into temporal action, and hence to ensure that narrative energy is repositioned as an effect of the controlling apparatus rather than as a vulnerable bodily intervention in filmic space. Filmic space will be dismembered, and narrative control will be located invisibly within the structure of the film, rather than in the over-anxious redundancy of the intertitles that had sought to secure discursive control through extra-diegetic language. Richard Abel actually cites the Film d'Art *Carmen* as an extreme example of this redundancy, suggesting that 'the narrative significance of each shot is so clearly tied to the expository intertitle [...] that the overall effect of the tableau's broad spectacle is merely to illustrate an essentially verbal text' (Abel 1994: 516n). The explanation for this must be that the extreme display of feminine bodily action in the film seems to require this re-imposition of linguistic (masculine, *pace* Lessing) control, in much the same way that Mérimée effected a secondary closure on his narrative through his final display of linguistic mastery over the language of his protagonist.

Notes
1. Observation made at the Carmen Conference, Newcastle, March 2002.
2. In her essay 'Women's Time' Julia Kristeva notes Freud's linking of hysteria to place (Kristeva 1986: 191).

References
Adorno,Theodor W. 1980. *The Philosophy of Modern Music.* New York: Seabury Press.
Abel, Richard. 1994. *The Cine Goes to Town: French Cinema 1896-1914.* Berkeley: University of California Press.
Benjamin,Walter. 1973. 'The Work of Art in the Age of Mechanical Reproduction in *Illuminations* (ed. Hannah Arendt.). London: Fontana: 219-252.
Blake, William. 1996. 'A Vision of the Last Judgement', in *Collected Works.* Oxford: Oxford University Press: 604-617.
Bowlby, Rachel. 1985. *Just Looking: Consumer Culture in Dreiser, Gissing and Zola.* London: Methuen.
Brewster, Ben. 1990. 'Deep Staging in French Films, 1900-1914' in Elsaesser (1990): 45-55.
Burch, Noël. 1990. *Life to Those Shadows* (tr. Ben Brewster). London: British Film Institute
Deleuze, Gilles. 1992. *Cinema 1: The Movement Image* (tr. Hugh Tomlinson and Barbara Habberjam). London: Athlone Press.
Elsaesser, Thomas (ed.). 1990. *Early Cinema: Space Frame Narrative.* London: British Film Institute.
Foucault, Michel. 1991. 'Space, Knowledge, and Power' in Rabinow, P. (ed.) *The Foucault Reader.* London: Penguin: 239-256.

Goethe, Johann Wolfgang von. 1959. *Faust: Part Two* (tr. P. Wayne). Harmondsworth: Penguin.

Hamilton, Andy. 2002. 'Iannis Xenakis' in *The Wire* 216: 68.

Hansen, Miriam. 1990. 'Early Cinema: Whose Public Sphere?' in Elsaesser (1990): 228-246.

Harvey, David. 1989. *The Condition of Postmodernity: An Enquiry into the Origins of Cultural Change*. Oxford: Blackwell.

Kracauer, Siegfried. 1999. 'The Establishment of Physical Existence' in Braudy, Leo, Gerald and Cohen, Marshall (eds), *Film Theory and Criticism: Introductory Readings*. 5th edn. New York: Oxford University Press: 293-303.

Kristeva, Julia. 1986. 'Women's Time' in Moi, Toril (ed.) *The Kristeva Reader*. Oxford: Blackwell: 187-213.

McClary, Susan. 1992. *Georges Bizet: Carmen*. Cambridge: Cambridge University Press.

Mitchell, W. J. T. 1986. *Iconology: Image, Text, Ideology*. Chicago: University of Chicago Press.

Oliver, A. R. 1947. *The Encyclopédistes as Critics of Music*. New York: Columbia University Press.

Panofsky, Erwin. 1999. 'Style and Medium in the Motion Pictures' in Braudy, Leo, Gerald and Cohen, Marshall (eds), *Film Theory and Criticism: Introductory Readings*. 5th edn. New York: Oxford University Press: 279-292.

Geraldine Farrar and Cecil B. DeMille:
The Effect of Opera on Film and Film on Opera in 1915

Gillian B. Anderson

This chapter explores the ways in which Metropolitan opera star Geraldine Farrar (1882-1967) changed the status of the motion picture and also changed the interpretation of the opera *Carmen* itself with her appearance in Cecil B. DeMille's film, *Carmen* (1915). Extensive use of contemporary accounts documents contemporary reactions to Farrar's Hollywood experience and her transfer of the film's overt sexuality and physicality to live performances of *Carmen* at the Met. The role of Farrar is revealed to be key to a wider moment in cultural history when the ultimate in theatrical grandeur was transferring from the opera stage to the movie screen. Reactions to performances of the restored original musical accompaniment arranged from Bizet by Hugo Riesenfeld with unrestored and restored versions of the film allow us to critique the contemporary accounts.

DeMille, Cecil B.: *Carmen*
Farrar, Geraldine
Musical accompaniment to silent film
Opera and film
Riesenfeld, Hugo

> There must hereafter be a recognized line between the
> Carmens who have feathers and scratch and those that
> have whiskers and bite. (*New York Sun* 1915)

1. Introduction

Since its inception the moving picture has been associated with grand opera. In 1893 in an article in *The New York Times*, Thomas Edison painted a futuristic vision that was not to be realized until the advent of television and the videotape recorder:

> My intention is to have such a happy combination of photography and
> electricity that a man can sit in his own parou and see depicted upon a curtain
> the forms of the players in opera upon a distant stage, and hear the voices of
> the singers.[1]

Edison went on to make a 22-minute *Parsifal* (1904) and a shorter version of von Flotow's *Martha* (1906) whose music had to be produced live with the mechanical image. These were only two of many subsequent examples of opera stories transferred to the screen by many different film directors. In 1916, taking a different tack, Thomas Dixon advertised his *The Fall of a Nation* with its completely original score by Victor Herbert as the first 'grand opera cinema.' In

almost every instance the association of opera with film was made by
film directors who were trying to capitalize on the status of opera to
elevate their movies. Even the term 'silent films' made its very first
appearance in association with opera. A 1918 headline for a review of
Hellcat starring opera singer Geraldine Farrar (1882-1967) read 'Two
Opera Stars in Silent Films.' The headline emphasized how ironic it
was to have opera singers working in a medium which could not
reproduce their voices.[2]

By the 1920s, the motion picture had reached such a level of
popularity that it was beginning to threaten the once unassailable
position of opera as the pinnacle of theatrical glamour. Geraldine
Farrar's entry into film in 1915 made a substantial contribution to this
shift in status. As one of the finest American sopranos of her time,
known for the mellowness and maturity of her voice, the breadth of
her vocal range, and her superb gifts as an actress, she was famous in
both Europe and America for her interpretations of Puccini, also for
her Carmen as well as many other major roles.[3] Choreographer Agnes
DeMille referred to Farrar in the following terms:

> Grand Opera meant far more in those days than it does now or possibly ever
> will again. It represented the ultimate in theatrical grandeur, honor,
> permanence and splendor and Farrar was among its most dazzling names.
> (DeMille, A. 1952: 22-24)

Farrar's appearance in Hollywood and her participation in a film lent
her celebrity status to the medium. It was part of a calculated attempt
to elevate the status of the motion picture, and it largely succeeded.

On 23 April 1915, Hollywood producer Jesse L. Lasky attended
Farrar's performance of *Madame Butterfly* at the Metropolitan Opera
House. He wanted to attract players from the legitimate stage to
motion pictures and with them a new, upscale audience. He also
wanted to make his company competitive with that of Adolph Zuckor
whose stable of players was led by Mary Pickford. After the
performance and an introduction by Farrar's friend, Morris Gest,
Lasky put his proposal to Farrar:

> I don't know whether you have even seen a motion picture, but my
> company makes them, and I'd like to persuade you to do the story of
> Carmen for us [...]. We have no trouble securing famous plays and
> engaging their stars [...] but they're always afraid acting in a movie will hurt
> their stage prestige. I could see by the ovation you got today that your
> prestige is such that whatever you do, your public will accept it as right.
> (Lasky and Weldon 1957: 116)

Although the Metropolitan Opera disapproved, Farrar went to Hollywood in the summer of 1915. Cecil B. DeMille's brother, writer William DeMille, described the terms of her engagement, emphasizing the economic demands that went with stardom – a house, a car, and 20,000 dollars (a very high sum for the time) for eight weeks' work.

> The idea of taking our most expensive star from the field of grand opera was, perhaps, more daring than the Company realized, because of the different standards and methods of acting in each medium. On the operatic stage 'Jerry' was known as a fine actress, which meant that she had more than two facial expressions, that she never tripped over her own feet and that her gestures were not semaphorical. But the long-sustained expression of emotion *a tempo* of the opera house, always subordinated to singing tone and orchestral rhythm, was quite a different problem from the smoothly flowing, intimate, silent and realistic acting which the screen demanded. It meant an instant translation from the most distant and artificial form of acting known to modern man to the closest and most naturalistic method that had yet been evolved. Facing a camera for the first time, an opera singer, more than the ordinary actor, misses his voice.

Despite studio fears of 'artistic temperament', DeMille noted Farrar to be an enthusiastic and cheerful hard worker:

> Tales were told of the utter unreasonableness of great singers; how impossible it was to get them to take direction; how they were liable to throw things and break furniture in order to express displeasure without hurting their voices; so that the whole plant awaited our distinguished songbird with definite but well-concealed anxiety.
>
> When she turned out to be an honest-to-God two-fisted trouper, strong as an ox and rejoicing in scenes of physical combat, the studio rubbed its eyes as if awaking from a bad dream. When it further developed that she was delightful to work with, kind, considerate and hail-fellow-well-met with the lowliest extra or the newest property boy, the studio turned over on its back and purred. (DeMille, W.C. 1939: 147-149)

2. Farrar's Carmen

Before going to Hollywood, in an interview that appeared in *The Music Lover* (1915) Farrar answered the question 'what manner of woman is your Carmen?':

> She isn't merely sensual. She couldn't be. The merely sensual woman is too transparent to be dangerous and, lacking mentality, she lacks power. Carmen couldn't have played havoc as she did except for the fact that there was a keen and subtle intelligence behind it all. She was deadly only because she could compel the highest as well as the lowest form of

admiration. Then, too, remember that in playing the role the sympathy of the audience is all with the other woman. How is one to gain a justifiable sympathy for Carmen unless she is capable of making more than a merely sensual appeal?

The Hollywood experience in the summer of 1915 seems to have tipped the balance of Farrar's interpretation towards the 'havoc' side.

Carmen, was premiered at Symphony Hall in Boston, Massachusetts on 1 October 1915. It was based more or less on the original story by Prosper Mérimée, and so there were substantial differences between it and the opera. Most significantly, in the film, Carmen is a less sympathetic character; in William DeMille's screenplay she is a manipulative, nomadic, tribal Gypsy with fickle sexual appetites rather than the unconscious force of nature one finds in the opera. Micaela does not play a role in the DeMille version, and in the movie there are realistic fights in the cigarette factory (musical aspects of which are discussed in detail in the final section of this chapter), in Pastias' tavern, and in a bull ring. Although the differences between the movie and the opera were remarked upon, the movie won good reviews. In *Musical America* Olin Downes said of the premiere that Farrar had managed to convey a sense of realism appropriate to the film medium, and particularly relished the fight scene that displayed Carmen's physical prowess (commenting as an aside that this enjoyment may reflect his own 'low character' and 'unaesthetic mind'). He then went on to ask:

> But is it Art? That is the question. To lovers of Bizet's opera, which so wonderfully avoids what is purely photographic and merely realistic and yet depicts with an eloquence perhaps never surpassed in a musical score the primeval passions and eternal sex antagonisms of Mérimée's story, the scenes on Friday night were not all inspiring. For those, on the other hand, with the liking for moving pictures of the more melodramatic variety, the spectacle was wholly satisfactory. Miss Farrar made love in a delightfully frank manner; she fought like a fiend and a guttersnipe and displayed abundance of devilry when, by every means in her power, she assisted José to kill his brother-officer—another stroke of breath-taking realism. All this she did, to a rearrangement of Bizet's music, which was here effective and there inartistic, and to the gratification of at least a majority of the spectators. Yet those who have often had occasion wholeheartedly to admire Miss Farrar's dramatic singing as well as her uncommonly finished histrionic art missed much that they had seen on the operatic stage, and some things that they had hoped they might see in the 'movies'.

Downes concluded:

> As for Miss Farrar, I would rather watch her and listen to her in opera, where she occupies a niche wholly her own, than to watch her in a far less artistic frame, where others less exceptionally gifted than she can appear with success as her rivals. (Downes 1915)

The Lasky executives were extremely pleased with the film's reception, as the *Boston Post* (1915) reported:

> Mr. Goldfish [Sam Goldwyn] was delighted with the success of the first presentation. He said to a *Post* reporter: 'I believe that Miss Farrar will supersede any human being ever seen on the screen and that she will bring into the moving picture house people who have never been there before. I am confident that she will elevate the moving picture drama to heights never dreamed of'.
>
> S. L. Rothapfel, who had personal charge of the musical adaptation, declared that the first presentation exceeded his greatest expectations. One of the most interested witnesses of the presentation [...] W. W. Hodkinson, president of the Paramount Picture Company [...] saw the realization of his dreams of years ago, when he first conceived the idea of presenting grand opera on the screen. (*Boston Post* 1915)

The premiere of *Carmen* at the Strand Theatre in New York a month later earned similar reviews, the following taken from an article in the *New York Sun*, entitled 'Farrar a Tiger as Screen Carmen—Gypsy Girl is a Slugger:'

> A Spanish cigarette maker is, to judge from what the audience witnessed yesterday, a combination of tigress and lightweight slugger, with a tendency to go about all the time in a state of undress. Miss Farrar emphasized the physical, not to say the bestial, note in the Gypsy, as these pictures reveal her idea of *Carmen* to a degree that leaves but little else in the woman's character. She lays about her with the vigour of a longshoreman when she does not care for the addresses of a swain and bites and scratches her fellow employees like a tigress. Miss Farrar was best in the scenes of comedy and her banter with the cigarette girls was very eloquently expressed by her facial emotions [...].

The reviewer went on to observe that:

> There must hereafter be a recognized line between the Carmens who have feathers and scratch and those that have whiskers and bite. At all events Maria Gay's Carmen seems all prunes and prisms compared with the Spanish Gypsy that Miss Farrar is revealing at the Strand Theatre. (*New York Sun* 1915)

On the evening of February 17, 1916 Farrar returned to the stage of the Metropolitan Opera to perform the operatic version of *Carmen*. Believing that 'art profited immensely from this work in silent pantomime', she incorporated certain elements from the cinema version of *Carmen* into her operatic performance. Without warning any of her fellow performers, she introduced a realistic fight in the cigarette factory into the first act of the opera. Then she stuffed her rose into don José's (Caruso's) cheek. In Act 3 she became so energetic and distracting while he was singing that Caruso grabbed her and would not let her go. After he finished singing, Farrar broke away and fell to the floor (Nash 1981: 191-192). Off-stage, Caruso directed a violent temper tantrum at Farrar.

A rather uncharitable account of this appearance was published in the music journal *International Music and Drama*:

> I don't believe there is one of our readers who has not read in the daily papers the reports of that memorable and historical evening, with all its accompanying details such as the incident with Caruso behind the scenes, the strange and pathetic vulgarities indulged in by Mme. Farrar, the slaps she administered the bewildered don José; the kicks and cuffs and catch-as-catch-can bout with the chorus girls, one of whom was valiantly thrown over by Madame and had to be surrounded by her companions to conceal her tears to the public, etc., etc..
>
> In the first act especially, Mme. Farrar seemed like an energumen seized and shaken either by the evil spirits or by several quarts of her ancestral beverage which rendered her entirely incapable to check and control herself. I am not mentioning her impossible make-up, her torn and tattered dress, her arm and right breast entirely naked, her boorish poses, her sudden sallies towards her fellow cigar-makers, and the rest with all its concomitants of altered or interrupted melodic lines which reduced the scene to the proportions of a Los Angeles film.
>
> I was staring in utter stupefaction at this extraordinary exhibition of stage diabolism, and being a very pious Christian, I was seized by a great, profound and inexpressible feeling of pity and compassion. (E.V. 1916)

In spite of this account and others like it, Farrar continued to be phenomenally successful. The huge salary she earned in Hollywood, the increase in the number of people she reached through the movies, and the constant publicity her pictures brought soon encouraged other stars of the legitimate stage to follow her lead. Her motion-picture work improved her box-office appeal rather than detracting from it. Although she dropped the business with don José in subsequent performances with Caruso, and although her athletic and blatantly sexual interpretation caused a scandal at the Met, a lot of her realistic, film-inspired business was incorporated into subsequent operatic performances of *Carmen* as I myself witnessed at Covent Garden fifty-five years later. Farrar reached the larger public she had hoped for. Lasky coopted her glamour and appeal and made them work for the less prestigious medium of motion pictures, and film shortly replaced the opera at the pinnacle of the entertainment hierarchy in the United States.

There is little doubt that DeMille's *Carmen* and Geraldine Farrar played important roles in the changing status of the motion picture in the United States, but twenty years later William DeMille, looking at the film without its musical accompaniment, perhaps projected at the wrong speed, and perhaps even without its original colour tinting and toning, was very critical:

> Just twenty years later I had occasion to look at our picture of 'Carmen'. It was hard to believe that what I saw on the screen was actually the same work upon which so much honest effort had been expended. As I had gone with the screen, step by step, in its gradual evolution, my memory tended to clothe our earlier efforts with technical attributes which had become essential and commonplace in the modern film. Their absence was startling. Our beloved 'Carmen', which had been hailed as an achievement in 1915, was as much like a modern motion picture as the little three-toed echippus is like Twenty Grand; or as the earliest 'horseless carriage' is like the streamlined, high-powered automobile of today. For the first time I actually realized what the constant pressure of millions of people who want a certain thing improved, can do to bring about that improvement. Looked at with 1935 eyes, our picture was badly photographed, the lighting was childish, the acting was awful, the writing atrocious and—may Allah be merciful—the direction terrible. [...] 'Carmen' would have lived in my memory as a fine picture if only I hadn't seen it again. But all things are relative to their times. (DeMille, W.C. 1939: 154-155)

3. The Restoration of the Music and the Film

By 1985 all that remained of DeMille's *Carmen* were these accounts and reminiscences, a battered black and white print of the film at the George Eastman House that had been Cecil B. DeMille's own copy (perhaps exactly the one his brother looked at in 1935), and a copyright deposit of the original musical accompaniment by Hugo Riesenfeld at the Library of Congress. The gradual restoration of both the music and the film over subsequent years and a number of performances at various stages in the restoration process provided a deeper insight into the meaning of the original sources and also a means of critiquing them.

The copyright deposit consisted of a piano conductor score and orchestral parts for flute, flute/piccolo, two clarinets, two trumpets, one trombone, percussion/timpani and strings. There were no parts for oboes, bassoons, French horns, harp or second and third trombones, maybe simply because these parts were not deposited for copyright (which happened often enough) or because only the copyrighted parts were played at the Boston premiere.[4] There were no vocal parts in the copyright deposit, but the newspaper reviews of the New York performances indicate that there were vocal soloists ('L'amour est enfant de Bohème' was sung when the Lilias Pastia scene was shown, 'La Fleur que vous m'avez donnée' accompanied don José's courtship, and the toreador's march was also featured (*New York Sun* 1915).[5]

Because it no doubt affected the reception of the work originally, something should be said about the imprecision of the piano conductor score and the indications it had for synchronization of the music with the film. A piano conductor score was made for the pianist and the conductor. It was cued so that the conductor knew that when an intertitle or action that was printed above a certain section of music appeared on the screen, the conductor was to begin that section of music. Usually there was an intertitle or dramatic action listed at the beginning of each new musical section of the score. The musical scores for D. W. Griffith's *Birth of a Nation* (1914) and *Intolerance* (1916), for example, (which were made at the same time as the score for *Carmen*) were minutely cued in this fashion even though they changed music and tempo continuously, about every twenty to thirty seconds for two and a half to three and a half hours respectively. In the score for *Carmen*, however, sometimes there was no indication of what was happening at the beginning of a new section of music. Sometimes the titles were not correct (or they had been changed after the score was made). The cues frequently read 'Play Until Title' which meant theoretically that one would keep playing and leap into the next section of music when the title appeared whether or not one had finished the section being played. Sometimes there was too much music. This lack of precision could not but have affected the quality of the synchronization and performance.[6]

The first time I performed *Carmen* was in Washington, DC with only ten instruments (members of the National Symphony). Although the first run movie palaces would have had at least a chamber orchestra, the smaller theatres would have used a ten-piece ensemble or smaller. The National Symphony players were not disturbed by the missing material: the pianist filled in a lot of the missing textures and harmonies, and they liked playing for a film. The print was Cecil B. DeMille's own black and white copy. The producer of a French television programme on opera filmed a fifteen-minute segment on the restoration. She was fascinated by Farrar and enthusiastic about the film. The reaction of the North American audience, by comparison, was tepid. The next performance was at the Pordenone Silent Film Festival with a chamber orchestra from Slovenia. There were three singers including a very statuesque young woman who did Carmen's arias sexily dressed (a North American colleague in the audience couldn't keep his eyes off the singer)—which was just as well, because the Italian audience didn't much like the film or the music. As a final insult, the projectionist started the film in the middle of the overture.[7] The film was still in black and white, and not yet restored; the orchestration minus the missing instruments left the accompaniment sounding thin, without the colour of Bizet's original; and in particular the French horn melody meant to go with a tremolo string accompaniment in the final scene (Carmen's death) was missing (neither transferred to the trombone nor to the piano part)—although the tremolo strings conveyed the tension, they sounded odd and senseless in isolation.

What I learned from that performance was that the 1915 Boston review was correct. The orchestration was bizarre. Nevertheless, the accompaniment was workable, and there were some powerful moments. In the fight in the cigarette factory, for example, one heard the strangeness of the arrangement, but otherwise the operatic music became good film music. At the beginning of the scene the music announced Carmen's entrance and through the use of pregnant pauses and a demanding percussiveness, it alerted the audience to the beginning of something important. Before the fight it even suggested the laughter of the factory girls at Carmen's expense. Then as Carmen took off her jacket, a shrill, insect-like motif in the strings heralded something more disturbing. Following this, the low strings, playing fast, off the beat (which was hard to do), carried its own tension. Something more violent was about to happen. Cascades of ever louder runs down the scale led up to a percussive chord when a bottle was broken over Carmen's head. Short punctuated chords suggested jabs and punches, then an antiphonal motif suggested the back and forth of the fight. When Carmen looked her adversary in the face, the antiphonal motive climaxed in a series of repeated phrases. The fight continued, but a new, repeated, static motif announced the switch of the scene to outside the factory. Don José was being urged to come in and break up the fight. This was the original music for the fight scene in the opera and its kinetic energy matched that of the screen without ever seeming to duplicate it.

My first performance in France took place in Strasbourg with ten members from the Strasbourg Symphony. That group of musicians thought that the accompaniment was going to be easy, because they knew the music so well. They were surprised when it turned out to be really hard to do with just ten players. They had the original Bizet orchestration in their heads and found it hard to make adjustments for all the missing material. Nevertheless, the French audience was enthusiastic. The film was still in black and white. A second performance in France, this time in Lille, was perhaps the best of all. The film's original tinting and toning had been restored, and the film looked sumptuous.[8] The ten-piece ensemble from the Lille Symphony had worked up the music over the summer, making adjustments for all the missing material. The final French horn melody that accompanied Carmen's death had been transposed to the trombone. But perhaps best of all was the context. The five, free performances were presented by the theatre in Lille as part of the national holiday devoted to the patrimony of France. Ordinary people came into the theatre for the five hour-long screenings. I normally respond to questions after a performance, but got none. Afterwards I received a note from one of the members of the public. She said she was sorry no one had asked any questions, but she thought the reason was that they were all so deeply moved by the film and its music that they could not snap out of the effect quickly enough to ask a question. In France one had the feeling that Carmen was truly theirs, no matter what the arrangement.

All these experiences led me to believe that the instrumental parts missing from the copyright deposit may have been missing because Riesenfeld the adaptor was not the musical genius he was reputed to be. For my recording with the London Philharmonic[9] and for bigger orchestral performances, I decided to take the missing parts from the opera's full score; and at the end of the film I restored the missing horn melody referred to above (arranged for the trombone for the purposes of the ten-piece ensemble performances). As at Pordenone (and as, indeed, in those 1915 New York performances of *Carmen*), vocalists were used on the London Philharmonic recording.[10] Again sonic texture added considerably to the visual and dramatic effects. The woman who sang Carmen listened to her first take while watching the video monitor and said, 'I have to make her sexier and more of a whore' and so changed the colour of her voice for the subsequent take. The effect was to highlight Farrar's facial expressiveness and, when the bass sang the toreador song during the bullfight the detail of the bull pawing the earth (in time to the music) was one of several to become newly noticeable. It was as if the vocal music intensified the movement of body and muscle on screen, in a different way, in fact, from the instrumental music.

4. Conclusions

So now let us return to William DeMille's assessment of *Carmen* in 1935. I think he was both right and wrong. Cecil B. DeMille's *Carmen* is a fragile theatrical property. It is considerably strengthened by the original tinting and toning. It is considerably strengthened by an orchestration closer to that of the Bizet original. It works with only ten players representing the Bizet orchestration but only when the ensemble is really superb, and the pianist makes up for a lot of the missing instruments. The imprecision of the cueing in the score makes for some awkward moments. On a program with Cavalcanti's *La P'tite Lili* accompanied by music by Milhaud, the DeMille seemed old fashioned.[11] On the other hand, particularly in France, the restored film with its restored score has a very powerful historic appeal. William DeMille forgot how much the colour and the music added to the film. He forgot what the intention had been in having Farrar play the title role, and he forgot how successful *Carmen* and Farrar were at changing the status of the motion picture and the performance of the opera itself. DeMille's *Carmen* is a historic milestone and under the right circumstances even with but a pale shadow of the original operatic music, it still has the power to move, particularly a French audience, deeply.

Notes
1. In *New York Times*, 13 May 1893. Quoted in Hendricks (1972: 104-105).
2. *New York Times*, 25 November 1918: 11 (col. 3).
3. Her popularity with the younger opera goers in New York earned them the nickname 'Gerry-flappers.' Farrar was in real life a strong, independent and unconventional woman. It is ironic that she made her reputation both on the opera stage and in film as Carmen, a character who according to offensive operatic convention had to die at the end because she was a strong and independent woman.
4. The use at the Boston premiere of only the copyrighted parts might partially explain the criticism of the orchestration in the *Musical America* review (Downes 1915). The usual copyright deposit for a smaller ensemble would have had flute/piccolo, clarinet, trumpet, trombone, percussion/tympani, piano and four strings. The viola would have been lacking.
5. *New York Sun*, 1 November 1915: 7. Although the flower song was mentioned, the music for it does not appear in the Riesenfeld adaptation of the Bizet deposited for copyright. This might mean that the journalist was mistaken, or that there might have been more than one arrangement of the accompaniment for the film. It raises the

possibility that the criticism of the Riesenfeld arrangement and the sloppiness of the indications for synchronisation led music directors outside of Boston to create their own arrangements.

6. So, were we dealing with a different version of the film? A simple miscalculation? Or perhaps the intention really was to have this music played unusually fast. In the restoration of the music, an attempt was made to have the orchestra keep playing until the nearest musical cadence, and the score was synchronized accordingly so there was not too much extraneous leaping (even so, there was still some). If there was a choice of how much music to use, a tempo that made sense musically and was within the opera tradition was selected. However, between 1892 and 1929 musicians played much faster than they do today, maybe because the bowing was really different, the tone production was much lighter, and the strings were gut strings. 'Made sense musically' therefore was extremely subjective. Sometimes cuts in the music had to be made because there was dancing on screen. One could actually tell how fast the music was supposed to be going, and as a result you could see that there was simply too much music. Actually Farrar did her scenes to music; her accompanist played to get her in the mood. She claims to have been the first movie star to have had such accompaniment—I asked Lillian Gish about this and she said it was very likely—and afterwards all of the female stars wanted music on the set. So the discrepancies in the dancing probably resulted from the cutting and the use of different takes. However, at other times it was clear that the dancing was in fact not made to music because it varied speed so wildly. In these cases the tempo was set to match the dancing and the synchronization adjusted when the camera moved to someone besides the dancer. At one point in the score there was a notation 'repeat over and over' and 'change tempo according to action' which was simply baffling. All the conductors who used the Riesenfeld score must have had the same challenges because of the lack of precision in the piano conductor score.

7. I had to cut the orchestra off, tell them where to begin again and then hope I could still remain in synch. The projectionist did, however, go down on his knees by way of apology at the end and offered me a chocolate bar.

8. The VAI video shown in Newcastle at the Carmen Conference was made from a restored version of the film from the George Eastman House in Rochester, NY which has the DeMille Collection; the tinting and toning was done to specifications found in DeMille's hand.

9. Cecil B. DeMille, *Carmen* (1915). Video Artists International 69222. The orchestra was recorded first. Then the singers sang to the prerecorded orchestral part. It was the only time that I was able to sit back and actually watch the movie and listen to the music being recorded.

10. A reviewer of the video called me before publishing his review because he was upset by the vocal music. He was sure that it was not authentic and had a very clear (but erroneous) idea of what a silent film accompaniment should sound like (and it shouldn't have singing!). I pointed him to the evidence of the New York showings, and to many other examples of silent film scores with occasional appearances by vocalists (*Way Down East* and *Intolerance* to name just two).

11. Normally, although only an hour long, *Carmen* appeared as the only item on a programme. In 2000 in a series of performances with the Het Residentie Orkest in the Netherlands, *Carmen* was put on a programme consisting of Cavalcanti's *La p'tite Lili* accompanied by Darius Milhaud's score, and a fifteen minute opera buffa by Raymund van Santen, *Moi, J'aime mon marie*.

References

Boston Post. 1915. 'Farrar Has Movie Debut. Famous Singer Greeted With Wild Applause as She Sees First Presentation of *Carmen* on the Screen' (2 October): 1 & 4.

DeMille, Agnes. 1952. *Dance to the Piper.* Boston: Little, Brown and Co..

DeMille, William C.. 1939. *Hollywood Saga.* New York: E. P. Dutton & Co..

Downes, Olin. 1915. 'Boston Sees Miss Farrar as "Carmen" in Moving Pictures' in *Musical America* (9 October): 4.

E.V.. 1916. 'The Fourteenth Week at the Metropolitan, A Farrar Movie Thriller' in *International Music and Drama* (26 February): 3-5.

Hendricks, Gordon. 1972. *Origins of the American Film.* New York: Arno Press and the *New York Times.*

Lasky, Jesse L. and Weldon, Don. 1957. *I Blow My Own Horn.* Garden City, NY: Doubleday and Co..

The Music Lover. 1915. [Unattributed interview with Geraldine Farrar] (May): 12.

Nash, Elizabeth. 1981. *Always First Class. The Career of Geraldine Farrar.* Washington, DC: University Press of America.

New York Sun. 1915. 'Farrar a Tiger as Screen Carmen—Gypsy Girl is a Slugger' (1 November): 7.

Carmen and Early Cinema: The Case of Jacques Feyder (1926)

Winifred Woodhull

How, in the context of early twentieth-century Europe, does *Carmen* take on meanings that are distinct from those that prevailed in Mérimée's time or in Bizet's? How does *Carmen* engage with social contradictions that have been central to modern life since the early nineteenth century, but that have greater or lesser significance at particular historical junctures in the century that follows? These are the main questions the chapter addresses in considering Jacques Feyder's *Carmen* (1926), a silent film that is based principally on the Mérimée novella, but that necessarily takes account of Bizet's opera as well, since the latter work was much better known to the mass audience that was targeted by the film's producers at Aubert Studios. The chapter will show how a historically-grounded analysis of Feyder's movie can illuminate the aesthetics, politics, and economics of French filmmaking in the first decades of the twentieth century, and how this particular film handles the tensions between commercial cinema and art cinema and, more broadly, between popular and elite cultural forms. Finally, the author suggests that Feyder's *Carmen* engages viewers in the pleasurable exploration of psychic, sensuous, and social experiences that could help them to imagine new and better worlds.

Feyder, Jacques: *Carmen*
National identity (French)
Gender and nation
Gender and space
Subjectivity

In the wake of World War One, disillusioned Europeans were hard-pressed to extol the virtues of their supposedly superior civilization, since technical rationality, put in the service of nationalist aggression, had wrought unprecedented destruction and had decimated the male population in many countries. In fact, the Great War inspired grave doubt as to whether the West could even consider itself to be civilized. Yet at the same time Europeans felt a greater need than ever to convince themselves of their own worth and to exercise their power in arenas that remained open to them, notably in their colonies. At the cultural level, this tension was strikingly conveyed in many popular novels and films that fostered escapist fantasies of travel to strange and beautiful lands, where readers and viewers could vicariously experience the adventure and unconventional love affairs that went with the imaginary territory.

A key film genre of the period was colonial cinema, whose prototype, Jacques Feyder's *L'Atlantide* (1921), enjoyed enormous success at the box office while also setting a new standard for French filmmaking by featuring breathtaking landscapes shot on location on the edge of the Sahara. Feyder's *Carmen* (1926) resembled colonial films insofar as its action unfolds in a place that was 'exotic' in the eyes of the French, and the primitiveness attributed to Spain enabled French audiences to see their own society as quite civilized by comparison. Yet as we shall see, Spain occupied an especially complex place in the French cultural imaginary in the early twentieth century. Since Spain was a rival European colonial power (notably in Morocco) as well as a 'backward', picturesque tourist destination—one that shared a long national border and a certain cultural history with France—its ambiguous cinematic representation registered even more ambivalence than representations of the colonies in films of the 1920s.

Feyder's *Carmen* is one of many early films based on Prosper Mérimée's novella or on the Meilhac-Halévy libretto of Georges Bizet's opera. A striking feature of the film is that Feyder did not intend it to be accompanied by Bizet's music, although there were plenty of precedents for film/opera productions by the time his version of *Carmen* was released in 1926, including feature-length films of actual staged operas. There were also many silent films based on libretti that presented opera narratives in abbreviated form, accompanied by singers and orchestra, as well as silent musicals whose narratives were contrived in such a way as to feature performances by opera singers, which could be accompanied by live or recorded singing and music. In the United States, there was a period when Vitaphone made a large number of shorts featuring opera stars singing popular arias (the 'Flower Song' from *Carmen* being a favourite), which were shown along with feature films in major theatres (Fawkes 2000: 1-55). And finally, there was Cecil B. DeMille's film, *Carmen*, adapted from the Meilhac-Halévy libretto and starring Geraldine Farrar—the most acclaimed opera singer to appear on film in her day—which had its début in 1915 at Symphony Hall in Boston (see Gillian Anderson's essay in this volume).

The most obvious explanation for Feyder's decision to make a film without operatic musical accompaniment is that he based his film principally on Mérimée's novella rather than on the opera, following the already established tradition of putting literary classics on the screen. I want to suggest, however, that it is precisely his choice to attend carefully to Mérimée's text that makes his film resonate so effectively with Bizet's music, which, as Susan McClary has compellingly argued, is much more complex than the Meilhac-Halévy libretto in its figuration of Carmen. According to McClary (1992: 44-110), the weave of musical discourses in Bizet's opera often moves outside the narrow frame of the Meilhac-Halévy narrative and works against it in socially significant ways. Likewise, Feyder's visual rendering of Mérimée's poetics is frequently at odds with the author's narrative, which the film adopts in abbreviated form. His *Carmen* makes clear that he wanted to experiment with 'art cinema', that is, to explore the potential of cinema's visual rhetorics, much as Bizet explored existing musical rhetorics (both operatic and popular) and developed new ones, not just as an aesthetic exercise, but as a way of engaging with current debates about modern life. Both Feyder and Bizet expanded the range of their respective artistic practices while at the same time satisfying the demands of the commercial projects in which they were involved.

Elements that mark Feyder's *Carmen* as commercial fare include the producers' decision to place an 'authentic', internationally-famous Spanish actress, Raquel Meller, in the title role and to have her perform in a way that would allow French audiences to 'recognize' her as a Spanish Gypsy according to the French (but also international European) acting codes of the time. As we shall see later, these elements also include adherence to narrative conventions of 1920s film melodrama. However commercial it may be, though, Feyder's *Carmen* bears witness to the lively and eclectic film culture from which it emerged, one that spawned, for instance, not only experimentation with technique, but also astonishing fluidity with respect to film genres and the social situations in which cinematic 'experimentation' played a part.

Experimentation and generic fluidity were by no means limited to 'art cinema' in the mid-1920s. For example, a well-known contemporary and collaborator of Feyder's, Jean Grémillon, produced an amazing variety of short films—industrial, scientific, documentary, and art films—that used similar techniques and challenged generic boundaries.[1] In 1926, the same year that Feyder's *Carmen* was released by Aubert Studios, Grémillon made a documentary on Italian immigrant workers (*La Vie des travailleurs italiens en France*), a project that indicates a need to expand and refine the long-established notion that Carmen embodies principally Gypsies and Jews as figures of France's internal 'others'. For in the early twentieth century, the range of 'foreigners' within had grown to include labourers and students from Southern Europe, the Caribbean, North Africa, and Indochina (the most famous immigrant of the time being a revolutionary who would later be known as Ho Chi Minh).

Grémillon's varied career in this period gives an idea of the dynamic context in which Feyder was working when he directed *Carmen*. It also casts light on Feyder's move to incorporate location shooting as well as innovative cinematography and *mise en scène* into commercial melodrama that capitalized on French interwar audiences' thirst for vicarious adventure in 'exotic' lands.

To be sure, Lazare Meerson's sets evoke the picturesque Spain that French audiences undoubtedly expected. But at certain moments, elements of the setting take on a life of their own, for instance when the immense wrought-iron gate of a Seville residence fills the frame, its graphic beauty commanding more attention than José's grudging replies to Carmen's teasing as she enters the house in order to sing, dance, and otherwise entertain José's commanding officer and his guests. In an analogous instance of innovative-filmmaking-on-display, Meerson uses a 'typical' narrow street in Seville as the setting for José's first submission to Carmen after the fight in the tobacco factory. In this street, Carmen's ties to the local community are thrown into relief as she runs to escape the soldiers who are escorting her to jail: the market women immediately take to the street to join Carmen in fending off her pursuers by throwing fruit and vegetables at them. However, as remarkable as the picturesque setting and the spunky resistance of Carmen's local female community may be, the camera work in this sequence does the most to capture viewers' attention. A long take registers Carmen's descent with José along the narrow street and her subsequent flight. This shot, which is unusual in 1926, establishes a parallel between José and the viewers, inasmuch as both hero and viewers are taken in at the same time, José by Carmen, and the viewers by the camera's entrancing 'take' on the scene of seduction. As these examples suggest, then, Feyder was working in concert with other filmmakers of the 1920s, such as Grémillon, in exploring cinema's potential as an artistic medium and a vehicle for social critique.

Like most film versions of *Carmen*, Feyder's follows the opera libretto in eliminating Mérimée's narrator, a character in the novella who, like José, is smitten by Carmen and sees her as a fascinating yet dangerous force. In Feyder, there are moments where an omniscient narrator comments on the action in intertitles, but for the most part the drama unfolds without direct intervention by the narrator. Among Carmen films, the notable exception regarding the handling of the narration is an early German version, Ernst Lubitsch's *Carmen* (1917) (also known as *Gypsy Blood*, and sub-titled 'A Love Tale of Old

Spain'), in which the narrator is a male Gypsy relating 'the tale of a man bewitched' to two other male Gypsies as they sit by a campfire at night. The opening titles in the frame narrative present the quintessentially European story that is about to unfold as authentic Gypsy lore, presumably in order to enhance the film's exotic appeal: 'From Gypsy lips... Gypsy love... from the days of yore'. I mention Lubitsch's handling of the narration because it makes explicit a key feature of the novella, the opera, and most film versions of *Carmen*, namely that *Carmen* is primarily a man's story, in almost every sense of the term: it is told by a man to other men, and deals with 'a man bewitched'. The Gypsy, Carmen, is the main problem in the story, but the story is not hers. Instead, it is mainly about her effect on José and other men.

Apart from the issue of the narrator, Feyder stays close to Mérimée's text in constructing his film narrative, in incorporating many lines from the novella into the dialogue displayed on intertitles, and in his visual rendering of the poetics of *Carmen*. He begins with an evocation of the murder committed by don José in Navarre, which prompts the hero's flight to Castile and launches the series of events that will lead to his obsession with Carmen and her death by his hand. Feyder does not depict the Navarre murder itself, but his technique of filming José in extreme long shot, running from the scene of the crime, establishes from the outset the social isolation that results from the hero's violent act. In confessing his crime to his mother, José does not mince words; he says, 'je l'ai tué' (I killed him). Feyder follows Mérimée, then, in presenting José as an outlaw from the time he leaves his native Navarre, rather than as an innocent whose purity is sullied only under Carmen's evil influence. This is important because it shows that José himself is responsible for his initial transgression, and it suggests that we should attend to the matter of his responsibility in future cases of criminal behaviour, rather than accepting the course of his life as being determined by a fatal attraction for which Carmen is implicitly to blame.

More important, at certain moments, Feyder, like Mérimée, grants Carmen an independent, vibrant, and appealing subjectivity, even if he follows the writer in openly condemning it in commentaries by José (and by his own omniscient narrator), and in attempting to control it at nearly every turn. Let's look first at the attempts at control, and then turn to the figurations of Carmen as a subject in her own right. The most obvious inscriptions of control occur in two scenes that are almost identically staged and shot, in which Carmen is brutalized first by her husband, García, and later by José. Naturally, these scenes are meant to underline the 'barbarity' of Gypsy life and to illustrate José's downfall, but they simultaneously do the ideological work of violently subduing a female protagonist who threatens male dominance in more 'civilized' societies. The principal cinematic means of constraining Carmen's subjectivity, however, is more subtle: sometimes deliberately, but often unwittingly (as in Mérimée), the film presents Carmen's subjectivity through José's conscious or unconscious experience of it, which usually results in reducing it to a blind force whose primary significance is that it resists the hero's will or eludes his understanding.

Key examples in Feyder's *Carmen* involve three parallel sequences in which a literally wounded José appears in a reclining pose, gazing up at an interlocutor standing near him, with a look of supplication on his face. In the first instance, he is looking at Dancaire; in the second and third, he is looking at Carmen. With respect to the first, José has just killed García, and Dancaire has indicated that García's death, as well as José's physical and emotional suffering were needless, since García would have gladly sold Carmen to him 'for a piaster' if he had only asked him. In this case, José's pain stems simultaneously from the dagger wound inflicted by García, his remorse over killing Carmen's husband out of jealousy, and above all his bewildered reaction to Dancaire's remark. Dancaire has certainly meant to suggest that José has killed needlessly for a woman whom he could have had for the asking: in her husband's eyes, she was worth so little that he would have gladly exchanged her for a paltry sum of money, in the same way that he would have sold a prostitute's services to another man. From José's perspective, on the contrary, he has righteously killed a cheat and a scoundrel who did not recognize in Carmen the treasure that José sees in her, a priceless object that he wants for his own. Either way, the male characters do not consider the implications of Dancaire's remark for Carmen as a potential object of exchange; they consider only García's venality, José's naïveté, and the question of Carmen's worth, which has been raised by José's murder of García. Has he not just killed García, Carmen's rightful owner, so to speak, in order to secure his own exclusive possession of her, using the quarrel over a card game as a pretext for murder?

More troubling than the male characters' blind spot here, however, is that it is not identified or reflected upon as such either in Mérimée's text or Feyder's film. There is no evidence of any conscious awareness of a problem in their outlook or in a social system based on the exchange of women (except in the 'uncivilized' form it is shown to take in Gypsy society, where all women are treated as chattel). In its supposedly civilized form in European society, this social system passes without comment: some women are chattel (the 'bad' women whom men believe themselves to be justified in selling to one another), while others are traded by men of 'honour' (the 'good' women who are supposedly exchanged with a view toward ensuring that they be loved and protected). The weighty implication of Dancaire's offhand remark about García's willingness to sell Carmen to José—namely that prostitutes and wives occupy structurally similar positions under current social arrangements in the 'civilized' world— are lost on writer and filmmaker alike. Both Mérimée and Feyder tend to ignore the consequences of the prevailing social arrangements for Carmen, and focus instead on José's suffering, at once underscoring its debilitating effects on the hero and inviting sympathetic meditation upon its meaning. Is it the result of an inescapable fate? Or is it instead a shameful moral weakness that José should have managed to overcome, but that is nonetheless quite understandable?

In the replay of the scene in which José is reclining on the ground, physically wounded and emotionally pained, the hero is talking with Carmen herself. He is looking up at her as she asks him anxiously, referring to García, 'Tu l'as tué?' (Did you kill him?). In addition to recalling José's earlier confession to having killed his Navarre countryman ('Je l'ai tué'), Carmen's question, together with the physical distance between the lovers as they are positioned in the frame, points to the emotional chasm that has been opening between them for some time. Her question also signals José's active part in producing the lovers' supposedly fatal circumstances. Yet Carmen's subjective presence and symbolic effectiveness are severely undercut by Feyder's visual rendering of the scene's dynamics. Feyder's *mise en scène* provides José with the alibi that he is a *victim* of circumstance: his helplessness, suffering, and martyrdom crystallize in his pose as a reclining, wounded figure dominated by Carmen and by the eye of the camera.

In the third sequence modeled on this pattern, José is reclining in an interior space, looking up at Carmen. Intertitles have informed spectators that Carmen has found a safe hiding place for him in a small village, where she is taking care of him 'avec adresse et constance' (skillfully and faithfully). At this juncture, José begs Carmen to go away with him to live elsewhere, his fantasy of another life being figured visually by a series of subjective shots of landscapes superimposed onto one another. Carmen refuses to go away with José, knowing that flight would put him in jeopardy because of the wanted poster she has seen at the nearby police station, which calls for the arrest of 'José Lizzarrabengoa, assassin, rebelle, et déserteur' (murderer, rebel, and deserter). We know that Carmen was dismayed when she first saw the poster because, after it is shown in close-up from her point of view, there is a reaction shot of Carmen recoiling in horror. Carmen's memory of this poster in the scene with José is conveyed in a subjective shot that stands, formally, in symmetrical relation to the subjective shots presented a moment before evoking José's dreams of escape. Both protagonists, then, are granted independent subjectivities that are clearly evoked in tandem by the same cinematic means.

At isolated moments such as this one, Feyder's film offers a view of Carmen as a subject in her own right, an equal of José in this regard. However, it quickly reverts to presenting Carmen only in terms of her effects on José. In this sequence, since José knows nothing of the wanted poster that signals his extreme vulnerability to capture, and further, knows nothing of Carmen's empathic emotional reaction to it, he imagines that Carmen refuses to leave with him because of a lover and for no other reason. The spectator is inclined to share José's view, not only because, barring some exceptions, the entire film concentrates on José's experience, but because the plot line has recently had Carmen meet Lucas, the swaggering toreador, in the street. Even though Lucas has behaved boorishly and has failed to impress Carmen, we suspect that he will become her next lover. My main point here is that in addition to inciting the spectator to share José's mistrust of Carmen, the narrative virtually obliterates Carmen's concern for José, which was quite apparent just moments before. In other words, the film narrative threatens to efface the nuances of Feyder's cinematography and *mise en scène*, just as, in the opera, the Meilhac-Halévy libretto narrative strives to tame and contain Bizet's score.

These nuances are the key to understanding the significance of the figurations of Carmen's subjectivity in various media and at various historical junctures. In spite of the film narrative's preoccupation with José and his torments, Feyder's film text, like the text of Mérimée's novella, provides meaningful inscriptions of Carmen's subjectivity. At several junctures Carmen has the opportunity of enacting and defending her 'freedom', insisting that her life and her sexuality are her own. The female protagonist never sacrifices herself to others, as the prevailing ideology of domesticity requires that women do. And of course Carmen asserts her liberty by moving at will from one lover to another. At the same time, she shares her enthusiasm for life and the rewards of her cunning with others: she cooperates with other Gypsies, helps them in their 'affairs of Egypt', and conceives many clever schemes on her own, from which they benefit. In addition, she breathes life into José, drawing him into an engagement with life in Seville that goes beyond policing the underclass. Carmen also nurses him when he is hurt, offers him reassurances when she herself is plagued by doubt, and provides the energy (which is almost completely lacking in our long-suffering hero) that drives the plot forward. All of these qualities help to account for the protagonist's appeal to so many readers, listeners, and spectators of *Carmen*, including many women.

One of the most powerful sequences in Feyder's film—one that sympathetically affirms Carmen's desire and agency—concerns the meeting between José and Carmen after José has been released from his first stint in prison. Shot on location in Spain and offering gorgeous views of the rugged Andalusian landscape, the sequence evokes the sense of adventure, pleasure, and danger associated with colonial cinema. It comes towards the beginning of the film at a point where, if one can believe the film script, Feyder intended to depict Carmen as José saw her when he was blinded by love. In it, we see the two lovers seated on the ramparts of the city of Seville. They appear in profile in a two-shot, symmetrically positioned in the frame, with an enormous bag of fruit between them. They are looking into each other's eyes and smiling, and we see that they are in love. Moreover, the rendering of the actions that follow offers a fleeting glimpse of a relationship characterized by harmony, equality, and reciprocity, one that the narrative never considers as a possibility and that, alas, quickly evaporates. Carmen reaches into the bag José is holding and begins eating a piece of fruit. José then reciprocates by pouring the fruit from the bag into a basket that Carmen is holding in her lap.

In his passion to possess her, though, José grabs Carmen's arms, upsetting the balance of things (as well as the symmetrical composition of the shot). In one stroke, he causes the fruit to fall over the wall on which the lovers are sitting and alters the mood of the scene from one of mutual sensuous enjoyment to one of sadness and strange foreboding. Next, in an extreme long shot taken from the surrounding countryside, we see the high wall on which they are seated and the enormous space below them, as if José and Carmen were teetering on the edge of the world. Their precarious position on the city walls marks their social marginality, the excitement and risk of their unconventional liaison, the wide-open spaces of possibility that seem to be open to them, as well as the threat of a huge void that could well engulf them.

The two regain their emotional equilibrium momentarily, but very soon are faced with the need to part, as José insists that he must return to the barracks. As the lovers walk off in opposition directions, we get a subjective long shot of Carmen's view of the plains below and the houses in the distance, their visibility fading in the evening light. It is at this moment, when the camera has just sympathetically registered Carmen's subjectivity, that the narrative abruptly intervenes in order to divert our attention from Carmen and redirect it towards José. A title reads, 'But what is love without folly?' Yet for a few moments longer, the images projected tell a different story from the one related in the titles. There is a cut to a shot of José turning around, eagerly yet tenderly joining Carmen, to her delight. Again, Feyder's visual rhetoric powerfully evokes the reciprocity between the two young people. As José walks towards Carmen, indicating his desire and willingness to stay with her as she has asked him to do, the long plume of his helmet is blowing in the wind, calling to mind a woman's hair or Carmen's fringed shawl.

At this stage, there is no visual indication that José has succumbed to the charms of a devil woman; on the contrary, he seems to have expanded and refined his means of interacting with a desiring and desirable person, of tuning in to her reality and responding to it meaningfully. Even José's sexual ambiguity at this moment poses no threat. When the sensuous, decorative plume of his helmet all but eclipses the headgear's martial aspect as an emblem of masculine authority, force, and duty, the effect is touching and beautiful. This is true despite the fact that the film script (which differs from the film in many basic respects) indicates that, at this point, José is seeing Carmen through his distorting fantasies of love rather than 'sous son vrai jour' (as she really is).[2] In other words, Feyder's visual poetics offers no indication that we are to adopt a sceptical view of José's perception and action in this sequence.

Not until the lovers leave the liminal space of the ramparts and descend into town do things start to 'look bad'. That is, chiaroscuro lighting, characteristic of the German expressionists and already familiar to French movie audiences, replaces the soft light of evening as the lovers move through the streets of Seville, their dark shadows cast on the brightly lit walls of the whitewashed buildings. José, the loving man in the plumed helmet before whom the whole world seemed to be opening a moment ago, now appears doomed to unhappiness and disgrace, thanks to the effect of the lighting. The eerie shadow cast by his body registers his subjective alienation (blind love versus duty) and the dark destiny that awaits him. Following a medium shot of barred windows in the street where Carmen and José are walking (on their way to Carmen's place for a tryst that is chastely elided from the film narrative) is a close up shot of the single barred window of the dark jail cell where José is confined as a result of disobeying orders and spending the night with Carmen. At this moment, Carmen appears to mean, and indeed to be, nothing more than the cause of José's downfall.

In Mérimée's novella and Feyder's film, Carmen is most clearly affirmed as a subject in her own right at the end of the narrative, as she is about to be killed by José. As we have seen, the narrative focuses mainly on José's experience of Carmen, his suffering, and his conviction that she has betrayed him. For him, her betrayal consists in refusing to stay with him on his terms. But it is important to recognize that neither Feyder's film nor Mérimée's novella has Carmen leave José for other men who may then possess her as José wrongly imagines he has done or could have done. She enters into relationships with other men for her own pleasure, and when she finally tells José that she no longer loves him and will never live with him, it is emphatically *not* because she has transferred her affections to the toreador, Lucas, as the Meilhac-Halévy libretto would have it.

By the time Carmen definitively rejects José, Lucas has been wounded, perhaps mortally. When Carmen later refuses to go to America with José after the two have left the bullring in Cordoba and headed for the hills, José thinks it is because of Lucas. But he is wrong, and Mérimée's text is absolutely clear on this point, as is Feyder's film. Carmen protests that she does not want to hurt José's feelings, but that everything is over between them. José then asks, 'Tu aimes donc Lucas?' (You love Lucas, do you?), to which she replies, 'Oui, *je l'ai aimé*, comme toi, un instant, moins que toi peut-être. A présent, je n'aime plus rien, et je me hais pour t'avoir aimé' (Yes, I *loved* him for a moment, as I loved you, maybe less than I loved you. Now I no longer love anything, and I hate myself for having loved you) (Mérimée 1930: 72; my emphasis and translation). At this stage, her love for Lucas is a thing of the past: the verb is in the *passé composé*. Feyder's film incorporates these lines of dialogue and drives home Carmen's declaration of independence from José by having her face the camera directly (facing away from José) when she speaks these words, to which José responds vengefully by drawing his dagger. So when Carmen insists on her freedom in the last lines of the film (and the novella), she is defending her right to choose to be with a man *or not*, to live and love as she pleases. After all, what sort of freedom would she have if it were defined exclusively in terms having the male partner of her choice, provided that she always be attached to a man? What sort of freedom rules out the possibility of a life that does not actually require a man's so-called protection, if one is a woman?

Yet it is precisely this travesty of freedom that is upheld in the opera narrative and in the myriad film narratives based on the opera. The Meilhac-Halévy libretto has Carmen affirm her love for Lucas in the present tense: 'Oui, je l'aime' (Yes, I love him). Hence the undue emphasis, in film narratives based on the libretto, such as those of DeMille and Lubitsch, on love triangles and betrayal, that is, on the meaning for José of Carmen's sexual relationships, rather than on their meaning for Carmen herself. For Carmen, by contrast, her sexual relationships mean independence, energy, material gain, and influence over the course of events; they mean an experience of sexuality that is for a woman's pleasure, rather than one that is subordinated to men's pleasure or to the supposed inevitability (and the duty) of childbearing for another. These things go a long way towards explaining Carmen's appeal in a bourgeois society that is fraught with ambivalence, not just about its 'others', but about itself—its possessive individualism, as well as its pervasive sense of the individual's impotence to make a significant mark in the world; the growing fragmentation and anonymity of a modern society organized by capitalist modes of exchange and exploitation, and the pound of flesh that modernity exacts in the name of Enlightenment, progress, and profits (Seigel, 1986).

Yet however much Carmen may embody a promise of freedom from the constraints of bourgeois modernity, she induces anxiety and even horror, as we see clearly in the Meilhac-Halévy libretto as well as in many films. DeMille and Lubitsch, for example, portray Carmen mainly as the 'demon' that José comes to see in her, a monster given to facial expressions and body movements that are excessive and grotesque even by the standards of early film melodrama. And in DeMille's *Carmen*, the vamp becomes a veritable vampire when Geraldine Farrar, looking directly at the still camera, fiendishly and

lasciviously licks the blood that spatters her face and mouth when José
murders his officer in a jealous rage. By contrast, in Mérimée and
Feyder, Carmen is unruly, impulsive, and vulgar (that is, low-born),
but scarcely monstrous. Both writer and filmmaker 'generously' allow
her a good measure of humanity and even a degree of grandeur when
she stakes her radical claim to freedom at the end. However
'Gypsified' they may be in this context, the heroine's words, 'Carmen
sera toujours libre' (Carmen will always be free), echo the
proclamation of the inalienable rights of woman by Olympe de
Gouges and other feminists in the wake of the French Revolution, as
well as recalling the rebellions of the French working classes
throughout the nineteenth century.

Regarding Feyder's task of working out a conclusion to *Carmen*
in interwar France, we can say that the filmmaker is faithful to
Mérimée in so far as he sustains the focus on José to the very end,
while also granting Carmen considerable weight and dignity in the
final scenes. Feyder brilliantly conveys José's remorse over the
murder of Carmen by means of a medium shot of the hero, on his
knees, stabbing his lover and then leaning back on his heels,
contemplating the horror of what he has done. On this shot he
superimposes a close-up of José in tears, thus providing a last visual
doubling of the hero to mark his alienation and the intensity of his
suffering. The tragedy of the scene is enhanced by its contrast with the
beautiful woodland setting and the soft daylight filtering through the
trees.

Feyder ends the film in a sentimental way that cannot fail to
astonish today's viewers. José dismounts from his horse in front of the
police station in Ronda, where he will surrender and accept the
consequences of his acts. The camera focuses our attention
momentarily on the horse's elaborate braided bridle, thus giving
spectators a final dose of local colour. Feyder then cuts to a two-shot
of José, now standing, and his horse. Here, the steed seems to serve as
an emotional substitute for Carmen, the passionate bond between José
and his mount being conveyed through caresses and the hero's visible
anxiety in the face of impending loss. A policeman then enters the
frame, tellingly positioning José between a representative of law and
order and an object of deep affection. In a last burst of emotion, José
kisses his horse goodbye before entering the police station. The film
then ends with a blackout. Since there is no humour or irony in the
treatment of José at previous points in the film, it is reasonable to
suppose that this ending is meant to be touching, and that it simply

conforms to the sentimental narrative conventions of early film melodrama, however campy it may be in the eyes of today's spectators. In any case, regarding the conclusion to Feyder's film, it is important to recognize that, despite its attention to José, it treats Carmen's last moments of life, as well as her death, with appropriate solemnity and respect. For example, by presenting an extreme close-up of Carmen's hands, folded calmly in her lap after she has tossed José's ring away, it underlines Carmen's reasoned determination in choosing freedom over a life of subjection. In his handling of this moment in the narrative, Feyder does not follow the example of other filmmakers who use Carmen's gesture of rejection (tossing away the ring which, we know from Mérimée, was bought from a Jewish merchant) as a pretext to emphasize her profound 'otherness' and utter intractability, thereby inviting sympathy for José as he stabs her. Also, after the stabbing and the superimposed images of José the murderer/José the remorseful lover, Feyder cuts to a long shot of Carmen's body lying motionless on the ground in the soft daylight, her hand on her heart. Two things are remarkable about this shot sequence. First, quite simply, Carmen's pose emphasizes that she does have a heart and thus is not the unfeeling demon that José has at times made her out to be. Second, the long shot of the dead heroine, which is at a ninety-degree angle from José's point of view, grants Carmen's body, and her life, a discrete existence, distinguishing them from José's body, life, consciousness, and angle of vision. The importance of this representation of Carmen is in no way diminished by its being posthumous, for as we have seen, there were other moments during Carmen's life when Feyder sympathetically acknowledged her separate existence in his visual renderings. If anything, this last figuration of Carmen is even more significant than comparable earlier ones because here, at the end of the film, the abrupt shift in the camera angle and the distance from the object of vision open a space of interpretation for spectators, who are implicitly enjoined to reinvent both their vision of the character and their understanding of *Carmen*.

I believe that Feyder's *Carmen* engages, wittingly or unwittingly, with a central feature of interwar French society that involved passionate debates in many arenas—from the National Assembly to the university and the mass media—about women's roles, the figure of the 'new woman', and the legacy of French women's widespread participation in public life during World War One. Moreover, Feyder's film reflects the dynamic analyzed by Mary Louise Roberts (1994), who argues convincingly that in interwar

France, many of the key issues of the day concerning class relations, the nature of national identity, and the future of the country were embedded in public debates about gender. In other words, according to Roberts, discussions of gender were not concerned solely with questions of 'women's place', but engaged the entire range of social and political questions facing France in that period. Feyder's *Carmen* takes on the fundamental questions of women's independence, subjectivity, and social agency, and as we shall see in the discussion that follows, it explores these questions in relation to French national identity.

Susan McClary has argued (1992: 29-61) that the character Carmen as well as the musical codes of Bizet's opera convey real or feared challenges to bourgeois dominance emanating from women, Jews, the 'dangerous classes' in France, and colonized peoples throughout the nineteenth century, notably in 1830 with the collapse of the July Monarchy (which coincides with the conquest of Algeria), in the Revolution of 1848, and in the Paris Commune of 1870-1871. I want to extend McClary's analysis by pointing out that in the first years of the Third Republic two new worries materialized on the sexual-political front, namely the blurring of visible class distinctions as a result of the mass production of inexpensive clothing modelled on the fashions of the élite, and the perceived threat to the sexual hierarchy by working women who were gaining economic independence as well as social respectability. These worries, which lingered well into the twentieth century, are crystallized in the figure of Carmen. Her much remarked on ability to move effortlessly from one social milieu to another, if not exactly to 'pass' as a lady, takes on new meaning in French consumer society, since she evokes the unstable social categories of the late nineteenth and early twentieth centuries, as well as attendant worries about the shift from an economy of production to one of consumption, and anxiety about the moral and political implications of this shift.

McClary's witty and insightful analysis of Carmen's fluid musical characterization in Bizet captures key aspects of the threat she embodies. Carmen 'slips unpredictably from the "exotic dance" of cabaret entertainment to high opera, throwing cultural boundaries of class, race and sexual propriety into confusion at a time when those boundaries were felt to be under siege' (McClary 1992: 57). Although Carmen sometimes speaks/sings privately in an earnest, unmarked fashion, McClary argues that

> her public persona is semiotically promiscuous: she sings 'Gypsy' music, but
> always in such a way that she might be understood as simply performing
> cabaret numbers (which Bizet actually gives generic names: 'Habanera' and
> 'Seguidilla' rather than expressing herself; she can converse fluently in José's
> musical tongue and seduces him in the 'Seguidilla' by dictating to him in his
> own histrionic style the terms of his passion; she sings duets with Escamillo;
> she banters with her fellow-smugglers. Like Mérimée's Carmen and the
> 'alien–at-home', Bizet's heroine has mastered the languages of those around
> her and can slip easily in and out of them without revealing 'herself'. (57)

Carmen is a threat, in short, because she blurs key boundaries within
metropolitan French society as well as crucial distinctions, established
through colonial domination, between the French and their cultural
'others'. Yet Carmen embodies more than a potentially revolutionary
threat coming from 'below', that is, the 'lower classes', showgirls, and
'aliens-at-home' such as Gypsies and Jews. Likewise, she incarnates
more than a threat arising from 'outside', notably from colonized
peoples whose 'alien' character seems to have prompted Camille
DuLocle, director of the Opéra-Comique when *Carmen* opened there,
to describe Bizet's music as 'cochin-chinoise' (as if from Cochin-
China; i.e. oriental) (Gaudier 1922: 32), and whose ongoing resistance
to French rule is registered in the Moroccan Rif War of the early
1920s (a conflict that coincides with the filming of Feyder's *Carmen*).
For in the new consumer society of late nineteenth- and early
twentieth-century France, Carmen also embodies a threat emerging
from within the bourgeoisie itself, namely the anxiety generated by the
new bourgeois ethic of consuming, not only as a means of increasing
national wealth and power, but as a source of personal pleasure. This
ethic will uneasily coexist for at least a century with the earlier
bourgeois ethic (zealously imposed on working-class people in
particular) of sacrificing pleasure, or at least delaying gratification in
the name of productive labour and 'morality'. In her aspect as a
pleasure-seeking modern woman who gives pride of place to personal
satisfaction, Carmen is a disturbing figure indeed.

The ambiguous social stakes of consumerism, individualism,
and 'new womanhood' find expression in Feyder's *Carmen* in a way
that is typical of many early French films: the star, Raquel Meller,
plays a Gypsy who wears dresses by Jeanne Lanvin, which are of
course identified as such in the credits and are advertised and modeled
in the film itself. Such tie-ins blur the line between culture and
commerce, as does the film medium itself, insofar as it is an
industrially-produced popular cultural form geared mainly towards
mass audiences. The peddling of designer gowns in commercial films

also blurs the lines between social classes insofar as it encourages 'low-end' spectators/consumers to see themselves as having the opportunity of fashioning a 'self' that suits them, of acceding to a higher social position, and of paving the way for their ascent of the social ladder by achieving the 'look' of a higher position through the purchase of cheap imitations of luxury commodities (Berry 2001). Yet however much the fashions modelled by Meller and other stars may spark spectators' desires and social ambitions, they hardly cause the prevailing hierarchies of class, gender, and ethnicity to melt away. In fact, these hierarchies figure prominently in Feyder's *Carmen* (the 'civilized' army officers versus the enlisted men and the Andalusian riff-raff) as well as in contemporary colonial films such as Feyder's *L'Atlantide* (*Lost Atlantis*, 1921) and Henri Fescourt's *La Maison du Maltais* (a.k.a. *Sirocco*, 1927).

Set in Sfax, Tunisia, Fescourt's film features Tina Meller, Raquel Meller's sister, in the starring role of the Bedouin belly dancer, Safia. Having temporarily escaped from Sfax and been incorporated into the Parisian bourgeoisie, Safia ultimately returns to her 'rightful' place in Tunisia, where she is subjected anew to the authority of European colonial power, figured by the titular house of the Maltese. Granted, Safia's class status improves by virtue of her marriage to the mixed-race son of the Maltese (his mother was a 'Bedouin'). Moreover, the union in matrimony symbolically mediates the colonial racial/ethnic divide as well. However, the marriage makes the gender hierarchy appear natural and legitimate at the same that it sanctifies the 'love' obscuring the persistent (albeit more permeable) barriers of class and ethnicity. Intractable social hierarchies figure as well in sound remakes of these films in the 1930s and early 1940s, such as G. W. Pabst's 1932 *L'Atlantide*, Pierre Chenal's 1938 *La Maison du Maltais* (1938) and Christian-Jaque's *Carmen* (1942). In the latter two films, Safia and Carmen, both played by Viviane Romance, are plagued by possessive men who feel that 'their' women have taken everything from them; both women understand that their lovers threaten them with a form of imprisonment that Carmen terms 'l'amour forcé à perpétuité' (a life sentence of forced love). Yet despite their keen awareness of the problems with prevailing gender arrangements, which are overdetermined by relations of class and ethnicity, neither Chenal's Safia nor Christian-Jaque's Carmen makes any headway on the sexual liberation front: Safia ultimately accepts domestication, while Carmen, who rejects domesticity, is nonetheless shown cooking meals over a campfire for the hungry troops in the Gypsy band.

The premium placed on national identity in early-twentieth-century France had the dual function of symbolically uniting the French against colonized 'others' while simultaneously encouraging the transcendence of potentially divisive regional identifications and loyalties. The gradual transformation of 'peasants into Frenchmen', as Weber (1976) puts it, was a difficult process that induced anxiety and generated widespread ambivalence. On the one hand, there was nostalgia for regional 'roots' and a strong connection to an idealized past, and on the other, a desire for the dynamic, modern, national life that looked towards the future. This ambivalence was registered in many cultural forms, a well-known example of which are turn-of-the-century postcards figuring women of the French provinces in traditional dress (the head-dress being the salient element in the image). Ironically, these symbols of waning regional specificities were put into mass circulation throughout France by a distinctly modern means that promised to preserve them, at least in memory.

French nostalgia for regional identity was a central concern in many films about the provinces, the most famous ones being those by Marcel Pagnol, set and shot in Provence. Noteworthy, too, in this connection are Jean Epstein's innovative silent films on Brittany. The relevance of this issue for a consideration of *Carmen* is twofold. First, French audiences could vicariously indulge in regionalist nostalgia not only in relation to cultural images of the French provinces themselves but also in relation to images of regions outside of France. In a sense, the *Normandes* and *Alsaciennes* pictured on French postcards, like Epstein's *Bretonnes* on celluloid, have counterparts in Feyder's *Andalusienne* as well as in the provincial Spaniards who appear in the bullfight scene filmed in the southern town of Ronda. According to Françoise Rosay (in Bachy 1968: 85), Feyder enlisted the people of Ronda as extras and asked them to come to the bullring dressed in whatever traditional costumes they had to hand, attire that, in 1926, had only a ceremonial function in their lives. By staging the bullfight scene in this manner, Feyder ensured its look of historical 'authenticity' and tapped a source of nostalgia for French spectators, while simultaneously positioning those spectators as modern national subjects in relation to the figures on the screen.

But there is another aspect of regionalism that has special relevance for Feyder's *Carmen*, namely the cultural particularity of the Basque region. This is expressed in the film's very first intertitle, which designates the location of the action as 'Elizondo, en Navarre espagnole'. In 1926, the qualification 'espagnole' was apparently still needed in order to distinguish Spanish Navarre from its French counterpart, and to align the northern and southern portions of the formerly independent kingdom of Navarre with France and Spain, respectively. The intertitle thus bears witness to the lingering power of regional identifications (both ethnic and linguistic) despite the pull of nationalism and modernization since the Renaissance, when Navarre was gradually annexed by the French and Spanish crowns. That the hero of *Carmen*, don José, is *navarrais* is significant for French audiences, who feel a greater affinity with a northerner from the Basque country than with the Spaniards of Andalusia. The latter are associated with several ethnic groups that are deemed 'undesirable' in France: Gypsies; Spanish Jews who fled to North Africa when they were banished by the Inquisition in 1492; and finally, Arabs who invaded and settled in southern Spain in the so-called Dark Ages, and whose descendants are openly defying French and Spanish rule in North Africa in the 1920s when Feyder is making his film. Feyder's Basque hero, don José, invites spectators' sympathy for another reason as well: as we saw earlier, his blind love for Carmen and the suffering it brings seem partially to absolve him of his complicity with the deceitfulness and criminality attributed to his lover and her Gypsy band. Together, then, don José's uncontrollable desire, suffering, and Basque identity provide an affectively-charged historical and cultural link between Spain and the supposedly more enlightened nation of France.

If don José's Basque identity provides an affectively-loaded point of identification for French viewers of *Carmen*, the alien nature of Andalusian identity (as the film construes it) carries a strong charge as well. In this connection it is interesting to note that *Carmen*'s concern with smugglers in Andalusia clearly mirrors the illicit activity of the French colonizing forces in North Africa and elsewhere. Like other colonial powers, the French arbitrarily confiscated huge tracts of land while also seizing and smuggling countless sacred and profane objects, enshrining them in the museums of Paris or selling them on the international market. Moreover, international smuggling by French criminals, ranging from low-class thugs to glamorous adventurers such as the one played by Edwige Feuillère in Jacques de Baroncelli's *Feu!* (Fire!, 1927), was a common theme in crime dramas and colonial films of the 1920s. Feyder's cinematic handling of the Andalusian smugglers enables French audiences to revel in the stagy drama of chases, gun battles, sword fights, and lethal stabbings without acknowledging the implication of their own compatriots in this type of violence. At the same time, his *Carmen* follows the pattern of colonial cinema in attributing unruly and criminal behaviour to ethnic and cultural 'others' while construing colonial violence as a just and rational response to that behaviour. If Navarre offers French viewers an idealized image of their 'noble' character and their nation's past as an assemblage of culturally-distinct regions, Andalusia provides them with an alibi for France's exploitative colonial ventures in the present.

The ambiguous relation between France and Spain, one which is frequently shaped by gender, assumes an especially disturbing form in Feyder's account of his relationship with the star of *Carmen*, Raquel Meller. Meller was a famous and influential actress when the film project was conceived, so much so that it was she who, having already been asked to play the lead role, persuaded the producers to hire Feyder as director. She had confidence in his ability to make a good film rather than a trite 'espagnolade'. The director's debt to Meller may go some way towards explaining his mockery of her in an interview he gave decades after the shooting of *Carmen*. According to Feyder (in Bachy 1968: 87-88), Meller refused to read the Mérimée novella in preparation for playing her role. Instead, she had her secretary tell her the story in fragments, with the result that she made up her own story and fabricated an idealized Carmen, the sort of heroine she wanted to play, as 'pure, noble, chaste'. When Meller balked at a kiss called for in the script, deeming it inappropriate for the Carmen she had in mind, Feyder impatiently reminded her that she was supposed to play the character invented by Mérimée. At this point the actress reportedly became furious with Feyder: 'Throwing up her hands and jingling her bracelets, she cried, "I don't give a damn about Mr. Mérimée. Where does he live, anyway, this Mr. Mérimée? I'm going to telephone him!"' (88).

Feyder apparently held quite a grudge against Meller, an independent woman with a successful international career in Hollywood as well as in various European countries. Did he belatedly ridicule her in print because of her ignorance of and indifference to the élite literary culture with which he sought, in this case, to associate his cinematic art? Or did he do so because of what he clearly saw as Meller's capricious and decidedly 'Spanish' femininity? In any case, it appears likely that he resented Meller's refusal to keep quiet and do as she was told, a refusal that was quite in keeping with the role she was charged with playing, provided that Carmen be interpreted as a subject in her own right rather than a blind force that must, at all costs, be 'directed' and controlled.

Mixed feelings about Spain in the early twentieth century played a prominent part not only in Feyder's *Carmen*, but also in many other films of the period produced in the industrial 'North'. A fellow colonizing power since the early-modern era (as we are reminded when José dreams of escaping to America), Spain appeared by turns as an ally in Europe's struggle against 'heathens', a formidable military and political rival, an attractive travel destination, and a backward country worthy only of pity or scorn. For example, *The Sheik* (1921) famously uses Rudolph Valentino's Italian ancestry, his cachet as a 'Latin lover', and his swaggering acting style to reinforce the view that southern Spain, like southern Italy, is barely distinguishable from Africa (Hansen 1991). Spain merges with Africa in a similar manner in Josef von Sternberg's *Morocco* (1930) which, through sets, costumes, jewelry, makeup and dialogue in various languages and accents, blurs or effaces ethnic and cultural distinctions between the various 'dark' women who are lovers and prostitutes of the Legionnaires (Spaniards, Italians, Maltese; Gypsies; North African Arabs or Berbers; women of mixed race) to make them, simply, undifferentiated 'others', rendered in grotesquely stereotypical fashion. Their function is to provide a foil to the Marlene Dietrich character, Amy Jolly, who is clearly a 'northerner', and at the same time to encourage viewers to see Jolly (a cabaret performer) as having an affinity with her 'dark' female counterparts after all. Especially in the final scene of the film, where Jolly tosses aside her elegant high heels and joins the 'southern' women (as well as their goats) marching in the footsteps of the Legionnaires, she is cast as the weak link in the evolutionary chain that ties the superior peoples of the North to the inferior ones of the South. That this same figure, again played by Dietrich, reappears in Sternberg's *Blonde Venus* (1932) suggests that it fascinated not only Sternberg himself, but many film spectators in the North as well (Doane 1991). Presumed to be less 'civilized' than the élite white man, the bohemian white woman is an ambiguous figure who blurs the boundary between northern Europe, southern Europe, and Africa.

By contrast with *The Sheik* and *Morocco*, Francesco Rosi's *Carmen* (1983), which of course emerges in a very different historical moment, makes use of ethnic ambiguity in a strategic, critical way that produces amazing results visually, musically, and politically. Rosi's is the only film I have mentioned that follows the Meilhac-Halévy libretto and incorporates Bizet's entire operatic score. The star of this film, Julia Migenes-Johnson, brilliantly 'works' the female protagonist's ethnic ambiguity in her performance, making of Carmen a clever, sensuous, and irrepressible Andalusian of utterly uncertain ancestry, a woman who ceaselessly reinvents herself ethnically and otherwise. Migenes-Johnson's virtuosity makes it impossible to assign a single, stable identity to this protean character, much less to control or possess her. Her performance is the only one I know of that does justice to the complexities of Bizet's music as analyzed by McClary. Although Carmen's vibrancy and dynamism are subdued within the frame of the narrative (since she is killed by José at the end), the remarkable potency of Migenes-Johnson's singing, acting, and dancing, in concert with Bizet's subversive music and Rosi's *mise en scène*, far exceeds the libretto narrative's power to contain it. Migenes-Johnson's achievement in this film is stunning (see also Mary Woods' essay on the Rosi *Carmen* in this volume). Like Feyder's film, Rosi's manages to attend to the texts of Mérimée and Bizet and to invent new modes of expression that enable his contemporaries to enjoy *Carmen*. Both films encourage spectators to reinterpret *Carmen* in light of the world in which they live—its problems, its possibilities, and its pleasures.

Notes
1. His avant-garde *La Photogénie mécanique* (1927) (Photogenic Machines) on the uncanny character of industrial objects consisted of a montage that drew on his industrial films, according to one newspaper account (consulted in the Fonds Jean Grémillon Bibliothèque de l'Arsenal, Paris: archive mark 48 [012]).
2. The script is held in the Fonds Meerson, Bibliothèque du Film et de L'Image, Paris: archive mark 06 (III).

References
Bachy, Victor. 1968. *Jacques Feyder: Artisan du cinéma, 1885-1948*. Louvain: Librairie Universitaire.
Berry, Sarah. 2000. *Screen Style: Fashion and Femininity in 1930s Hollywood*. Minneapolis: University of Minnesota Press.
Meilhac, Henri and Ludovic Halévy. 1970. *Carmen* (libretto) (tr. Ellen. H. Bleiler). New York: Dover Publications.
Doane, Mary Ann. 1991. *Femmes Fatales: Feminism, Film Theory, Psychoanalysis*. New York and London: Routledge.
Fawkes, Richard. 2000. *Opera on Film*. London: Duckworth.
Gaudier, Charles. 1922. *Carmen de Bizet: Étude historique et critique/analyse musicale*. Paris, Librairie Delaplane.

Hansen, Miriam. 1991. *Babel and Babylon: Spectatorship in American Silent Film.* Cambridge, MA: Harvard University Press.

McClary, Susan. 1992. *Georges Bizet: Carmen.* Cambridge and New York: Cambridge University Press.

Mérimée, Prosper. 1930. *Carmen.* Paris, Editions Fernand Roches.

Roberts, Mary L.. 1994. *Civilization without Sexes: Reconstructing Gender in Postwar France.* Chicago: University of Chicago Press.

Seigel, Jerrold. 1986. *Bohemian Paris: Culture, Politics, and the Boundaries of Bourgeois Life, 1830-1930.* Baltimore: The Johns Hopkins University Press.

Weber, E. 1976, *Peasants into Frenchmen: The Modernization of Rural France, 1870-1914.* Palo Alto, CA: Stanford University Press.

Shadow and Substance: Reiniger's Carmen Cuts Her Own Capers

Harriet Margolis

Lotte Reiniger's silhouette-animated *Carmen* (1933) prefigures later cinematic attempts to challenge popular patriarchal narratives by rewriting them in revisionist feminist modes. This chapter traces how Reiniger, a pioneer in animation, reinterprets the Carmen narrative so that Carmen herself takes up the position of subject rather than object of her own story, while the male characters—don José and Escamillo, and even the bull—become the objects of her gaze that can only react to her desire and her control. In this revisionist take on the story, Reiniger provides us with an unusually happy ending to the story, as Carmen and Escamillo ride off together at the end. Reiniger's reworking is paralleled by the musical accompaniment of Peter Gellhorn. Although Reiniger herself claimed to be apolitical, aiming above all to charm through her animation, the chapter elaborates the different ways in which her *Carmen* functions as feminist comedy, in which the delicacy of her silhouettes ultimately cannot disguise the strength of a woman to undercut patriarchal values.

Animation
Female gaze
Gellhorn, Peter
Music and film
Parody
Reiniger, Lotte: *Carmen*

Defying the tragic fate that Carmen usually meets, Lotte Reiniger's *Carmen* (1933) rewrites her story, ending on a happy and comic note. This time, Carmen literally removes herself into a better situation, her physical strength and dexterity as well as her sexual powers overwhelming the males she encounters, human and bull alike. From a male point of view she may still seem to be a dangerous *femme fatale*, but since this version is her story as she might tell it, we can forget about don José's desires. As a result, no one dies. Once Carmen nimbly escapes don José, her would-be assassin disappears from the picture, his story taking a back seat to hers. Short and deceptively simple, Reiniger's *Carmen* marries music with silhouette figures in a film that one could easily dismiss as enjoyable but slight, but which, seen in the context of tellings of the Carmen story and in Reiniger's own time, takes on its own interest.

It isn't just that Reiniger playfully marries 'high' and 'popular' art forms (opera, on the one hand, and cinema, on the other);[1] she also changes point of view. Carmen is now not just nominally but also structurally the protagonist, and don José is no longer her victim but simply a means to an end. Needing to escape don Jose, Carmen subdues the bull in the ring: at a time when Picasso's Minotaur was terrorizing men, women, and horses alike, Carmen merely looks at the bull and he bows. When Escamillo finds himself bested by her on his own ground, the bullring, he at least has the sense to join her, graceful in his defeat. The change in perspective in conjunction with the change in tone allows Carmen to reject the nineteenth century and embrace the twentieth. It does so insofar as it rejects the sort of romanticism in which the male hero can lament the tragedy of his fate while his female counterpart dies: meanwhile, with a twentieth-century self-awareness of power struggles between males and females,[2] it also rejects the traditional mythological relation between Zeus and Europa, on the one hand, and the Minotaur and humans, on the other. Playful as it is, it not only engages with the earlier Carmen vehicles, but also with the work of some of Reiniger's more serious contemporaries such as Bertolt Brecht and Pablo Picasso.

Although significantly shorter than Bizet's opera, Reiniger's *Carmen* manages to be amusing, charming, beautiful, and satirical as well as parodic. Her version is also revisionist, especially as regards her jaunty presentation of male/female relations. Although there is no external evidence to suggest that Reiniger considered herself a feminist, 'her female characters are especially lively and original, displaying wit, sensuousness, and self-awareness' (Starr 1999: 348). The parody is clear from Reiniger's title, subject matter, and soundtrack: the satire exposes male heroics at the expense of female lives. In offering such a different ending to the story from that to be found in either Mérimée's novella or Bizet's opera, Reiniger carries her film beyond parody to challenge patriarchal narrative imperatives.

Although Reiniger (1899-1981) made experimental shorts while working 'within the Berlin avant-garde milieu' (Wedel 1999: 202), primarily she took as the subject of her films 'fairy tales, myths and opera librettos' (Strobel 1999: 16). Reiniger herself said that fairy tales were a path to truth, that she 'love[d] fairy tales [...] I believe more in the truth of fairy tales than the truth in the newspapers'.[3] Reiniger matured in a Germany increasingly threatened by forces that would wreak havoc on her world. She was, by all accounts, a non-political person who enjoyed the escapism of her chosen material. Her films in general are non-threatening and amusing, technically breathtaking and visually charming. While she did not publicly confront Nazi policies, from the mid-1930s she and her husband Carl Koch preferred to live in England. Her friends, among them the wealthy banker Louis Hagen and the French filmmaker Jean Renoir, also included many figures from the Weimar avant-garde, including eventual exiles such as Brecht and Peter Gellhorn. In the 1920s Reiniger had worked with composers such as Kurt Weill and Paul Dessau; for Reiniger's *Carmen*, Gellhorn arranged the music. According to one biographer, Reiniger was an introverted wit who gathered around her at different times various circles of friends who were pleased by her company and fascinated by her ability to cut beautiful silhouettes.[4] These silhouettes made their way into *Silhouettenfilme*, the cinematic art form that she pioneered. It involves cutting out dozens and thousands of images (depending on the length of a film) and painstakingly moving them about from shot to shot so as to create the impression of movement.[5]

Animation itself existed before Reiniger was old enough to work, and she discovered it early in her career. Even 'silhouette animation existed before 1919, but Reiniger was its pre-eminent practitioner, transforming a technically and esthetically bland genre to a recognized art form' (Starr 1999: 348). Reiniger tells an amusing anecdote about the difficulties crew experienced trying to get first rats and then guinea pigs costumed like rats to follow the Piper in Paul Wegener's *The Pied Piper of Hamelin* (1918), explaining why it eventually took wooden rats and stop-motion cinematography to achieve the required effect. She was not responsible for this particular bit of animation, but, as she says, 'this was my first encounter with animation,' and the film 'gave me my first film job, cutting out silhouette titles for each reel' (Reiniger 1970: 84). For most of her life she cut figures destined to become part of at least forty films that she completed (Strobel 1999: 18), including the first animated feature film, *The Adventures of Prince Achmed* (Milestone, 1923-1926). Even after the sound era, Reiniger's films rely mainly on her ability to tell stories through her visuals rather than through a voicetrack.

Reiniger's *Carmen* runs for less than ten minutes. Its function, both socially and in its makers' careers, differs greatly from that of both Mérimée's novella and Bizet's opera. By 1875 the story had already been altered in order to make it available to a more general audience that could be expected to include women young and old. Shocking as *Carmen* may have seemed to nineteenth-century bourgeois France, especially in the context of the prudish Opéra Comique, 'the music's tendency to throw a glamour over its subject' smoothed some of Carmen's rough edges and the story's 'savage brutality' (Parker 1926: 212). By the time Reiniger and Gellhorn made their version, the figure of Carmen was so well known as to be ripe for parody. However, since the film's images follow the narrative until the finale, for the parody to work Reiniger needed something to cue her viewers' expectations. That is what Gellhorn's arrangement accomplishes, functioning to establish the film's tone.[6]

Weimar Germany, of course, was alive with artistic endeavours. By the end of the 1920s various theatrical classics had been restaged and/or filmed, incorporating the latest in visual and musical trends. In 1928 Brecht and Weill had had a major critical and commercial success with their revision of *The Threepenny Opera*, in which Weill's atonal music helps to establish the jarring mood of the piece, a story at least as sordid and brutal as that of Carmen. While *The Threepenny Opera* was part of the cultural context in which Reiniger's *Carmen* came into being, it is still an opera, at least in terms of its scale and ambition. It is also meant very much to be a social critique of its day, forcing its audiences to engage with its message. In contrast, while embedded within that same artistic and cultural context, Reiniger's *Carmen* does not use its music or imagery in so blatant a way, and its relation to its audience is gentler, less coercive.

Necessarily, Gellhorn's musical arrangement for *Carmen* involves much omission, reordering, and re-instrumentalisation, although it remains completely within the original framework. That Gellhorn made changes comes as no surprise, for he worked with a limited palette and in a genre widely divergent from the *opéra-comique* that Bizet had found restricting. Instead of a full orchestra, Gellhorn relies mainly on a piccolo or two, some trumpets and percussion, a piano, guitar, violin, and an alto saxophone. His orchestra belongs to the era of jazz and tea dances, and to the Berlin avant-garde. And so, in some ways, the film's musical accompaniment is ambivalent in terms of its relation to high and low culture. Are we to take this *Carmen* for a 'serious' recreation of the text within technical limitations, or is this *Carmen* an opportunistic free reading? Given that the only information on the soundtrack comes from the music, as the soundtrack carries nothing but the music, what can the relation between sound and image tell us about the film?

In the spirit of the times, the film begins with a 25-second barrel organ rendition of the 'flashy, pseudo-Spanish music' first heard at the beginning of the opera's prelude and again in Act IV (McClary 1992: 62). The film's music thus begins in congruence with the original, at least as far as the notes go. However, the difference of tone provided by the barrel organ associates the film more with popular than élite culture.[7] We can expect the opera in some way to be altered, to speak differently, and to speak differently to different audiences. After the opening, though, the barrel organ is replaced with a contemporary jazz orchestra, speaking to a further audience, setting up different expectations. From the beginning, we know that this *Carmen* will not set itself up as High Art, but the presence of a jazz orchestra might, in 1930s Germany, suggest that one should expect something unexpected. In a sense, Gellhorn's instrumentation sets up a sort of fusion (see McClary's essay in this volume) among the various levels of popular, traditional high, and contemporary avant-garde art of its day.

In the same way that Bizet himself created music with a Spanish flavour rather than the thing itself, Gellhorn's arrangement re-orchestrates, reorganizes, and reassigns best-known bits of the opera to re-create its flavour in a way that suits Reiniger's purposes. The most obvious omissions are the melodies in minor keys associated with fate. In this version, there is no sadness. Don José has brought his troubles upon himself through his own foolishness, and Carmen determines her own fate. Between them, Reiniger and Gellhorn have provided Carmen with a more level playing ground. Carmen is no longer a victim, either musically or narratively, not of her own sexuality nor of anyone else's desire. Yet at the end, Gellhorn's version retains significant aspects of Bizet's interweaving of themes in the finale. Conjoined with Reiniger's different ending, the music changes its meaning. Gellhorn's reweaving of Bizet's pattern of themes in conjunction with his orchestration of those themes creates subtleties not immediately apparent to those only casually familiar with the opera. What seems on the surface to be simple turns out to be complex, much like the end result on screen of Reiniger's painstaking behind-the-scenes work, cutting and capturing images.

A structural breakdown of the film runs as follows. After the credits, the film divides the story into five sections. The music guides us through the transitions, announcing each new section with new music, or even a trumpet fanfare. The music also helps to make the first four sections coherent in that each has its own signature tune from the opera. The final section, set mainly in the arena, brings various themes together, as does the opera's final scene. There are thus moments when the film's soundtrack is faithful to the opera, but ultimately the film's soundtrack plays the opera's subtleties against itself.

Immediately after the credits, when we meet Carmen and don José, we have the *choeur d'enfants*. This first section not only retains the impudent attitude to the soldiers of the original, but also enhances that attitude by making all the soldiers the subject of the voyeuristic gaze of Carmen and of three better-dressed women who survey them from above. Carmen jauntily climbs down from the parapet in pursuit of don José. (She sees him, she knows she wants him: the way to a better future lies in his uniform).

Section Two, appropriately, uses the 'Seguidilla', for in this section don José sits down for a drink at a table outside a café after dismissing his troops. Carmen immediately joins him and jumps up to dance on the tabletop. While she is there, she moves her foot in a gesture that the bull will echo near the film's end. In the course of her campaign, Carmen will give don José three kisses and beckon him with her finger three times, in time with the trumpets. Meanwhile, it becomes obvious that don José's drinking has affected him and Carmen's efforts at seduction are successful.

She leads him off in Section Three to the Gypsies' mountain hideaway, accompanied by the 'Habanera'. The smugglers dance around their campfire; don José continues to be seduced by Carmen; eventually he sleeps and she strips him of his clothes. The 'Habanera' continues, the images dissolve, and we rediscover Carmen at a city pawnbroker's, exchanging José's uniform, including spurred boots and sword, for a proper lady's dress complete with mantilla. She is now uniformed for what she hopes will be her next conquest. The 'Habanera' is beginning to thin out as this section progresses until it is down to a guitar with some bits of percussion and brass highlights.

When we return to don José as he wakes up in the mountains to discover Carmen's deception, the music is slower, softer, and limited primarily to the guitar until the last seconds, when don José finds a knife to add to the peasant's costume he has cobbled together for himself. That last portentous gesture is accompanied by the harsh burst of a piccolo playing the notes for 'l'amour est un oiseau rebelle' in a dying fall. Where Bizet is indulgent, this portentousness is the only opportunity Gellhorn and Reiniger allow don José to seem in control of the narrative imperative.

The fourth section begins brightly with the trumpets from just before the original appearance of the *choeur d'enfants*, to be followed immediately by the Toreador's song. Escamillo makes his proud entrance, followed by the three ladies whom we first saw watching don José on the parapet. Carmen approaches Escamillo, but he rejects her so violently that she falls to the ground. As she picks herself up, don José approaches her, and the scene ends as he follows her to the bullfight.

The final, fifth section takes place in the arena and its environs. The music announcing the beginning of a new section is the allegretto moderato sung in the opera by the chorus as the Introduction in Act 1, Scene 1. This scene, in opera and film, presents a public space filled by a busy crowd. Then the music briefly shifts to the 'To your toast' of Act 2, Scene 2 before it grows into the Toreador's song. This transmutes into a complex medley in which each figure or group gets its own musical theme and instrumentation associated with it. For Carmen, there is the main toreador music associated in the opera with Escamillo. The three toreros are represented by piccolos playing the last lines of the chorus ('et que l'amour t'attend') (and love awaits you). The bull gets the 'Habanera' in the form of the melody for 'L'Amour est un oiseau rebelle' (Love is a rebellious bird). Played by a saxophone, the bull's notes add a sardonic presence. As the bull and Carmen dance together, a reversal of musical themes occurs to parallel the characters' situations on screen. Carmen has tamed the bull: through her presence in the arena in conjunction with the Toreador's song, Carmen has taken on Escamillo's role as top dog of the bullfight. Yet, as the music indicates, gender relations are more complex than a simple role reversal. On the one hand, a saxophone had previously represented Escamillo, but now it plays for the bull. On the other hand, the music it plays was associated earlier with the scene in which Carmen played the seductress. The saxophone, of course, was linked by Adorno with an uncivilised degree of sexuality,[8] so it is apt that this bull comes complete with an un-Disney-like erection. The erection may be read as the bull's attempt to seduce Carmen, but it also suggests that he has already been seduced by her. As with don José, all it has taken is for her to accost the bull, stand in front of him, and move about a little. So far, only in the case of Escamillo has her charm failed her.

After the bull prances around Carmen, she offers him her rose, presumably the rose that, in the opera, would have gone to don José and that symbolized for him the love between himself and Carmen. In Reiniger's film the bull comes to Carmen to accept the rose she carries. Then he subordinates himself to Carmen, allowing her to jump onto his back and conduct him triumphantly around the arena. Once the bull succumbs to Carmen's powerful attractions, we see that Escamillo has as well. He approaches and the bull allows Escamillo to join Carmen. The three then prance happily out of the arena. The curtain that rose with the barrel organ's introduction once again falls.

The sheer beauty of Reiniger's silhouettes, their delicacy and grace, is so overwhelming that her films initially strike viewers in purely visual terms. Reiniger's images don't seem like the type to go slumming it, even when she made silhouette films for advertising or public service purposes.[9] So what we see dominates our perception until the images themselves prompt us to be consciously aware that what we are watching includes a narrative as well as beautiful images. Yet how beautiful these images are, how amazing that they move with such convincing grace! Once the viewer is prepared to move past that level of perception and take in the story, the bare elements of *Carmen* seem to be proceeding straightforwardly until the bullfight. Still, even up to that point something about the occasionally somewhat off-key musical notes and the cheeky orchestration complicates the reception of Reiniger's telling of the Carmen story.

Carmen was shown during the Berlinale in 1934 (for the first and the last time)[10] and until recently the film has not been referred to in anything but specialist catalogues. A copy of the film is available in Wellington, New Zealand, as part of the Federation of Film Societies' collection, and another copy exists in Australia. There is also a copy in London at the British Film Institute. Inquiries in 1999 to the then copyright-holder Louis Hagen[11] led me to believe that the film was unavailable for purchase in any format. However, it is now available through German sources. Meanwhile, many people had the opportunity to see it when a retrospective of Reiniger's work toured parts of the world in recent years under the aegis of the Goethe Institut Inter Nationes.

The précis provided in a booklet accompanying that tour concludes that Reiniger's *Carmen* is a 'not very serious parody of a popular opera story' (Ferber and Ströhl 1999: 57), so the curatorial view would seem to be that Reiniger's *Carmen* is a mere bagatelle. Perhaps this is so compared with her heavyweight sources. Indeed, it isn't easy to argue that this *Carmen* has had any significant or specific influence. Yet it is possible to argue for the significance of the existence of such a vision. Such an argument rests on a basic premise of feminist ontology, that the existence of an alternative poses a challenge to the dominant view. This sort of reversal of fairy tales, myths, and popular stories, it might be argued, suggests that it should be considered as a standard among feminist strategies for challenging patriarchal representations of women, given that it occurs in examples that can be drawn from different eras and places.[12]

To argue for this film's significance and to care that it has survived in collections around the world is to take the film seriously. The film has its intrinsic merits, based on the aesthetic characteristics previously referred to. It is of historical interest both as part of its *Zeitgeist* of 1930s Germany and as part of the history of women filmmakers. In this latter context, its rereading of a well-known story, its response both to Mérimée and to Bizet, makes it a part of feminist film studies, of a recovery of lost history and of what the pioneer women filmmakers had to say. Like McClary, I read the Carmen story as engaging primarily with the discourse of power and submission (McClary 1992: 4). In Mérimée's original, this struggle plays out through nationality and gender. Nationalism—which McClary identifies as so important to Mérimée's story and its context—isn't an issue, perhaps oddly enough, given the era of Reiniger's *Carmen*. The battle between a local population and an imported military force is absent, and the specific identities of the characters involved have also disappeared.[13] For example, since we no longer have verbal or visual clues to tell us that don José is Basque, we have no reason to connect Carmen's seduction of him with a cliché of Spanish culture: that northern men are particularly vulnerable to seduction by southern women.[14]

What remains as much a basis for Reiniger's story as for those of her predecessors is the generic battle between the sexes. Social changes related to gender were an aspect of Reiniger's era, and 'the New Woman' was as much a phenomenon in Germany as in Britain or the United States. New women could do and were doing anything, just as Reiniger herself was pioneering a new type of filmmaking. Thus it is not surprising that Reiniger's Carmen could be resourceful enough to survive, even triumph, physically intact and more than equal to the men around her. And Reiniger's film presents this survival as making better sense than that the male characters should triumph. If we re-examine *Carmen* in terms of its narrative structure, the visual/narrative text as well as the musical text reveal a reshuffling of powers associated with gender. The balance of power tilts toward Carmen on the basis of an equality evident in the combination of actions and events. For example, Reiniger makes Carmen the active subject rather than object of the narrative through the agency of her gaze. The film begins, after all, with Carmen as voyeur, at the moment that she watches a procession of men led by don José. Unlike the other, higher-class women who also watch this procession, however, she does more than simply observe: she goes after her prey by climbing down from her observation post, moving quickly and lithely. In the next two sections of the film, Carmen goes beyond controlling don José through the gaze to master him through her physical qualities. What she wants from him is not the man himself, but his wealth, which she wishes to have for her own goals. That her goals have so little to do with don José himself contributes to the process of belittling a male subject elsewhere set up as heroic.

It soon seems that Carmen's targets also include the pompous, self-satisfied toreador, Escamillo, whose posturing suggests his high opinion of himself, probably expressed in thoughts that he is a veritable bull of a man. In his own way, Escamillo may be as much a fool as is don José, but Carmen wants him for his own sake rather than as a means to an end. There is no sense that she thinks of belittling him, even though, when she postures in front of him in her guise of middle-class femininity, he sweeps her away from him. As a member of the audience at the bullring she again becomes a female voyeur whose object is a man in uniform playing a public role. She is initially unaware of don José's presence, but as soon as she realizes that he is there she moves to escape from him. She climbs down from a wall to the ground below, as she did in the opening section, but this time, instead of climbing down in order to take don José as her prey, she moves in order to avoid becoming his prey. In so doing, she leaves behind any false gentility that might cling to her dressier clothes and reverts to the physicality that characterized her at first. In this guise she tames the bull, not because she particularly wants anything from the bull but simply because he falls under her spell. Here, in this urban public space, the Gypsy Carmen conquers man and beast, not for a man, nor even her family, and certainly not for her country—wherever that may be—but for herself.

Once Gellhorn's reorganization of the musical themes comes in to support Reiniger's narrative reversal of relations between Carmen and the men, that reversal grows more complex. In conjunction with the music, these visual images, including their components of costume and performance, tell us that things are not always what they appear to be. Don José performs the role of an officer until he loses the costume that makes him one. While Carmen desires the costume that she thinks will change her status, her own strength and innate character get her what she wants. The role reversal Reiniger sets up rests on the distinction between 'gender' and 'sex', between something that is conditioned and performed versus something that is apparently innate.

Since antiquity the bull has been associated with ferocious sexuality, as when Europa finds herself riding the back of a bull who is really a randy Jove in disguise. Reiniger's Carmen, however, is not so likely to be taken in by such a disguise. Consider, too, the story of the Minotaur. In Reiniger's version, Theseus is unnecessary: Ariadne can do the job. In the original, the Minotaur terrifies through his otherness as part man/part beast as well as through his habit of eating people. Carmen, though, tames the bull's violence. On the one hand, there is her physical appeal, her sexual strength or life-force; on the other hand, there is her kinship with the bull as other, for this Carmen is part man/part woman, and the bull stands still before her in immediate recognition. In Reiniger's own lifetime, artists had reanimated the theme of the 'bull-man', most particularly Picasso, as a commentary on the animalistic side of man. Yet Carmen not only triumphs where the men had yet to do so; she can be strongly associated with sexuality—both the bull's and her own—and still the story can end happily.[15] And while she has the strength, the agility and the ability to dominate that any toreador would require, the toreros are mincing around the arena in their elaborate costumes. They have become effeminate, another trio of chorines supporting the major players, like the group of three female figures. Almost supernumerary, Escamillo bows to the obvious and accepts second billing to Carmen when the bull allows the previously scornful toreador to join them on the ride out of the arena.

It would seem that Carmen's sexuality is potent where her femininity is not. Carmen's desire is associated with her femininity and with her posing as feminine. When she plays at behaving according to her 'proper' gender, she loses; when she is true to herself, she wins. Is there a message here about the essence of being female? Not necessarily. Carmen's sexuality derives from her physical activity and her physical power. That is the same source on which Escamillo draws for his attraction. In other words, gauged in terms of sexuality, they are equals. In contrast, although the opera sets Carmen up as a *femme fatale* who makes don José her victim (McClary 1992: 18), the film dismisses the association of any tragic element with him because he doesn't merit it. *Pace* Parker (1926: 227) and Dean (1975: 213 and 226), don José simply isn't as interesting as Carmen, nor is his story. He prances about—and Reiniger's silhouettes for don José at this point are particularly delicate and his legs particularly ethereal. Yet don José also sits pompously, drinks heavily, falls for flattery, and is easily misled. Why does an opera exist about this fellow? For, despite the novella and opera's title, the original Carmen narratives focus on don José's story, even when he isn't present, as when Carmen and Zuniga discuss his imprisonment. Certainly his attempt to control Carmen dominates Bizet's opera, perhaps in no version so obviously as in Cecil B. De Mille's film (1915) with opera star Geraldine Farrar.

McClary argues that *Carmen*'s hold on audiences derives from its narrative strategy: 'Virtually all of the elements that compose the structure of the [original] story are intimately linked to questions of control and mastery, as the major narrative strategy aptly illustrates' (1992: 3). McClary finds 'the paradigm of control and subsequent threat to its hegemony' to be thoroughly interwoven through narrative structure, episodes, and anecdotes (1992: 3). In her analysis, Carmen is the object to be investigated because her 'resistance' to don José and her generally threatening quality as seductress attract the male desire to control. Mulvey (1988) has famously argued that Hollywood's classic realist text rests on a sadistic paradigm in which the female character is investigated and punished, primarily through the gaze: the traditional versions of Carmen's story would seem to fit this paradigm.

In various ways, though, Reiniger has altered the traditional version. Her *Carmen* engages in satire, and even more heavily in parody. It is less interested in the individuals themselves. After all, in ten minutes it is difficult to engage in deep character development. Instead, through its use of a particular narrative Reiniger's *Carmen* comments on the unfixed quality of gender itself. Physically, Reiniger's Carmen is as solid as she is dainty; emotionally, she would seem to be a law unto herself. What matters is her sexuality, a physical quality that enables her role reversal a reversal of gendered roles in which the parody involves Carmen's besting the men at their own games. The tragic story gets rewritten so that the male protagonist just disappears while the female protagonist lives rather than dies. Dean notes the unique status of Carmen in that for the first time 'the heroine and the villain are combined in one person' and that person is female (1975: 226). Yet no one is punished in Reiniger's film. If no characters die in this film, it is because there is no longer a narrative imperative for death. After all, the story has become a feminist comedy.

Notes

1. As essays elsewhere in this volume attest, this distinction needs refinement, for the status of both opera and cinema, especially the sort of cinema that Reiniger produced, is more complicated, both historically and in terms of the particular works associated with stories about Carmen.
2. See Petro (1989) for a discussion of the Neue Frau/New Woman phenomenon in the Germany of Reiniger's twenties.
3. In the Diarama film *Lotte Reiniger: Homage to the Inventor of the Silhouette Film* (Katja Raganelli, 1999), included in the Milestone/BFI video edition of *The Adventures of Prince Achmed* (BFIVD523). (Milestone often goes beyond distribution of films to help reclaim film history by reconstructing and restriking prints of old films).
4. In Raganelli's *Lotte Reiniger*, see note 3. In return, Reiniger sometimes included these friends in her films. For example, Carl Koch is to be seen in the arena (the spectator with the binoculars), Jean Renoir is the little, stout innkeeper Lilas Pastias and Catharine Hessling is Carmen (Alfred Happ, personal email, 13 February 2004).
5. Schobert states that Reiniger's feature, *The Adventures of Prince Achmed*, required '300,000 individual camera shots' (1999: 6), although her eightieth birthday notice in *Die Welt* spoke of 250,000 shots over three years.
6. Much as the music in *Sweetie* (1990) does, according to Jane Campion: 'If I think the tone is not clear I can try to clarify it [...] At the beginning of [*Sweetie*] I felt there was an ambiguity [...] People had to know that the voice of the filmmakers was that we knew we were being ironic. In the end we chose to do it with music' (Hawker 1989: 30). Dean argues that the opera 'is rich in dramatic irony, a quality never so potent as when expressed through the suggestive powers of music' (1975: 223).
7. According to my colleague the composer Jack Body who has written his own Carmen piece, in this era barrel organs frequently played the most popular operatic tunes on the streets for general audiences, and eventually these versions were themselves recorded. Given *Carmen*'s popularity, it seems likely that recordings of barrel organ versions of the opera's best-known tunes would have been made.
8. His best-known and most controversial statement on the subject is the following: 'In truth, the instrument to which so much modernistic infamy is attributed and which is supposed to perversely subject the over-stimulated Western nerves to the vitality of blacks [*Negervitalität*], is old enough to command respect' (2002: 471). Editor Richard Leppert's 'Commentary' on this essay and Adorno's other references to the saxophone in jazz clarifies the context of Adorno's argument and argues convincingly against assuming that Adorno is expressing his own racism (2002: 350-352). For one thing, Adorno looks to the instrument's history, noting that it appears in Hector Berlioz's *Treatise on Instrumentation* and that Bizet uses it in his *L'Arlésienne* Suite (2002: 471 and 492n).
9. The Milestone video of *The Adventures of Prince Achmed* includes the short but brilliant Nivea ad called *The Marquise's Secret* (1923).
10. Alfred Happ, personal email, 13 February 2004.
11. Son of the Louis Hagen who financed Reiniger's *Carmen*.
12. Along with Reiniger's film from 1930s Germany and Sally Potter's *Thriller* (1979) from Britain, there is Anne Sexton's poetry from 1960s America, for example. Feminist rewritings of fairy tales have occurred in movies (*Ever After* (1998) for a recent example), but Potter's film rewrites *La bohème* via *Psycho* (1960) in order to critique narrative itself as much as any particular narrative. Potter is particularly critical of the narrative imperative that so often leaves female characters dead.

13. However, Reiniger introduces a gratuitous stereotype, in that her pawnbroker physically resembles Nazi caricatures of the 'greedy Jewish moneylender' type and its predecessors elsewhere in Europe.
14. My thanks for this information to my colleague Nicola Gilmour. Parker (1926) does not mention the cliché as such, but he stresses Micaela's blondeness and her native costume, which would make her identifiably northern. He also describes the don José of the opera's opening as 'a country fellow [...] He was rather afraid of Andalusian women' (Parker 1926: 227).
15. My thanks to classicist Arthur Pomeroy for reminding me of the bull-man theme in early twentieth-century European art and to Jungian film scholar John Izod for assistance with some of the complications of European associations between the bull and sexuality.

References

Adorno, Theodor W. 2002. 'On Jazz', in *Essays on Music: Theodor Adorno* (ed. Richard Leppert). Berkeley: University of California Press: 470-495.

Dean, Winton. 1975. *Bizet*, rev. edn. London: J. M. Dent.

Ferber, Carola and Strohl, Andreas (eds). 1999. *Lotte Reiniger: Films*. Munich: Goethe-Institut.

Hawker, Philippa. 1989. 'Jane Campion' in *Cinema Papers* 73: 29-30.

Leppert, Richard. 2002. 'Commentary' in Adorno (2002): 327-372.

McClary, Susan. 1992. *Georges Bizet: Carmen*. Cambridge: Cambridge University Press.

Mulvey, Laura. 1988. 'Visual Pleasure and Narrative Cinema', in Constance Penley (ed.) *Feminism and Film Theory*. London, Routledge: 69-79.

Parker, D. C. 1926. *Georges Bizet: His Life and Works*. London: Kegan Paul, Trench, Trubner.

Petro, Patrice. 1989. *Joyless Streets: Women and Melodramatic Representation in Weimar Germany*. Princeton: Princeton University Press.

Reiniger, Lotte. 1970. *Shadow Theatres and Shadow Films*. London: B.T. Batsford.

Schobert, Walter. 1999. 'Tribute to Lotte Reiniger' in Ferber and Strohl (1999): 5-13.

Starr, Cecile. 1999. 'Reiniger, Lotte: British Animator', in Unterburger, Amy L. (ed.) *The St. James Women Filmmakers Encyclopedia: Women On the Other Side of the Camera*. Farmington Hills, MI: Visible Ink Press: 348-349.

Strobel, Christel. 1999. 'Lotte Reiniger and Her Films', in Ferber and Strohl (1999): 15-18.

Wedel, Michael. 1999. 'Reiniger, Lotte', in Elsaesser, Thomas. with Wedel, Michael. (eds) *The BFI Companion to German Cinema*. London: British Film Institute: 202.

A Carmenesque Dietrich in *The Devil Is A Woman*: Erotic Scenarios, Modern Desires and Cultural Differences Between the USA and Spain

Hilaria Loyo

Although Josef von Sternberg's *The Devil Is A Woman* (1935) is not allegedly based on Mérimée's novella or Bizet's opera, many elements in the film bring the devilish character of Marlene Dietrich, Conchita Pérez, close to the figure of Carmen as sexual and ethnic other. The film is based on Pierre Louys's novella *The Woman and the Puppet (La Femme et le pantin),* in which an explicit connection is established between the love story of don Mateo with Conchita and that of don José with Carmen. This clear reference to Carmen story in Louys's story is reinforced in the film script, written by John Dos Passos and S. K. Winston, by its departure from the original story to include events and scenes from the Carmen story. This chapter examines the extent to which the character of Dietrich follows, and the extent to which it departs from, the Carmen myth of female otherness. To achieve this goal, an analysis of the erotic scenarios portrayed in both narratives serves to reveal the differences in the power relations established across gender and race lines and in the desires elicited. A consideration of some relevant features composing Dietrich's star persona as well as a general overview of the different historical contexts of the USA and Spain will provide further insight into Dietrich's defiance of Carmen's fate as well as some explanation of the Spanish government's condemnation of the film.

Dietrich, Marlene
Gender power relations
Othering
Race
Star persona
Sternberg, Josef von: *The Devil Is A Woman*

Josef von Sternberg's *The Devil Is A Woman* (1935) is allegedly based on Pierre Louys's novella *The Woman and the Puppet (La Femme et le pantin*, 1898), a work whose title was taken from one of Goya's Tapestries, XLII: 'In the meadow of Manxannares four young Spanish women toss a [male] puppet in a blanket' (Symons 1935: 13).[1] Louys's novella clearly derives from Mérimée's *Carmen*: don Mateo meets Concha in similar circumstances to those of don José and Carmen—in a brawl between women; both Carmen and Concha, the two devilish female figures, work at a tobacco factory as *cigarreras*, they both have animal qualities and both prostitute themselves to the English. In Louys's novella, at a certain moment in don Mateo's narration of his story to André, the French traveller and the other narrator of the story, don Mateo, makes an explicit reference to

Mérimée's tale when he tells how he and Concha moved to a *palacio* in Seville, in the same street 'where your Carmen received don José' (Louys 1935: 184).

The Devil Is A Woman, written by John Dos Passos and S. K. Winston, highlights those features and references that easily identify Concha Pérez, the character of Marlene Dietrich in the film, as a variation of the well-known figure of Carmen, mainly through the allusions to the heroine's youth in a tobacco factory and the brief appearances of the bullfighter, Morenito. But the title, *The Devil Is A Woman*, imposed by the film's producer, Ernst Lubitsch, against Sternberg's original *Caprice Espagnol*, also strengthens the connection between Concha/Dietrich and Carmen in the film. With these literary references this last Sternberg-Dietrich collaboration acknowledges its indebtedness to the erotic sensibility of the nineteenth-century Romantic tradition and reinforces the continuity of Dietrich's onscreen persona with the *femme fatale* figure, a figure that enjoyed a privileged position in the European social imagination of that century. According to Benedetto Croce, Romanticism as a moral phenomenon, as *mal du siècle*, is rooted in the transition from an old traditional faith to a new belief in the liberal ideals, which were still partially and poorly assimilated (Praz 1969: 11). In a similar way, Evlyn Gould has noted that at the heart of Mérimée's *Carmen* lies the question of the European community, 'a Europe caught between, on the one hand, the idealistic dreams of a youthful Romantic nationalism [...] and, on the other, the stodgy resistance to change of a modern bourgeoisie sympathetic to imperial ideology but also decidedly pan-European in nature' (Gould 1996: 10). This ideological conflict and the difficulties of the new liberal faith demanded a new type of virility, which was often defined and dramatized through erotic fantasies.

Like his Romantic predecessors, Sternberg places the devilish figure of Concha/Dietrich in erotic scenarios to articulate male desires orchestrated by clashing contemporary cultural values. That the perception of these conflicting values may differ from one country to another seems to be proven by the Spanish government's condemnation of the film and its demand that all copies should be destroyed, forcing the Paramount studios to withdraw the film from distribution and exhibition everywhere. Here I will examine the extent to which the character of Dietrich follows and departs from the Carmen myth of female otherness. To this purpose, an analysis of the erotic scenarios portrayed in the nineteenth-century narratives will serve to identify the differences in the power relations established across gender and race lines and in the desires elicited. A consideration of some relevant features of Dietrich's star persona as well as a general overview of the different historical contexts of the USA and Spain will provide further insight into Dietrich's defiance of Carmen's fate.

At the very beginning of *The Devil Is A Woman* a title card, announcing that 'the action of the story takes place during a carnival week in the south of Spain, at the beginning of the century', frames the story in an imprecise time and location, which reinforces the fantasy dimension of a story bearing little resemblance to its real life equivalents. Not only this film, but all Sternberg's cinematic *oeuvre*, characterized as it is by its two-dimensional and metaphorical visual style, have been discussed by critics like Laura Mulvey (1988 [1975]) and Gaylyn Studlar (1988) who use semiotic-psychoanalytic models as melodramatic fantasies playing out visual pleasures and unconscious desires. In this general contextual framework, the narrative of *The Devil Is A Woman*, as in its two indebted literary sources, is from the start driven and motivated by desire. If the journey of the narrator of Mérimée's *Carmen* is apparently stimulated by scientific curiosity, his participation in the *angelus* bathing scene and his encounter with Carmen soon reveal that his narration is motivated by the same desires that the local men sublimate voyeuristically (McClary 1992: 6-7). Voyeuristic pleasures also elicit the desire that drives, as in Louys's original, the narrative unfolding of the film's story. In the film, the carnival starts by introducing a masked Antonio (César Romero) surrounded by images of macho virility: an enormous rooster and a person in a bull costume being teased, encircled and overpowered by a group of women. In this atmosphere of images of sexually threatened and teased masculinity, a close-up of Antonio's masked eyes, avidly searching for pretty women, finally reveals Concha/Dietrich on a carriage, extravagantly dressed and surrounded by balloons. Antonio's first move to attract Concha's attention is significantly an aggressive one, as he bursts several balloons with his sling shot (in the novella, André throws apples at Concha). This first scene introduces three related themes that are also present in the Carmen story: the importance of the voyeuristic male gaze in erotic scenes of seduction, and the carnivalesque reversal of class, racial and gender relations, as well as the association of male violence and sexual contact with these female figures, a violence that is recurrently stressed in the film.

The power of seduction of these two female figures, Carmen and Concha, is ascertained by the desiring gaze of men, a necessary presence in the seduction scenarios that is ironically commented on by Concha's mother with the apparent intention of flattering don Mateo/Pasqual: 'what makes young girls go wrong [...] is the advice of women, not the eyes of men'. Like Carmen, the character of Concha as the object of male desire is a product of male fantasy, since our knowledge of these female figures is given through the subjective narrations of don José and don Mateo, respectively. In the film a number of flashbacks render visually don Pasqual's narration of his relationship with Concha/Dietrich, thus providing a different perspective from that of the male protagonist (Jacobowitz 1987: 33). What makes these two female figures overwhelmingly attractive and repulsive is their antithetical personality that confers upon them a mysterious halo and a disturbing beauty, a paradoxical personality that converts them into irresistible monsters, products of men's minds.

Carmen's paradoxical personality is made manifest in her ambiguous origins: she is a Gypsy but also a Basque ('de Etxalar') who can even speak the Basque language (Mérimée 1989: 139). As for her physical appearance, she seems too attractive and clean for a Gypsy, which casts doubts upon the purity of her race (123), but has features that identify her as a non-white beauty described as strange and savage (124). Carmen's uncertain origins and physique are also associated with her sexual behaviour and freedom, which do not seem to be controlled by anything more complicated than her animal instincts. This association induces don José to describe her as a woman of an evil beauty and as the devil's handmaid (122), driving men to their own emasculation and moral chaos. Only Carmen's death at the hands of don José will restore order from chaos, a fatal destiny that she knows in advance through her fortune-telling skills, and accepts paradoxically to preserve her freedom. This is a tragic ending that makes impossible the fantasy of miscegenation, so frequently exploited in the early Francoist folkloric musicals (*folklóricas*) such as *Carmen la de Triana* (Florián Rey, 1938). In the socio-political context of Mérimée's France, 'the Carmen narrative', as Gould (1996: 67) has noted, 'is a tale of desire, and of human degradation primarily concerned with the nefarious effects of bohemian life on the moral fabric of modern society'. But in the socio-political context of nineteenth-century Spain, the Carmen story can be interpreted as the impossibility of achieving national unity, represented in the failed fantasy of miscegenation between the female Gypsy singer-dancer, brought up by bandits, and a white, northern army officer. As Jo Labanyi reminds us (1997: 224), 'the paramilitary Civil Guard set up in 1844 to bring the regions under central control was explicitly charged with suppressing bandits and policing gypsies'. The difficulties of integrating the irrational racial (regional) others into the central national project through the repression of the military, symbolising the rational order, can be read as the political subtext of *Carmen*'s tragico-romantic story.

No doubt, Louys's Concha, as a successor of Carmen created a few decades later, would introduce variations in the romantic story eliciting a different political subtext. Written in 1898, the year of the Disaster (when Spain lost the last of its colonies), *The Woman and the Puppet* portrays an equally ambiguous but even more devilish female figure as the object of desire of a more dubious representative of the military male order. Don Mateo Díaz, like don Pasqual Castellar (Lionel Atwill) in the film, is a middle-aged man, an idle ex-army officer and reputed womanizer and gambler involved in a masochistic relationship with Concha. Don Mateo/Pasqual's aggressiveness, associated with the vulnerability of male narcissism induced by sexual contact with Concha, is directed towards himself. As he admits at a certain moment in his narration, Concha, 'the toast of Spain', has been the cause of the ruin of his military career and of his poor health, but he chooses his submission to her regardless of his own suffering.

In a series of episodic visual narrative fragments a number of masochistic scenarios are played out in which don Pasqual is involved in repetitive rituals of seduction and rejection, of self-abasement and suspended desire. The transgressive potential of male masochistic desire lies in its challenging of a more aggressive, more virile and socially sanctioned form of masculinity—represented in the film by Antonio, significantly a Spanish Republican and not the French traveller of the original—since masochistic desire is seen, from the psychoanalytic perspective, as an unconscious desire to be released from the Law of the Father, to be relinquished from the bondage of patriarchy (Silverman 1992: 185-213). The power inversion along gender, class and race lines in Louys's novella can be related to the anxiety about virile masculinity provoked by the loss of the war against the USA in 1898. Identifying the national crisis as a crisis of masculinity, these discourses centred on the need for a new man—a disciplined, self-restrained, brave, virile man of strong character—to regenerate the Spanish nation (Vázquez García 2001). In a period when national identity was inextricably linked to imperialism, the loss of the last colonies, along with the problems generated by the difficulties of modernizing the country, was interpreted as a sign of racial degeneration (Álvarez Junco 2001: 503-504).

The differences between Mérimée's Carmen and Sternberg's Concha were even greater not only because almost a century separates their creation, but also because the latter originated in a non-European country. In Sternberg's *The Devil Is A Woman*, the character of Concha is based on Dietrich's star persona, which shares the stigma of female otherness with the Carmen figure and her successor. Departing slightly from *The Woman and the Puppet*, Sternberg abandons in this film the youthful, innocent aspect of the character in Louys's novella that Buñuel would exploit in his last film, *That Obscure Object of Desire* (1977). In line with Dietrich's star persona, Concha displays a sexual knowingness that differs from the image of sexual innocence of the original's eroticized virgin girl, although at times she puts on an act of a capricious, spoilt child while calling don Pasqual by the diminutive 'Pasqualito' in the same vein. The seductive power of Dietrich's screen persona is gained through her knowingness and control of costume and cosmetics, which become a masquerade with which she skilfully constructs herself as spectacle of sexual desire.

Through masquerade, Dietrich could adopt any identity across gender, class, and even race lines, a mobility of identity that bestowed upon her an antithetical personality, similar to that seen in Carmen. Dietrich incarnated culturally irreconcilable extremes: feminine and masculine, mother and whore, passive and active, blonde but with a strong affinity with non-whites. In her Sternberg films, Dietrich often wears masculine attire and adopts male mannerisms while she also appears dressed in notably feminine costume (apron, long night-dress) and makes the most feminine gestures. Offscreen, her habit of wearing male clothes in the early thirties was often seen as part of her scandalous behaviour (Shaffer 1933). In *The Devil Is A Woman*, Dietrich does not use cross-dressing but her masculinity, as in Carmen, is suggested in her active role as the seductress rather than that of the seduced—the passive role usually associated with women and femininity. Feminine beauty is combined here with an independence and sexual activity that is usually associated with masculinity, recurrently connoted in the phallic symbolism of her cigarettes.

Likewise, Dietrich's mobility of identity enables her to cross class barriers: on screen she frequently moves from poverty and destitution to the wealthy exclusiveness gained through the success of her performances (stardom), often suggested in Sternberg films as another form of prostitution—a similar association between dancing and prostitution is made in Carmen. Off-screen, fan magazines articles also reinforced her social mobility in romanticized biographical information that presented her as a cultured, middle-class German girl who, despite her dislike for the job, had to work in the cinema business for economic reasons (Kaiser 1931). In *The Devil Is A Woman*, when don Pasqual first meets Concha on a crowded train, we immediately identify Dietrich, who once again is using a masquerade that bestows on her culturally incongruous meanings. The innocence and virtue suggested by her nunnish attire and her circumspect pose are betrayed by her exaggeratedly made-up eyebrows and increasing irritability. Through costume Concha/Dietrich shows her capacity to transform herself by using the most extravagant costume she ever wore on screen, a capacity that allows her to escape from the poverty of her lower-class status.

The racial elements in Dietrich's persona also show an antithetical nature, whose cultural significance not only differs from that of Carmen but has to be related to the cultural context of the USA in the 1930s. Carmen's racial alterity is marked by her dark Gypsy features, which match up with her transgressive manners and behaviour, but with a beauty that casts doubt on her racial purity. This ambiguity was further highlighted in later Spanish versions of Carmen which almost collapsed the white/non-white opposition, thereby disavowing racial difference. Labanyi (1997: 230) has compared this mechanism of denying/affirming racial difference with the use of blackface in Hollywood musical comedies, in which the otherness (blackness) represented seems to be simply the result of makeup (white actors with painted charcoal faces). For her, the other-race roles played by white Spanish stars in the early Francoist folkloric musicals like Florián Rey's *Carmen la de Triana* can be seen as a kind of 'whiteface', in which the white skin of the performer allows a disavowal of racial difference. In this 1938 Carmen version the double function of masquerade is reinforced by the ambiguous origins of Imperio Argentina, the female star playing Carmen: her father was English and her mother was Spanish but she became famous as a child star in Buenos Aires (hence her last artistic name), and worked in Paramount's Paris-based Joinville studios where she met Marlene Dietrich in 1931 (Argentina 2001: 70-71).

However, Dietrich's racial otherness is manifested in her unmistakable, excessive and artificial whiteness, her 'blinding blondeness'. This form of whiteness juxtaposes the moral and sexual connotations traditionally associated with whiteness and blackness, but it never threatens to collapse them, as in the case of Carmen. On screen, Dietrich's racial persona was constructed through specific lighting techniques that combined the use of 'northern' light, or the 'Rembrandtian' north light, with that of the chiaroscuro. The former connoted the symbolic meanings of superiority and coldness of the Aryan ideal (Dyer 1997: 118), but also the meanings of white femininity as purity (reinforced by her character names such as Lily, Mary, Blonde Venus or Maria). Offscreen, fan magazines usually characterized Dietrich ethnically and racially as a German girl 'of purest Aryan stock' (Lee 1933). With the exception of *Blonde Venus*, her German origin was veiled in her films, where she played French or Austrian characters. But, the chiaroscuro technique symbolically hinted at the duality of her persona, while it ultimately served to highlight her whiteness. A parallel function can be seen in the use of racial masquerade in her films.

The meaning of Dietrich's unmistakable whiteness, however, is problematized by its close association with blackness. In *Shanghai Express*, for instance, she shares a train compartment with a Chinese prostitute, suggesting symbolically her affinity with the degeneration of racial others while being distinctively white. This racial tension is more intensely presented in *Blonde Venus* (1932), where the racial masquerade performs a twofold function: on the one hand, the racial emblems connoting blackness appear to be the necessary accoutrements to indicate her active sexuality, while, on the other, they serve as contrasts that highlight, rather than blur, her whiteness, both physical and symbolic. In the famous 'Hot Voodoo' number of the film, a beautiful, blonde Dietrich emerges out of a gorilla costume, a disguise of primitive, male blackness. Then she exchanges the gorilla head for a strikingly white Afro wig, thus exchanging a black masquerade for a stunningly white one still showing some 'black' attributes. Thus, the black attributes in Dietrich's persona are present not only when she mimics blackness, but also in her white masquerade, her 'blinding blondeness', an excessive and artificial form of whiteness that makes the absence of blackness conspicuous, as it hints at a mode of female sexual activity that can be associated with masculinity and blackness.[2] This special form of 'whiteface' differs from that of Imperio Argentina, discussed by Labanyi (1997), since the black and white opposition, suggesting culturally divergent meanings of legitimate and illegitimate femininity (mother/whore), never threatens to collapse in Dietrich's star persona.

Dietrich's racial personality is one of the features that makes the version of Concha in *The Devil Is A Woman* depart most significantly from Mérimée's and Louys's novellas. In *The Woman and the Puppet* Concha's racial otherness is marked by the contrast established between her skin colour and the whiteness of the snow covering the landscape all through the long train journey where don Mateo first meets Concha (Louys 1935: 82-83). The blondeness of Dietrich's persona was too strong to disavow racial difference, thus becoming an important point in the film. As the press book clearly stated, Paramount's research department had investigated 'the blonde situation in Spain', and, in an attempt to undermine the incongruity of Dietrich's playing a Gypsy, the writer remarks that the large number of blonde women in Spain 'differ[s] with the popular conception of Spanish señoritas as dark-eyed, raven-haired misses'.[3]

To understand the cultural significance of Dietrich's racial imprint, her 'blinding blondeness', as well as her sexual and gender mobility, it is necessary to place this imaginary almighty female figure within the cultural context of consumer modernity in the USA during the Depression years and its reshaping of Americanness. Her contradictory star persona incarnates the cultural clash between the female desires of sexual and social mobility promised to women by consumerism, or 'Americanization', and the traditional moral codes upon which US national identity was based. Hollywood usually resolved these internal cultural conflicts by displacing the dangers of US consumerism into exotic places like Spain, or by using a sexual-ethnic register that bestows an imprecise ethnic and racial otherness upon those film stars who represented potentially disturbing behaviour on screen (López 1999). Dietrich's illicit sexual behaviour is clearly connoted by her mark of racial and ethnic alterity: her blinding blondeness and Germanness.

The allegedly dangerous freedom of the Carmen figure has specific meanings in this Carmenesque Concha/Dietrich. If Carmen's freedom, her refusal to be subjected to any bourgeois law of the liberal project of civilization, is attributed to the primitivism and degeneration of her Gypsy race, Concha's dangerous freedom is understood here as her refusal to exchange herself in any sexual-economic transaction, thus breaking a basic rule in the capitalist culture of white civilization: as Jacobowitz has put it (1987: 38), 'one should get what one pays for'. She refuses to be an object of exchange even when she has proved her ability to create herself as an object of desire through fashion and other new merchandise, and she has accepted the money and gifts offered. From their very first encounter don Pasqual takes Concha as an object of exchange that he will incessantly try to get by offering her money, and even marriage. At first, he assumes that Concha, being a poor, innocent, lower-class girl, would accept his proposal of financial help in exchange for sexual favours. As Concha becomes more beautiful and more desirable for other men, her exchange value increases, a surplus value that impels don Pasqual to transgress social conventions by offering her respectability through marriage. In return, don Pasqual must be 'content with very little', as Concha states at a certain point in the film. Concha/Dietrich's refusal to participate in these sexual-economic transactions regulating relationships between men and women in consumer culture hints at another danger. Like Carmen, Concha/Dietrich moves from one lover to another in a potentially endless sequence. But unlike Carmen, Concha's aimless, unmotivated desire epitomizes the spirit of modern consumerism, whose satisfaction is by definition impossible, thus making men interchangeable and expendable (Felski 1995: 78). As she explicitly puts it in her song 'Three Sweethearts I Have', 'To all three I'm true / And I could be as true to you'. Thus, the dangerous freedom of Concha cannot be attributed, as in the case of Carmen, to the primitivism and degeneration of non-white others, but rather to the collapse of traditional moral values brought about by modern consumerism in an industrially advanced white civilization.

Concha epitomizes the dangers of a feminized modernity associated with consumerism: the mesmerizing allure of new merchandise that undermines masculine qualities of rationality, productivity and repression, while empowering women (Felski 1995: 4). Don Pasqual's masochistic desire for Concha displays this danger of men's submitting to the seductive powers of women as erotic commodities. Moreover, Concha's empowerment enables her to be in control not only of her fate but also of that of her male lovers, finally saving Antonio—and the Republican cause—from submitting to her mesmerizing charms. She convinces Paquito, the governor, to supply her with passports to escape with her lover, Antonio, and she also makes her final decision to abandon him, once saved, a decision that would help preserve his virile masculinity as well. The final scene, in which she asks for a cigarette and lingers alone as if deciding on her next move, reinforces her control of her fate and of that of the male characters.[4] This ending clearly challenges Carmen's tragic end, dictated by a supernatural force that rules both her will and don Jose's. In Rey's adaptation, Carmen will equally escape death but at the price of containing her erotic power and accepting her marginal assigned role—symbolized by the iron gate that keeps her away at the end of the film—after having contributed to restoring the virile masculinity necessary for the military heroism required to win the Civil War for the Nationalist cause.

When *The Devil Is A Woman* was released in 1935, Spain was undergoing a significant process of economic modernization, although it was far behind the US standards of modernity in consumer culture, and in fact, Marlene Dietrich, like other Hollywood film stars, was associated with a world of impossible dreams (Pizarro 1933). However, the myth of Carmen, as an external and condensed version of a problematic Spanish national identity, was already charged with conflicting meanings in Spain (Serrano 1999: 14). For the Spanish advocates of enlightened liberalism, *Carmen* projected a debased image of Spain, an artificial, picturesque and foreign image of the country, within the tradition of *casticismo* (cultural nationalism), the world of *majos*, *majas*, and *toreros* (beaux, beauties, and bullfighters) that opposed the rationalization necessary to modernize the country. For the conservative sectors, it was unacceptable that a woman like Carmen, with such morally transgressive behaviour, should be taken as representative of Spain (González Troyano 1991: 23). Moreover, the prominence given to Andalusian culture and symbols throughout the rest of Spain came to be resented by those who felt these cultural elements as foreign (99). However, with the modernization of the country, the figures of Carmen and Andalusia were eventually restored as a kind of memorial to a type of life that the cultural homogenization of modernity was helping to make disappear. In the world of music, Spanish composers such as Albéniz, Falla, Granados, and Turina adopted the Romantics' orientalized version of Spain to create their own 'Spanish' music. Bizet's *Carmen* was the anthem of the 1992 World Exhibition of Seville (Álvarez Junco 2001: 265-266). Spanish cinema would also re-appropriate the Carmen myth to portray a view of the nation dealing with the ideological conflicts prevailing at key historical moments, before and after Franco, as the current volume shows.

Modernization and the ensuing changes in legislation occurring during the 1930s Spanish Republic brought about a new concern about the gender inversion associated this time with 'a national decline' centred on the masculinization of women, rather than on the loss of masculinity in men. However, the changes induced by modernization pulled women in divergent directions. On the one hand, Spanish women in urban areas were imitating female Hollywood stars like Jean Harlow (another 'blinding blonde') and dyed their hair platinum blonde—a clear sign of modernization that troubled the Nationalists, defenders of traditional moral codes. On the other hand, Nationalist sectors (groups like Catholic Action) aimed their discourses at resituating women in their place, the home, and at procuring their recognition of their husband as the *pater familias*, for the masculinization of women was seen as an aberration of modernization that undermined any eugenic project (Bussy Genevoise 1993). Thus a pure Hispanic race had to be cleansed of racial and sexual impurities as well as of biological and degenerating effects (Cleminson 2000).

The question of the Hispanic race ('la estirpe hispánica') and its associated issue of gender inversion, which occupied a central position in the contemporary Spanish nationalistic discourse after the Disaster of 1898, were also raised in the discourses surrounding *The Devil Is A Woman*. José María Gil Robles, Minister of War in 1935 and founder of the 1933 centre-right coalition CEDA, instigated a series of protests against the insulting representation of the Spanish armed forces in the film, using the Spanish Ambassador in Washington, Luis Calderón (*Washington Times* 1935). In a letter addressed to the foreign manager of the Motions Picture Producers and Distributors of America the Spanish Ambassador wrote that the essence of their objections was 'the influence possessed by a woman of doubtful reputation over Spanish Officials, judges, politicians and persons of different social spheres.' This was seen as 'detrimental to Spanish social and official life.'[5] In *La Prensa*, a Spanish newspaper published in the US for the Spanish-speaking community, an article encourages other Latin American countries to follow Spain's example and forbid those Hollywood films considered offensive to the Hispanic race (*Prensa* 1935a); films that had been invading their countries' own media, a commercial and cultural influence that the writer calls, curiously enough, 'la historia de la "penetración" de nuestros medios' (*Prensa* 1935b) ('the history of the "penetration" of our media'), a sexual metaphor referring to the US aggression, this time a cultural and economic one, perpetrated on Spanish virility/Spanish nation, rather than to Spain's masochistic desire for submission to a powerful US.

In this brief analysis I have intended to highlight the similarities and differences between Mérimée's Carmen and Sternberg's Carmenesque Dietrich in *The Devil Is A Woman*, two female figures created at very distinct periods. The power of seduction in both provokes similar emasculating effects on their white male social betters, reversing gender, class, and racial relations. But the difference in their racial/sexual otherness marks a clear distinction in the liability of these female figures to be subjected to their assigned roles in their contemporary dominant project of civilization. If Carmen's non-white imprint represented those features that opposed the nineteenth-century liberal project in Europe, Dietrich's blinding blondeness stood for the USA's burgeoning economic and cultural world power that in the 1930s Spain was taken as an act of aggression to their national identity. Spanish cinema, however, gave a prompt response by creating more racially ambiguous and less threatening Carmen figures to deal with the cultural conflicts of their time.[6]

Notes

1. More well-known is the same image in the oil painting 'El pelele', in the Prado Museum, Madrid.
2. I have previously studied in detail the construction of Dietrich's racial persona in her films with Sternberg and in other extra-cinematic discourses during the early thirties (Loyo 1998).
3. *The Devil Is A Woman*, press book (Paramount Pictures, 1935): no pagination.
4. Kathleen M Vernon (2004) makes a different reading of Concha/Dietrich's defiance of public male authority. For her, the country represented on screen does not keep any resemblance to the 'real', historical Spain, but it offers both Dietrich and Sternberg the opportunity to express their ambivalence towards Nazi Germany, the homeland from which they were exiles. The problem with this argument is that both Dietrich and Sternberg cannot really be considered exiles since they left Germany for economic rather than political reasons, and despite the fact that some of their films were prohibited in Nazi Germany.
5. Letter dated July 11, 1935 and sent by the Spanish Ambassador, Luis Calderón, to Major Frederick L. Herron, of M.P.P.D.A at New York.
6. I would like to thank Vicente Sánchez-Biosca, Juan José Carreras, Richard Cleminson, Francisco Vázquez García, Joaquín Díaz, Timothy Bozman, and Ann Davies for their various contributions to the writing of this paper.

References

Álvarez Junco, José. 2001. *Mater Dolorosa. La idea de España en el siglo XIX*, Madrid: Taurus.
Argentina, Imperio. 2001. *Imperio Argentina. Malena Clara*. In collaboration with P. M. Villora. Madrid: Ediciones Temas de Hoy.

Bussy Genevois, Danièle. 1993. 'El retorno de la hija pródiga: mujeres entre lo público y lo privado (1931-1936)' in Folgera, Pilar (ed.) *Otras visiones de España*. Madrid: Editorial Pablo Iglesias: 111-138.

Cleminson, Richard. 2000, 'En torno a sexualidad: "desviación sexual", raza y la construcción de la nación' in *Reverso* 3: 41-48.

Dyer, Richard. 1997. *White*. London and New York: Routledge.

Felski, Rita. 1995. *The Gender of Modernity*. London and Cambridge, MA: Harvard University Press.

González Troyano, Alberto. 1991. *La desventura de Carmen: una divagación sobre Andalucía*. Madrid: Espasa-Calpe.

Gould, Evelyn. 1996. *The Fate of Carmen*. Baltimore and London: Johns Hopkins University Press.

Jacobowitz, Florence. 1987. 'Power and the Masquerade: *The Devil Is A Woman*' in *CineAction!* 8: 32-41.

Kaiser, E. 1931. 'The Real Life Romance of Marlene Dietrich' in *Picturegoer* (November).

Labanyi, Jo. 1997. 'Race, Gender and Disavowal in Spanish Cinema of the Early Franco Period: The Missionary Film and the Folkloric Musical' in *Screen* 38(3): 215-231.

Lee, S. 1933. 'Is Marlene in Love for the Second Time?' in *Motion Picture* (June).

López, Ana M.. 1999. 'Hollywood-México: Dolores del Río, una estrella transnacional' in *Archivos de la Filmoteca* 31: 12-25.

Louys, Pierre. 1935. *The Woman and the Puppet* (tr. Arthur Symons). London: Thornton Butterworth.

Loyo, Hilaria. 1998. 'So White that it Hurts: Marlene Dietrich and 1930s US Culture'. Paper presented at *4th Seminar on Culture and Power: Cultural Confrontations* (University of Zaragoza, September 1998)

McClary, Susan. 1992. *George Bizet: Carmen*. Cambridge: Cambridge University Press.

Mérimée, Prosper. 1989. *Carmen* (ed. and tr. Luis López Jiménez and Luis Eduardo López Estévez). Madrid: Cátedra.

Mulvey, Laura. 1988. 'Visual Pleasure and Narrative Cinema' in Penley, Constance (ed.) *Feminism and Film Theory*. London, Routledge: 69-79.

Pizarro, José. 1933. 'La venus rubia' in *La Voz* (21 March).

Praz, Mario. 1969. *La carne, la muerte y el diablo en la literatura romántica* (tr. Jorge Cruz). Caracas: Monte Ávila.

Prensa, La. 1935a. 'El cine anti-hispano' (18 October).

— 1935b. 'Una lección utilísima' (11 November).

Serrano, Carlos. 1999. *El nacimiento de Carmen. Símbolos, mitos, nación*. Madrid: Taurus.

Shaffer, R. 1933. 'Marlene Tells Why She Wears Men's Clothes' in *Motion Picture*, 45(3): 54-55 and 70.

Silverman, Kaja. 1992. *Male Subjectivity At The Margins*. London and New York: Routledge.

Studlar, Gaylyn. 1988. *In the Realm of Pleasure: Von Sternberg, Dietrich, and the Masochistic Aesthetic*. Urbana and Chicago: University of Illinois Press.

Symons, Arthur. 1935. 'Introduction' in Louys, Pierre *The Woman and the Puppet*. London: Thornton Butterworth.

Vázquez García, Francisco. 2001. '"En busca de hombres": Regeneracionismo y crisis
    de la masculinidad (España 1898-1915)'. Paper presented at *Colloque ETILAL*
    (University of Montpellier, December 2001).
Vernon, Kathleen M. 2004. 'Remaking Spain: Trans/national Mythologies and
    Cultural Fetishism in *The Devil is A Woman* (Sternber, 1935) and *Cet obscur
    object du désir* (Buñuel, 1977)', in *Journal of Romance Studies,* 4/1: 13-27.
Washington Times. 1935. 'US Stops Dietrich Picture' (12 November)

Rehispanicizing Carmen: Cultural Reappropriations in Spanish Cinema

José F. Colmeiro

The chapter examines the different forms of cultural reappropriation that the myth of Carmen has undergone in Spanish cinema, with particular attention to Florián Rey's *Carmen la de Triana* (1938), Tulio Demicheli's *Carmen la de Ronda* (1959), and Carlos Saura's *Carmen* (1983). At key historical moments in the modern reshaping of the nation—in the middle of the Spanish Civil War, under Franco's dictatorship, and during the post-Franco process of European integration—Carmen's myth is reappropriated and made a site of struggle for cultural identity. Spain's position in this process was singular and contradictory, for as an integral part of European culture it participated in this exotic venture in search of the picturesque, at the same time that its own eccentric cultural construction was highly mediated by orientalism. The chapter traces throughout the three films the ways in which the reabsorption and reproduction of these foreign-made constructs responds in large measure to the process of commodification of Carmen, already a well-known cultural product of continuing valuable currency in foreign markets, but also allows the reappropriation and contestation of those constructs for the purpose of internal national identification.

Cultural reappropriation
Demicheli, Tulio: *Carmen la de Ronda*
Myth (of Carmen)
National Identity (Spanish)
Rey, Florián: *Carmen la de Triana*
Saura, Carlos: *Carmen*

I would like to examine some of the different forms of cultural reappropriation that the myth of Carmen has undergone in Spanish cinema, with particular attention to Florián Rey's *Carmen, la de Triana* (1938), Tulio Demicheli's *Carmen, la de Ronda* (1959), and Carlos Saura's *Carmen* (1983). At key historical moments in the modern reshaping of the nation-state—in the middle of the Spanish Civil War, under Franco's dictatorship, and during the post-Franco process of political transition and European integration—Carmen's myth is reappropriated and made a site of struggle for cultural identity. The colonized marginal figure of the Gypsy woman is symbolically relocated to the centre in the process of reconfiguration of national identity, revealing the cultural anxieties provoked by the complex conflicts of gender, race, ethnicity, and sexuality in the formation of the modern self.

The mythical construction of the Gypsy in the European imagination is directly related to the orientalist discourse of exoticism. The conflation of orientalism with the exoticized and idealized images of Gypsies have also been intimately linked and con-fused with the modern construction of Spanishness. Spain's position in this process was singular and contradictory, for as an integral part of European culture it participated in this exotic venture in search of the picturesque, at the same time that its own eccentric cultural construction was highly mediated by orientalism (Colmeiro 2002). This contradiction engendered the creation of an internal other in the figure of the Gypsy, and through the absorption and reproduction of the foreign orientalist perspective, the establishment of the Gypsy as a privileged symbolic representation of national culture. Spain occupied in the European imagination the same space that the Gypsy occupied in the Spanish self-image: that of an exotic internal other. As cultural critics such as Mitchell (1994) and Charnon-Deutsch (2002) have shown, Spanish artists, musicians, and writers of all political inclinations have been complicit in the perpetuation of this mythologized and exoticized vision of Spain since the dawn of modernity. In reaction to the perceived dangers brought by modernity, many artists and intellectuals searched for ancestral and 'authentic' notions of *la raza*, a racialized cultural construction of the nation. Through this myth, radical differences are sublimated and Gypsies become symbolic token figures in the process of constructing a national identity. The mythical figure of the Gypsy is then reduced to a discursive trope, a convenient synecdoche for Spanishness.

The representation of the Gypsy followed a consistent pattern from the nineteenth-century *costumbristas* (writers treating traditional local customs and types) through to the modernist mythical re-elaborations of Falla, Manuel Machado, Martínez Sierra, and García Lorca, to the endless exploitation of the spectacle of Gypsy flamenco in national folkloric cinema beyond political or ideological orientation, during the silent film era and the Second Republic, on both sides of the Civil War, and on through Franco's nationalist regime. The Gypsy was dependent on an ambiguous Romantic vision of the natural, instinctual individual, necessarily marginal and outcast. Moreover, the Gypsy enabled a symbolic construction of a Spanish cultural identity predicated on a racial figure at once affirming and denying difference, an ambiguity for which the Carmen myth, forever entangled in a European/Spanish, Gypsy/*payo*, self/other battle for cultural definition, would be perceived as an ideal instrument.

Curiously, it is the international recognition of the Carmen story beyond Spanish borders that explains the internalization of the myth in Spanish culture throughout the twentieth century. Clearly, the reabsorption and reduplication of these foreign-made constructs, the topical 'typical Spanish' images endlessly reproduced, responds in large measure to the process of commodification of Carmen, already a well-known cultural product of continuing valuable currency in foreign markets. But, by the same token, the universal familiarity of the myth also allows the reappropriation and/or contestation of those constructs for the purpose of national identification according to different ideological currents and political currents. The interface between national and international economies, internal political struggle and international relations, European and Spanish cultures, is replayed in the new rehispanicized film versions of the story of the Gypsy Carmen, as the cultural struggle of North/South, white/Gypsy, impostor/authentic is reenacted in the process of market commodification, cultural reappropriation and national reconfiguration.

While the adaptation of Mérimée's novel to opera definitively crystallized the modern cultural icon of Carmen as the rebellious and exotic Spanish Gypsy woman, its numerous adaptations to the screen clearly strengthened the firm hold of those images in the realm of twentieth-century mass culture. Indeed, the film industry firmly established Carmen in the collective imagination very early on, as the democratic affordability of cinema enabled it to reach popular audiences worldwide. Cecil B. DeMille's version of *Carmen* in 1915, and its subsequent burlesque parody by Charles Chaplin the following year, are clear indication of the audience's familiarity with these images, indeed of their status as a widely recognizable set of stereotypical constructions of Spanish and Gypsies, and therefore subject to subversive parody.

Perhaps this opportunity for subversive parody is what led Luis Buñuel to play the part of a *bandolero* in one of the early major productions of Carmen, directed by Jacques Feyder in 1926, starring the well-known Spanish singer/actress Raquel Meller. Fully embodying onscreen as well as offscreen the fictional role of Carmen the independent, free spirited, and fiery, markedly ethnic woman untamable and uncompromising with rules and scripts, Meller is remembered as constantly at odds with the French director, arguing for her own particular version of scripted scenes, and even asking one day to speak on the telephone with *Mesié* Mérimée to convince him to change the script (Moix 1993: 11). This defiantly rebellious attitude was no doubt due in part to the clout of her international diva status, as much as to the nature of the character represented on screen, already well commodified in many earlier productions. But ultimately, this tension underlines a recurring theme in future Spanish screen adaptations of Carmen: the dissatisfaction with a pre-scripted cultural construction reflecting French attitudes and values, more than with Gypsy culture or Spanish realities. It suggests the need and desire to rehispanicize Carmen, while showing at the same time the difficulty of disassembling those inherited images and, ultimately, the unfeasibility of such a project when a white 'Gypsy' assumes the leading role.

These cultural tensions are prominently displayed in the German-Spanish co-production of *Carmen, la de Triana* directed by Florián Rey, a particularly fascinating version, given the exceptional historical circumstances of its production. This new *Carmen*, filmed in Berlin in 1938 during the Spanish Civil War at the invitation of the Nazi propaganda minister Goebbels, featured Imperio Argentina in the role of Carmen and the technical support of German specialists. It is well known that Adolf Hitler was an admirer of Rey and Argentina's earlier folkloric film *Nobleza baturra* (Aragonese Virtue, 1935), one of the most successful films of the 'golden age' of Spanish cinema during the Second Republic. Imperio Argentina was already an international star who had made films in Argentina and Cuba, and co-starred with Carlos Gardel and Maurice Chevalier in Paris, at a time when Nazi Germany's propaganda machine was eager to increase its presence in foreign film markets. Built upon the international marketability of Carmen, this new version offers proof of the basic ambiguity and adaptability of the myth to different temporal, political, and historical circumstances. In the same manner that Gypsies frequently are valued as exotic performers while marginalized as real life people, Rey's *Carmen* further proves that the language of exoticism—safely removed from reality—did not pose any real threats to Fascist ideology. In fact, it could be employed to reinforce the sense of cultural and racial superiority.[1] Similarly, the sexual and political threat represented by the figure of Carmen could be easily neutralized by relegating her to a marginalized space of exclusion and accentuating her self-imposed submission, thus ultimately reinforcing patriarchal order. As a result, the figure of the Gypsy is constructed as an internal other, a symbolic mirror where the cultural and political dominant forces project their own particular representations of the nation according to the rules of the new order.

Not surprisingly, the key political subtext of the story is the overbearing presence of the military machine from the first to the last scene. The quintessentially hierarchical and patriarchal institution of the army embodies in the film the power of the law, its enforcement, the enactment of justice, and its repressive capacity to discipline and punish, but also to reward and honour those sacrificed in the name of the nation. Clearly, the political context of the civil war sweeps through the film's narrative. The commanding officer of the occupying army announces to the newly arrived brigadier José

Navarro that their presence is needed to fight a war against the enemy, the local smugglers (for, as in a civil war conflict, the enemy is within). He further advises José to have no contact with the natives, but contact is exactly what takes place in the following scene when he meets Carmen. Predictably, José falls for Carmen and then falls into disgrace as he subsequently joins the smugglers; but in a reversal of the scripted story, Carmen finally submits to patriarchal order allowing José to break free and follow his own conscience, thus restoring the honour lost. He eventually surrenders, thus saving the army of Dragoons from a sure defeat by revealing the smugglers' plan to blow up the bridge they must cross. José dies from a smuggler's bullet, but through his sacrificial heroic gesture his honour is finally restored and he is posthumously re-awarded his lost stripes. Neutralizing the subversive potential of the myth, Carmen is made to conform to the Fascist ideal construction of femininity as submissive and resigned and is spared her life in the end, as a heroic death is reserved for the male soldier, the self-sacrificed martyr hero of Fascist ideology. Interestingly, José's public disavowal of his Basque ethnic background, so carefully constructed by Mérimée and maintained in Bizet's opera, is particularly fitting here, as he affirms 'No soy vasco, soy de Navarra' (I am not a Basque, I am from Navarre). For the purposes of creating a nationalistic hero in the political context of 1938, it is important that José reject his Basque identity (since the Basque Country supported the Republican side during the Civil War, but Navarre was a stronghold of Francoist support). As in the case of Carmen—who had been conveniently neutralized as threatening other and transformed into a devout Catholic, subservient woman—José is made to sacrifice his conflicting ethnic identity in order to be a politically suitable national hero.

Rey's folkloric version of *Carmen*, despite its German-constructed papier mâché Andalusia, is one of the first partially successful attempts at the rehispanicization of Carmen, largely due to his well established experience behind the camera and Argentina's strong screen presence. Bizet's score disappears completely, replaced by the more appropriate Spanish *coplas* filling the film soundtrack ('Los piconeros' and the García Lorca-influenced 'Antonio Vargas Heredia').[2] In this unusual version, the folkloric aspects and comic situations are accentuated while its subversive subtext is completely neutralized. Comedy prevails over drama, as Carmen's *duende* (mysterious and tragic aura) is transformed into mere Andalusian *gracia* (witty charm). She is definitely a tamer Carmen, a devout Catholic and white 'Gypsy' Carmen, not involved in the deaths of any men. Nevertheless, Falangist critics in Fascist Spain criticized the co-production for using as inspiration a 'cheap foreigner' such as Mérimée (Kinder 1993: 461). While on the Republican side, not only was it not shown in theatres, but the former and immensely popular film *Morena Clara* (White Gypsy) made by Rey and Argentina during the Second Republic was banned as well.

In the first two decades of Franco's dictatorship, the autarchic years of political, economical and cultural self-sufficiency, foreign models were frowned upon with suspicion by nationalist ideologues. Thus, Carmen underwent a new transformation. She had to be exorcised and re-imagined, made to conform to the new nationalist rules of the game, as in the popular *copla* 'Carmen de España' by Quintero, León and Quiroga originally sung by Juanita Reina and later identified with the appropriately re-baptized actress/singer Carmen Sevilla. According to the nationalist ideology of the new order, Carmen was now truly Spanish at last, a Spanish Gypsy *but* 'Christian and decent' nonetheless, devoid of all excesses. Thus, the 'authentic' Spanish Carmen can reclaim her own identity, which, in her own words, is definitely not a product of Mérimée's imagination:

> Carmen de España,
> manola,
> Carmen de España,
> valiente,
> Carmen con bata de cola,
> pero cristiana y decente.
> [...]
> Yo soy la Carmen de España
> y no la de Mérimée.
>
> (Carmen of Spain,
> proud,
> Carmen of Spain,
> brave,
> Carmen in a Gypsy costume,
> but Christian and decent.
> [...]
> I am the Spanish Carmen
> and not Mérimée's.)[3]

This Spanish Carmen, as rebellious and strong willed as ever, defiantly affirms her 'authentic' identity with nationalistic pride, while condemning the foreign construction of Carmen, the cultural text that Carmen has become, either in print or on stage, as fundamentally inauthentic, a simulacrum of the real thing, almost foreshadowing future postmodern Carmen figures who reject or resist the traditional 'script':

Me han cantado en el teatro
lo mimo que a la traviata,
mas le aviso a más de cuatro
que voy a meter la pata,
pues me tiene hasta lo pelo
que ande suerta por ahí
una Carmen de camelo
que en na se parece a mí.

(They've sung my song on stage
just like they've sung La Traviata,
but I am warning you all
that I am going to butt in,
for it gets on my nerves
that some fake Carmen
who has nothing to do with me
is roaming around free.)

The Spanish Carmen was resurrected again on screen in 1959, when the process of defascistization was already completed but before the more open political climate of the 1960s had developed, this time as *Carmen, la de Ronda* (AKA *The Devil Made a Woman* and *A Girl Against Napoleon*), directed by Tulio Demicheli. Interestingly, this exuberantly rehispanicized version of Carmen resorts to classical Hollywood visual codes and characteristically big-studio production style. This fact can be explained by economic as well as political and cultural forces at play. The film was produced in the heyday of the studio system and it attempted to create a product capable or competing in foreign markets, banking on the international status of its leading star, Sara Montiel. We should also remember that the 1950s marked the definitive entrance of Spain into the area of American political and cultural influence, after the military and economic pacts between Franco and Eisenhower. It is not surprising then that this re-enactment of Carmen, in a constant tension between Spanish referents and Hollywood codes, reveals the process of cultural reinscription. Thus, while the film unequivocally rejects French political domination it appears to openly embrace American hegemony.

The film was conceived from the start as an international production, with the veteran director Benito Perojo in the figure of the executive producer, hiring an accomplished but obscure Argentinian director to bring to life his revision of Carmen. The international cast included the French actor Maurice Ronet as José, the veteran Italian Amedeo Nazzari as the Colonel, and in the role of Carmen the Spanish actress/singer Sara Montiel, the new Hispanic mega-star of her generation already triumphant in Latin America and Hollywood (and arguably the greatest diva produced by Spanish cinema in its entire history).

This rehispanicized version of Carmen reveals the cultural paradox of many other Spanish productions of the Franco years, affirming nationalistic values while adopting and adapting the dominant patterns of American cinema. Thus, the hegemonic Hollywood style is prevalent in the glamorous close-up shots of Montiel, the exuberant makeup and costumes, the use of colour saturation in full Hollywood fashion, and in the emulation of the visual style and musical rhythm of western epics. The well commodified myth of Carmen served as an appropriate vehicle for Sara Montiel to exploit and export her eroticized Spanish image, but demanded from the viewer a supreme act of suspension of disbelief in her role as Andalusian Gypsy, only neutralized by the implicit pact of accepted fictiveness in the musical genre.

In line with the nationalist political agenda, this rehispanicized version of *Carmen* combines the two most popular film genres of the 1940s and 1950s: the folkloric musical and the historical film. In order to better serve the needs of the present, both Mérimée's story and Bizet's music had to be adapted and recontextualized. Bizet's score is substituted through a process of musical rehispanicization by a score evoking Manuel de Falla's *El amor brujo* and, as in Rey's *Carmen*, an anthology of popular Spanish *coplas*, whose greatest miracle is threading the diverse musical numbers through the pre-scripted narrative line. The film also rewrites Mérimée's story in the context of the shifting of the prevailing post-Civil War nationalist, Francoist ideology of resistance against foreign discourses, at a crucial time when the need to open up to new modernizing forces in order to survive became increasingly clear. The regime's characteristic ambiguity towards modernization during that period, struggling to achieve economic modernization without political modernization—in the form of the democratic ideals represented by other European nations and the United States—was also reflected in the film's ambivalent attitude and tension between national/foreign models, and symbolically represented in the passionate love/hate relationships between the main characters.

Through a convenient process of recontextualization, the film resituates the story in 1808 in the southern city of Ronda during the Napoleonic occupation, which marked the birth of modern Spanish nationalism. Demicheli's Carmen is used as a symbol of resistance against the occupying forces and the bandits are reconfigured as guerrilla freedom fighters against the French invaders. José, a Basque from Lizondo enlisted in the occupying French army, is portrayed as an unpatriotic *afrancesado* (supporter of French ideas) willing to change alliances with the enemy and betray the motherland (a reminder that Basque nationalism was considered one of the traditional 'enemies of Spain' in Francoist discourse). The situation, however, develops in a more ambiguous way than it appears at first sight. From the beginning, the spectator is supposed to distrust José, as a betrayer siding with the foreign invader; but later the situation is reversed when he falls in love with Carmen, kills the colonel and escapes to join the guerrilla in the mountains. The initially despised invading soldier is transformed into a more sympathetic fugitive, and the viewer is expected to empathize with him, with his suffering, his noble character and capacity for love and sacrifice. José's transformation for the viewer is parallel to Carmen's shifting desires, as seen in her trajectory from lover of a Spanish freedom fighter (the brutal and vindictive Antonio) to lover of a French ex-soldier (the honourable José). Carmen's new love for José is indicative of the allure of the new and foreign, and of the danger that it represents. In a reversal of the mythical free independent woman, she is willing to sacrifice her life for his love and succumb to an impossible doomed relationship.

Paradoxically, Carmen's nationalist affirmation coincides with her embrace of the foreigner. In the final scene, Carmen and José are killed by the French soldiers and die in each other's arms, both sacrificial victims of unattainable freedom and unfulfilled desires, as the Spanish people prepare the uprising against the invaders. In a single shot, the foreigners are collectively rejected and physically embraced at the same time, a curious juxtaposition that sums up the ambiguous nature of the film. Its hyperbolic affirmation of national identity is countered by its subliminally stated need to open up to the world outside and come to terms with the new cultural currents outside the national borders.[4] It appears to suggest that resisting outside influences, instead of opening up to them, would amount to a futile collective suicidal act. This is, of course, the economic and cultural crossroads Spanish society was facing in the late fifties, a critical turning point in its history which eventually would give way to the intense process of cultural change of the sixties and early seventies marked by internationalization (of capital investment, labour and tourism) and economic development.

The long list of folkloric variations of Carmen and its imitations, particularly fruitful and politically useful during the Francoist period, finally came to an end with a final exorcism; the ideologically loaded *españolada* (the stereotypical representation of the exotic Spain of bullfights and castanets), always anathema to the intellectual anti-Franco resistance, was to be contested by the new forces of modernity unleashed with the political changes following Franco's demise. The spirit of historical revision of the new democratic culture would be more prone to challenge the traditional usurpation of Gypsiness by non—Gypsies, the appropriation of Spanishness by foreign cultural colonizers and authoritarian nationalist discourses alike, while denouncing their essential falsification. This new spirit led Spanish soprano Teresa Berganza to reclaim for the opera in 1977 a new rehispanicized Carmen: 'Mi mayor deseo en este momento es el poder borrar para siempre de la mente y de la fantasía de los públicos la falsa idea de Carmen [...] con mi interpretación buscaré también el poder entregar al público la imagen de una España auténtica' (My greatest wish at this moment is to be able to erase for good from the public's mind and imagination the false idea of Carmen [...] I shall also do my best to present to the public the image of a real Spain) (Berganza 1978: 8, 9).

From a similar perspective, Carlos Saura's flamenco dance film *Carmen* (1983) attempts to return Carmen to the Gypsy roots of flamenco culture from where she was originally abducted. This rehispanicization of Carmen has at its core a quest for cultural 'authenticity', reclaiming Carmen's roots in Spanish flamenco dance and song, while at the same time being fully conscious of the constructed nature of cultural identity, presenting it as a complex performance within a performance.[5] This film adaptation was the second part of a well-known trilogy in collaboration with choreographer Antonio Gades, probing into the well established tradition of artistic idealization of the Gypsy myth and its use in the construction of Spanishness. Saura's *Carmen* exposes the contradictions and conflicts of this stereotypical artistic stylization serving the ideological purpose of imposing an identity from outside (by a Romantic foreign sensibility to the exotic), from above (by a centrally designed project of political unity, typical of the Franco years) or from within (by accepting and absorbing that imposed identity). Saura's work functions as a collective exorcism of exoticism, a cathartic process of self-questioning in search of an authentic collective identity. It explores new symbolic forms of national identity in a socio-historical moment of necessary cultural redefinition following the collapse of Franco's regime. It constitutes a cathartic process of interrogation and liberation of images tied to the past, rescued from their old ideological use (with a homogenizing and integrating effect inside the country, and outside it an exoticizing effect that is overdetermined by alterity). It provides a renovated vision that has exorcised the stale, typical Spanish images of *l'espagnolade*, resignifying their false 'Spanish' content by exposing their constructedness. It is for this reason that, while basically agreeing with the sound analysis of Saura's *Carmen* offered by Fiddian and Evans (1988: 83-92), I would argue that at the core of Gades and Saura's collaborative project we find not the 'europeanization of Carmen', but, on the contrary, we witness her rehispanicization, through the deconstruction of the ideological underpinnings of the European formation of the Carmen myth.

In this version Mérimée's and Bizet's texts undergo a process of specular confrontation in an intertextual set of reflections in search of an ideal, uncorrupted form, the reflection of an identity assumed as one's own. This process of self-questioning is accompanied as well by a great deal of self-reflexivity underlining the processes of identification in artistic creation and filmic representation, as well as in the construction of the spectator as subject. The vehicle and visual metaphor for all these processes of identity construction in Saura's *Carmen* is the specular reflection, and the mirror functions as the basic structuring principle in the construction of subjectivity (Colmeiro 1995; D'Lugo 1991: 203-213).

Saura's *Carmen* foregrounds the search for identity in alterity, revealing in the last instance the fictive and imaginary nature of that homogeneous representation of Spanishness. The unifying element of this whole enterprise is the structure of split specularity, or specular reduplication. This structure frames the search for an autonomous and coherent identity manifested in a variety of registers through the encounter of self and other. The double framing of the film—narrating the process of preparation and rehearsal for a dance performance— blurs the clear demarcations between both narratives, between actors and performers, presentation and representation. Thus, this search for identity mirrors the fictional director's search for the perfect Carmen throughout Seville's dance studios and the difficult if not impossible process of imposing a ready-made identity on his chosen dancer (not a Gypsy). The spectacle of the struggle between personal identity and cultural construction is played out before and behind the camera, as the new Carmen, in a mismatch of realities and expectations, is forced to conform to the scripted role. Another older and much more experienced flamenco dancer Cristina, who has the racial look of a Gypsy, is denied the role of Carmen that she felt entitled to portray— on the grounds that her physical appearance does not conform to the idealized stereotype. Cristina is relegated to training Carmen for the role she is not allowed to perform, a casting choice that disavows her ethnic and professional identity, and, ultimately, fatally undermines the authenticity of the final project.

The cinematographic construction also reveals the process of supra-individual identification. The film mobilizes the notion of filmic spectacle as a mirror reflecting the images of a collective identity. In this respect, particularly representative is the scene where Gades, alone facing the mirror in a climactic moment of self-questioning, conjures up the stereotyped image of Carmen ('with the fan, the comb, the flower, the mantilla, all the clichés') before she materializes precisely in front of the mirror. Here the mirror reflects the vision provided by the other, a foreign image of an exotic and pseudo-romantic Spain, the picturesque and archetypal Spain of *l'espagnolade* that has been internalized. The ubiquity and force of this deep-rooted image imposes itself upon the weary Antonio, as he surrenders and finally submits to its exoticism: 'So who cares anyway? Why not?', perhaps anticipating his final defeat.

This false identification is recognized as a case of mistaken identity and is publicly destroyed in the following scene where the cast performs a parodic inversion of the French *espagnolade*: the clichés of the sensual Gypsy girl, the macho toreador, and the national fiesta are performed and ridiculed as empty signifiers at a cast party ending with an impromptu flamenco Gypsy *fiesta* as grand finale. This festive performance enacts the return of the oppressed, including the 'Gypsy revenge' of Cristina, the self-reflexive caricature of Romantic clichés, some ludic gender bending, and a parodic inversion of authority. This collective oppositional act, which Bakhtin would define as 'carnivalesque', subverts the cultural paradigms through the performers' exorcism of *l'espagnolade* in front of the disarmed director. Saura exemplarily demonstrates that laughter can indeed be a powerful instrument for upsetting long-established conventions. The resistance to an imposed ready-made image parallels the affirmation of an identity that looks to the collectivity for its authentic roots. The film thus becomes the mirror reflection of the collective self, rejecting the constructed foreign image provided by the Other and re-imagining the self, opposing popular to high culture, the Gypsy flamenco music, dance, and songs to *bel canto*, and self-definition to a definition imposed from outside.

In the final analysis, Saura's self-reflexive re-enactment of Carmen remains an illusory proposition, for Carmen ultimately escapes representation. The attempt of Antonio, the director-within-the film, to create an 'authentic' Gypsy Carmen is bound to fail and in the end Antonio finds Carmen impossible to represent (as she rebels against performing the stereotypical role of Carmen and eventually dies for not conforming). Nevertheless, in spite of the metafictional mirroring of Antonio standing in for the film director, as earlier the French narrator for the author of the novella, Antonio's defeat is ultimately Saura's success. As long as Carmen is not allowed to speak herself, the film seems to suggest, she will always be misread. Carmen's final ambiguous death (killed by Antonio the dancer portraying don José or by Antonio the director?) has a symbolic meaning beyond the literal sense: the illusion of recreating an 'authentic' Carmen, mediated through a French Romantic orientalist mould, becomes an impossible representation. Carmen's death ultimately signifies the need to exorcise once and for all the exotic construction of Gypsiness and Spanishness.

The spectacle seen through the mirror of Gades/Saura presents an individual and collective identity in a continuous tortuous process of self-questioning, involving at different moments rejection, supplantation, reabsorption and parodic inversion. The film's high degree of specularization reiterates its imaginary composition and mobilizes the spectator's awareness of the constructed nature of that identity. The explicit foregrounding of the specular framing conditions and restrains the spectator's identification with the image reflected—in a manner reminiscent of Brecht's *Verfremdunseffekt* or 'alienation effect' on the audience—which can only take place on the basis of its acceptance as an imaginary construct. In the mirror of infinite citations and endless recycling of received images of Spanishness, Saura calls attention to the way those images have been constructed, rather than having a direct correspondence to some essential reality. As we have seen, the enduring repetition of the cliché images, like the endless reflexive citation of orientalist discourses and the multiple resurrections of Carmen, have authorized a long chain of appropriations, misrepresentations, and distortions, used as sites for negotiating the political and cultural anxieties of hegemonic groups in different times and locations. What all of the Carmen films analyzed here have in common, although espousing quite different artistic and ideological objectives, is their attempt to rehispanize Carmen, by reappropriating the cultural capital invested in the myth. Rey's folkloric version of Carmen successfully negotiates the German and Spanish Fascist ideologies during the Spanish Civil War; Demicheli's nationalist epic with Hollywood undertones constructs a more ambiguous rendering of Spain's changing post-war cultural climate and political realignment in the context of the cold war; finally, Saura's postmodernist work in the art film tradition deconstructs Carmen during the post-Franco process of European integration. The mirror of infinite citations might prove impossible to shatter, but, as

Saura's film seems to suggest, only by recognizing the romanticized mistaken identity, by questioning the cultural assumptions underlying the Carmen myth and by exorcizing their exoticism is it possible that the mythical notion of the Spanish Gypsy might be finally confronted and put to rest.[6]

Notes

1. A metafictional version of this historical episode was re-enacted by Fernando Trueba in his 1998 *La niña de tus ojos* (The Girl of Your Dreams), featuring Penélope Cruz and Jorge Sanz, which was publicly denounced by Imperio Argentina, disavowing the sexual and political undertones of the film and its relation to the factual events represented.
2. A German version of the film, entitled *Andalusische Nächte* (Andalusian Nights), was directed simultaneously by Herbert Maisch, also with Imperio Argentina in the leading role, phonetically saying her lines and singing her *coplas* in German.
3. The Spanish text is from Vázquez Montalbán's *Cancionero general del franquismo* (2000: 65). The English translations are my own.
4. The ambiguous nature of the movie is reflected in the duplicitousness of José—both Spanish and French—and in Carmen herself, maneuvering between her alliance with the fighters and her apparent friendship with the invaders. As her archrival Micaela puts it: 'Es el juego de Carmen. Queda bien con Dios y el diablo' (That's Carmen's game. She's on good terms with both God and the Devil). A somewhat similar ambivalent figure is Lucas, the bullfighter, another political *afrancesado*, who is publicly scorned by the people for his political allegiance when not a single soul in Ronda attends his bullfight. But Lucas is also ultimately redeemed when he gives up the money received from the French to the Spanish fighters: 'Al servicio de España, aunque parezca amigo de los franceses' (At the service of Spain, even though he looks like a friend of the French).
5. Saura effectively underlines those 'performative aspects of gypsy spectacle' that Charnon-Deutsch appreciates in flamenco dance and song, debunking the myths of 'authenticity' and 'spontaneity' (2002: 29-30). As she points out, spontaneity and authenticity were perceived from early on as assets that Gypsy performers actively and consciously cultivated. Yet, the transformation of flamenco performers into professionals in the nineteenth century also parallels the progressive transformation of Gypsies into symbolic commodities of Spanishness for the consumption of the native bourgeoisie and foreigners alike.
6. Vicente Aranda's *Carmen* (2003), although a Spanish-British-Italian co-production, effectively adds to the list of Spanish Carmens. His intention is to challenge Bizet's story, which constitutes in his own words 'una falsedad literaria con buena música', 'a literary falsification with good music' (Martí).

References

Berganza, Teresa. 1978. Letter to Peter Diamand, 7 July 1977, in Booklet to *Carmen* by George Bizet. Deutsche Grammophon 419 636-2.
Charnon-Deutsch, Lou. 2002. 'Travels of the Imaginary Spanish Gypsy' in Jo Labanyi (ed.) *Constructing Identity in Contemporary Spain*. Oxford: Oxford University Press: 22-40.
Colmeiro, José. F.. 1995. 'El espectáculo tras el espejo de Gades/Saura' in *Siglo XX/20th Century. Critique and Cultural Discourse* 13(1-2): 161-175.

—— 2002. 'Exorcising Exoticism: *Carmen* and the Oriental Construction of Spain' in *Comparative Literature* 54(2): 127-144.

D'Lugo, Marvin. 1991. *The Films of Carlos Saura: The Practice of Seeing*. Princeton: Princeton University Press.

Fiddian, Robin and Evans, Peter William. 1988. *Challenges to Authority: Fiction and Film in Contemporary Spain*. London: Tamesis Books.

Kinder, Marsha. 1993. *Blood Cinema: The Reconstruction of National Identity in Spain*. Berkeley, CA: University of California Press.

Martí, María H.. 2002. 'Aranda recupera a la "violenta y agresiva" "Carmen" de Mérimée' in *El País digital* (25 October). On line at: http://www.elpais.es/suple/cine/articulo.hmtl?xref=20021025 (consulted 5.01.2004)

Mitchell, Timothy. 1994. *Flamenco Deep Song*. New Haven: Yale University Press.

Moix, Terenci. 1993. *Suspiros de España*. Barcelona: Plaza & Janés.

Vázquez Montalbán, Manuel. 2000. *Cancionero general del franquismo, 1939-1975*. Barcelona: Crítica.

Putting the Blame on Carmen:
The Rita Hayworth Version

Peter William Evans

Coupled again with Glenn Ford (as in *Gilda*, 1946 and *Affair in Trinidad*, 1952), Rita Hayworth in *The Loves of Carmen* (Charles Vidor, 1948), is caught between, on the one hand, late 1940s Hollywood versions of sexual difference and ethnic/racial otherness and, on the other, what Richard Dyer (1978), writing about *Gilda*, has defined as the star's 'resistance through charisma'. *The Loves of Carmen* links its interest in the otherness of the Spanish/Gypsy settings with anxieties over sexual difference focussed, above all, on its star vehicle, Rita Hayworth, in whose languid, mocking and treacherous sensuality this film, as in other Hayworth vehicles such as *Blood and Sand* (1941), *The Lady from Shanghai* (1948) or *Salome* (1953), gets more than it bargained for. The essay explores the various competing discourses of *The Loves of Carmen* mainly through questions about the shifting and contradictory meanings of the persona or 'masquerade' of Rita Hayworth. After a theoretical and historical introduction it moves to discuss Hayworth's Carmen in terms of the erasure of Gypsy ethnicity through Americanization, and Carmen's betrayal of don José as another example of the betrayal of the *femme fatale* of American noir. The essay concludes by positing both Hayworth and her Carmen in terms of mimicry and masquerade.

Ethnicity (Gypsy), cultural representations of
Femme fatale
Hayworth, Rita
Masquerade
Star persona
Vidor, Charles: *The Loves of Carmen*

Introduction

Rita Hayworth's transformation from Margarita Carmen Cansino—her real name—into 'Rita Hayworth', the revered 1940s sex goddess, crystallizes in miniature the larger processes of narrativization of gender and history in one of her most characteristic films, *The Loves of Carmen* (Charles Vidor, 1948), the principal role in which her own middle name seemed to make her destined to play. My essay is divided into four parts; a historical and theoretical introduction that will also point ahead to ways in which I shall focus discussion as a whole, followed by three sub-headings, Americanization, Betrayal, and Mimicry or Masquerade, beneath which I shall consider Rita Hayworth's persona and its adaptation to her role as Carmen.

Born in 1918 in New York, she was the daughter of Eduardo Cansino and Volga Haworth or Hayworth (biographers differ on the point), the latter an Irish/English American, the former a Spaniard and

Spanish and Latin American dancing teacher. Taking after him, Rita Hayworth—the name she adopted pretty soon after she was contracted by her first studio, Fox—began her performing career as a dancer. From Fox, where in a tiny dancing role she made her first film, *Dante's Inferno* (Harry Lachmann, 1935), closely followed, in an acting part, by *Under the Pampas Moon* (James Tinling, 1935), she moved under the tutelage of her manager and first husband Ed Judson to Columbia, the studio of her greatest triumphs. The first few films saw her in support roles, a period important not only in building up a respectable film CV but also, while at Columbia, in transforming her physically from the raven-haired, low-forehead, Latin-looking 'B' actress into the auburn-haired, electrolysis-improved hairline American beauty with a *soupçon* of exoticism. Her first real break— though still in a support role—came with Hawks' *Only Angels Have Wings* (1939). After further exposure in films where she was loaned out to other studios, for instance to Warner Brothers for *Strawberry Blonde* (Raoul Walsh, 1941), and perhaps especially to Twentieth Century Fox for *Blood and Sand* (Rouben Mamoulian, 1941), a key film as a sort of precursor to her *Carmen*, Columbia finally recognized her enormous potential, and set up productions for its timely fulfilment. Fred Astaire and Cole Porter combined on *You'll Never get Rich* (Sidney Lanfield, 1941), Astaire again and Jerome Kern on *You Were Never Lovelier* (William A. Seiter, 1942), Gene Kelly and Kern again on *Cover Girl* (Charles Vidor, the director of *Carmen*, 1944), to provide her with 'A' movie musicals that paraded her versatility as a dancer and icon of sensual, exotic-American beauty that would turn her into one of the studio's most bankable stars.

But it was perhaps *Gilda* (1946), again directed by Vidor, that truly established the meaning of Rita Hayworth, a film that added further sexual experience and betrayal (already detectable in *Blood and Sand*) to all the more wholesome ingredients of fun and vivacity associated with the major earlier films.

Around the time of *The Loves of Carmen* the aura of peaches-and-cream beauty crossed with exotic, self-conscious sexual difference is being further nuanced not only through her roles in *The Lady from Shanghai* (Orson Welles, 1948), *Affair in Trinidad* (Vincent Sherman, 1952, a film in which she teamed up as in *Gilda, Carmen* and *The Money Trap*, 1965, with Glenn Ford), and *Salome* (William Dieterle, 1953), but also through her chaotic offscreen life, characterized by her marriages and divorces from Ed Judson and Orson Welles, followed by her elopement to Europe with Aly Khan, the latter defined by *The People* newspaper in a headline as 'An affair that is an insult to all decent women', a further instance in the public's eyes of Rita Hayworth's brush with the tar of the exotic.[1]

As the Rita Hayworth story from 1953 to her death from Alzheimer's in 1987 has no bearing on the production and reception of *The Loves of Carmen*, I shall progress now to consideration of some theoretical questions that might help to focus discussion of the film.

The transformation of Margarita Cansino into 'Rita Hayworth', and her casting in *The Loves of Carmen*, complex enough issues in themselves, provide a fitting overture to the discussion of gender, ethnicity and identity raised by the film. Michael Wood's characteristically fine chapter on *Gilda* in *America in the Movies* nevertheless glides over what in my view is the significantly Hispanic element in Rita Hayworth's origins: 'she looked like a very attractive American woman—even if she started out in life looking Spanish' (Wood 1975: 58). Even though neither as Margarita Cansino nor as Rita Hayworth does she ever approximate to Mérimée's prototype of the Gypsy as 'Calé' or swarthy (Mérimée 1998: 333-334), with almond-shaped, darkly fringed eyes and the demeanour of a beast covered in greasy unkempt air, the very hybridity of Hayworth—part Irish/English American (through her mother), part Spanish (through her father), part white, part hybrid (through the construction and complication of Spanish ethnicity by Jewish, Arab, Gypsy as well as European Iberian heritage)—highlights even more the variegated issues of ethnicity and identity attached to the meanings of Carmen.

Carmen's exoticization can be read through Said's and Bhabha's discussions of, in the case of the former, 'Orientalism' (1978) and, in the latter (1994), of more psychoanalytically-inspired notions of ambivalence, fantasy and fetishism. Though not strictly speaking an 'Orientalist' subject, Carmen's gypsiness—with its Asian/Egyptian roots (in the Lubitsch version, the intertitle reads that Carmen goes to Gibraltar on 'business of Egypt')—qualifies as another site for the clash between East and West.

As Carlos Serrano argues in *El nacimiento de Carmen: símbolo, mitos y nación*: '[…] la Carmen romántica y sus herederas fueron más que españolas, ya casi "orientales" para la imaginación europea, que asoció entonces "España", "Sur" y fantasía erótica.'(Serrano 1999: 54) (the Romantic Carmen and her inheritors were more than just Spanish, being already almost 'oriental' for the European imagination of the time, which associated 'Spain' with 'The South' and erotic fantasy).

Mount Carmel (etymologically the root of the name 'Carmen'), the Asian/Egyptian origins of the Gypsy, all blend together in the construction of the mythic, quasi-Oriental figure who became attached to the cult of the Blessed Virgin of the Sea, María del Carmen, Our Lady of the Sea, the patron saint of mariners.

On this reading, Carmen's gypsiness becomes the space for the dominant European culture's exercise of power, a Western projection onto the Eastern exotic—in this case not far afield, but in its very midst—of ambivalent desires. Bhabha's engagement with such issues in the wider field of postcolonial studies casts doubt on what he considers Said's notion that power rests entirely with the colonizer. The colonized in *The Loves of Carmen* is Carmen's body and, through her, all Gypsies, not the exoticized reality of a remote country and civilization, but a local community, a minority group, colonized by the prejudices of the *payo* majority. In Bhabha's argument, though, this process is not one-dimensional. Rather, it leads to a profound ambivalence towards otherness on the part of the colonizer, something that, as Robert Young notes in *White Mythologies*, indicates that 'colonial discourse is founded on an anxiety, and that colonial power itself is subject to the effects of a conflictual economy' (Young 1990: 142).

This argument is later developed by Bhabha to the point where hybridity both undermines colonial authority and actively promotes the resistance of the colonized, whose natural complexity disturbs the processes of stereotyping to which they are subjected, processes that in Bhabha's view are analogous to those advanced in Freud's theory of the fetish. Bhabha writes in 'The Other Question', in *The Location of Culture*:

> In this spirit I argue for the reading of the stereotype in terms of fetishism. The myth of historical origination-racial purity, cultural priority—produced in relation to the colonial stereotype—functions to 'normalize' the multiple beliefs and split subjects that constitute colonial discourse as a consequence of its process of disavowal. The scene of fetishism functions similarly as, at once, a reactivation of the material of original fantasy—the anxiety of castration and sexual difference—as well as a normalization of that difference and disturbance in terms of the fetish object as the substitute for the mother's penis. Within the apparatus of colonial power, the discourses of sexuality and race relate in a process of functional over-determination [...] Fetishism, as the disavowal of difference, is the repetitive scene around the problem of castration. The recognition of sexual difference—is disavowed by the fixation on an object that masks that difference and restores an original presence. (Bhabha 1994: 74)

The Americanization of Margarita Cansino, in line with Hollywood practice to erase ethnicity from the names of its star performers (e.g. Daniel Kaminsky becoming Danny Kaye, Spangler Arlington Brough becoming Robert Taylor), to some extent conforms to this pattern. Margarita Cansino—an unWASPish, name that is Hispanic, Spanish or Latino, tainted perhaps by Latin American as well as Spanish *mestizaje*—must give way to Rita Hayworth, the Americanness teased out of her looks, remodelled to conform to mainstream ethnic norms. But while 'Hayworth' (retaining the Irish semantics of her mother's surname 'Haworth/Hayworth'), proclaims the triumph of colonization, 'Rita' (though in the child-like mutilated form of 'Margarita') is allowed to retain the memory of hybridity, just as the self-conscious sexual roles rooted in exoticism—Salome, doña Sol (in *Blood and Sand*) and Carmen—disturb the wholesome innocence of her parts in *Cover Girl* or *You Were Never Lovelier*.

And yet, this botched fetishization, designed both to control its object and to disavow its difference, fails to eradicate the threat of difference since, through what Richard Dyer in a Max Weber-inspired discussion of Gilda called 'charisma' (1978: 91-99), but also through her residually exotic, un-American part-identity, Rita Hayworth defies her wholesale colonization.

2. Americanization

The rescue of 'Rita Hayworth' from Margarita Cansino is self-consciously dramatized no more spectacularly than in *Down to Earth* (Alexander Hall, 1947). Here, the Greek muse or goddess of the dance, offended by what she considers the vulgarization of her story and character by a Broadway musical producer (Larry Parks), is eventually obliged to surrender to American taste, admit her error and recognize the values of the Broadway aesthetic. Terpsichore, goddess of the dance, effectively becomes a Broadway hoofer. At the end of the film she informs her heavenly minder Mr. Jordan, who has authorized her terrestrial visit to put the musical's producer straight, 'I don't want to be a goddess—I just want to be a human being'. The remark, of course, resonates beyond the narrative into the offscreen life of this and many other screen goddesses, trapped by their onscreen personae, the most notorious of whom is Marilyn Monroe, eternally seeking security, only ever finding partners or husbands looking for glamour-girl trophy wives. Rita Hayworth herself once said her husbands went to bed with Gilda and woke up with her. But within the limits of this film's narrative, being a human being meant being

American, not some exotic European Olympian. By the time she makes this plea, she has learnt to concede, to abjure elitism and to embrace the vulgar charms of *The Swinging Muses'* demotic lyrics: 'Take a chick like me/They call me Terpsichore.'

But it was precisely its garish, brassy all-Americanness that in the opinion of many reviewers led to the critical, though not box office, failure of *The Loves of Carmen*. The *New York Times* suggests that 'With all due regard for Rita Hayworth's abundant and evident charms bestowed upon her by nature and the make-up department equally, it must be surmised that the lady simply hasn't got what it takes to play the role of Carmen' (*New York Times* 1970: 2275).

In England, the *Daily Mail* picks up on the way Rita Hayworth is shod: 'A remarkable feature of this perversely amusing travesty is the way Carmen's one pair of high-heeled shoes stands up to the mountains'. The *Evening News* notes that 'such gleaming white teeth, such pale, well-manicured fingers, never lingered over a *gitana*'s stew-pot; nor did such snow-white off-the-shoulder blouses, such a generous variety of Paisley shawls, such flaming, flaring skirts and high-heeled shoes (again!) with double-ankle straps ever grace the rocky heights of Granada'. Finally, The *Daily Graphic* tells its readers of how 'Miss Hayworth sways her hips, flashes her eyes, clicks her castanets, shouts, spits, fights, bites, tosses her mahogany (sic) mane, stamps her feet (shod in elegant, high-heeled little numbers with the fashionable crossed-ankle strap) [...] she just about breaks her back to be a tempestuous Spanish Gypsy—and she remains throughout a luscious Hollywood star, fresh from a foam bath'.[2]

None of this mattered to audiences brought up on Hollywood, who came to see Rita Hayworth more than Carmen, who were far less exercised by the authenticity or historical accuracy of the narrative than by the spectacle of an idolized star in a colourful setting. At one level, the production values of the film make it absolutely essential for the all-American Rita Hayworth to be on display. So, the ever-changing colours on this nineteenth-century Cover Girl's gaudy costumes, and the supposedly authentic *flamenco, fandanguillo* (a sort of Can-Can Dance) and *chufla* (a burlesque dance) numbers, all highlighted in the Studio's Production Notes for the film (1949) and choreographed by her father Eduardo Cansino, belong more securely to the Latin American song-and-dance ambience presided over by such as Xavier Cugat in South of the Border musicals, like her own *You Were Never Lovelier*. As the film was produced by her own recently formed Beckworth company, though still made at Columbia, she was able to employ some of her own friends and family in the production, such as her father, and her uncle José and brother Vernon in small roles (De La Hoz 2002). Elsewhere the film offers loving, sometimes lascivious close-ups of Hayworth's face, the back of her head to show her luxuriant Gilda-defined head of hair, poses that demand legs peeping out from her flaring skirt, as she sits dangling them on stone walls or window ledges, or in *a tergo* positions, like some latter day clothed Rokeby Venus to titillate her inflamed worshippers. After the failure of *The Lady from Shanghai* this was the film, as Jeremy Tambling notes (1987: 29), that was intended to restore her status as a sex-goddess.

Acknowledging its debts to Mérimée, the film's publicity leaflet boasts of its neglect of Bizet's score, preferring to use original compositions by the celebrated composer Mario Castelnuovo-Tedesco. While the music itself is unremarkable, the sinuous, fluent Latinate limbs of Rita Hayworth as she dances confirm the radiant, dream-like sexuality of a star in her prime. Early on in the film Glenn Ford's don José watches her—bedecked as she is, as ever, in one of her interminable collection of deep-décolleté blouses, free-flowing flaring skirts, pendulous earrings and multiple layers of bead necklaces—through the bars of a wrought-iron gate. Don José, in contrast, is dressed in the stiff, ultra-virile uniform of his regiment: the phallic steel helmet, with its chin strap and visor almost enveloping and imprisoning his face, and the starchy, rigid sheen of his doublet and hose are as if mocked by the sexually liberated, performative, loose-limbed femininity beyond his reach. The polymorphously sexualized body of Rita Hayworth/Carmen is given further piquancy by her repeated clicking of her castanets, an insistent, mocking awareness of his tumescent desires as well as of her power over him. Yet, even at this early stage, we are warned—though the audience comes to the film knowing its tragic end— that Carmen's powers of sexual enslavement are ephemeral. As she coquettishly summons her captivated admirer, a shot-counter-shot sequence revealing the two in conversation through the bars of the gate suggests that both are trapped by the circumstances of self, social conditioning and heritage, and that while don José betrays his masculinity in his pursuit of Carmen, Carmen's betrayal in her momentary infatuation with don José represents an affront to the destiny of women in 1940s America as much as in nineteenth-century Spain.

3. Betrayal

In Manuel Puig's novel, *La traición de Rita Hayworth (Betrayed by Rita Hayworth)* (1975: first published 1968) characters endlessly chatter about the relative merits of their favourite Hollywood stars. Rita Hayworth is here often described as the character with 'la cara traicionera' (treacherous face), or the star who 'pone cara de mala, es una artista linda pero que hace traiciones' (has a look of evil, she's a pretty star but she betrays). There is an extended discussion of *Blood and Sand* and her betrayal of 'el muchacho bueno' (the good guy), Tyrone Power (Puig 1975: 88-89). Within the framework of Puig's novel Rita Hayworth's betrayals relate, specifically, to her roles as faithless lover and, more generally, both to her own conversion from Latin-identified Margarita Cansino to American-defined 'Rita Hayworth', and to the novel's interest in questions of sexual, political and cultural betrayals in Argentina (see also Jeremy Tambling's essay in this volume). The duality of Rita Hayworth—as distinct from the more one-dimensional innocence of her early musicals—may be seen in a variety of films, including *Carmen,* but even a scene from one of her lesser-known films, *Affair in Trinidad,* stresses the point. Here this duality is clearly stated when she sings a song entitled 'I've been kissed before', or through often-used chiaroscuro lighting that gestures to the mystery, melancholy and pain that also informs the sexuality of the star.

Michael Wood argues that in *The Lady from Shanghai*, another of her famous devil-of-the-flesh caricature incarnations, Hayworth, as he puts it, 'doesn't come off as a natural predator [...] she embraces treachery in the way that she faked whoredom in *Gilda*, as the only way out of the trap' (Wood 1975: 61). The air of detachment, of what Bhabha calls 'mimicry', or of Rivierian 'masquerade'—two concepts I shall return to in the final part of this essay—is indeed important in Hayworth's attitude to sex, but her aura of betrayal, beyond the literal and metaphorical senses noted and highlighted by Puig also includes in *The Loves of Carmen* an assault on social constructions of femininity.

The publicity Production Notes for the film point directly to this, and interestingly in a way that places some of the blame not just on Mame/Carmen but on Johnny/don José:

> *The Loves of Carmen* not only captures the spirit of femininity; it also shows what happened to a man who, too late, found out the truth about Carmen—and himself [...] Glenn Ford has [...] the most difficult role of his distinguished career, portraying the proud, possessive, perplexed don José. It's an arduous

characterization because although within the man there has to be a moral weakness, there is a latent savage streak.[3]

Don José's savagery—controlled and redirected in his professional life as a soldier—surfaces in his relations with Carmen when ardour concedes to possessiveness, when he comes to loathe his own emotional dependence on her, when the courtship of an independent woman becomes the frustrated expectation that she will be satisfied with domesticity. Don José's attraction to Carmen is the Anglo-Saxon American's fascination (Ford was Canadian) with the exotic. But it may also be motivated by perversion in the form of masochism (from his very first contact with her, we see him as if humbled beneath her in the frame, while she sits eating her orange above him), as well as by both the challenge to domesticate a free spirit, and to rescue what Freud (1977) refers to in the essay on 'A Special Type of Object Choice Made by Men', a woman of ill-repute or of dubious fidelity. Following Freud, the mother-fixated don José is turned on by infidelity, and rescues a betrayer, the woman who as the song has it, has 'been kissed before', and in doing so punishes the father—here represented (in keeping with the Mérimée original) not only by Carmen's husband García, but also by the various other men who have been her lovers, including José's patriarchal commanding officer, whom he kills. But when Carmen fails to live up to the fantasy of the rescued, domesticated mother-figure her punishment is a foregone conclusion, and love's martyr becomes the scourge of desire. The relations between the two are more defined by hostility than libido, by jealousy fed by hatred.

Rita Hayworth's Carmen belongs to the monstrous regiment of film noir anti-heroines, rebels against their domestic heritage, sirens whose libidinal victims crash on the rocks of fatal desires. Barbara Stanwyck (*Double Indemnity*, Billy Wilder, 1944), Joan Bennett (*Scarlet Street*, Fritz Lang, 1945), Ava Gardner (*The Killers*, Robert Siodmak, 1946), or Jane Greer (*Out of the Past*, Jacques Tourneur, 1947), all played deadly women who, like Cathy in *Out of the Past*, could be described in the words of Jeff, the latter's lover-victim as 'a leaf that the wind blows from gutter to gutter'. Carmen, like her own Gilda or, say, Phyllis Dietrichson in *Double Indemnity*—though obviously unlike her in many other ways—abhors marriage, an institution opposed to love, morality's vain effort to impose permanence on the changeability of desire, a contract that in her eyes leads only to abuse, above all of women. In a very early scene she exclaims, as a wedding party passes by, that the groom will soon be beating his wife, a remark that may be inspired by her own marriage to García, and that also heralds don José's beating of her until, he threatens, she is black and blue. When relations between these two become strained, her insistence on independence eventually leads to explosions of anger that seem in line with 1940s noir-related female resentment of contemporary attitudes in America: 'I won't sit on my hands and wait for you like the wife of a *payo* stirring a pot of stew. I've been my own woman and a Gypsy too long my friend [...] I'm not your slave. I am Carmen, and nobody tells me what to do. I do as I please'. The discourse here—writer Helen Deutsch's code–switching between screen-foreigner and recognizably colloquial English— transgresses against notions promoted in the heavier climate of South American machismo, of Latin female submissiveness. For all her ethnicized English, Carmen here steps out of role and speaks for all 1940s women. She is the woman who refuses to be Oedipalized by her patriarchal lover, but who for her insubordination is first physically abused—when she refuses to divulge the identity of the benefactor who has bought her a new navy dress—and then finally killed when he cannot endure her defiance any longer. Through don José the film reflects the mental condition of a man whose savagery is innate, but also to some extent prompted by self-loathing and despair, a tormented lover finally destroyed by his uncontrollable descent through passion into the very depths of psychological hell.

4. Mimicry and Masquerade

The demise of don José, shrouded in the pathos of the film's final moments as, beside Carmen, he lies shot by a soldier, will dim perhaps only fleetingly the memory of earlier moments in the film that celebrate human brio and vitality. In that respect—in its sense of life as a game, a ludic, regressive, almost childish challenge (we note the diminutive 'Carmencita'), to free the spirit before the call of a final destiny—is perhaps most strikingly marked by Carmen's laughter, so vilified by the reviewers of the day, and yet, originating in Mérimée's novella, so accurate a measure of her essence.

"'Carmen", declares the film, "likes to laff"', *The Observer* reported:

> and under the circumstances, one does not blame her. Miss Hayworth laffs almost all the time from the moment when Mr Glenn Ford, as don José, discovers her sucking an orange in the lunch-break at the local tobacco factory, to the moment when he plunges a knife into her chest because she

will not fly with him to Mexico. Every time she laffs, all the gentlemen within sight are supposed to swoon with longing.[4]

This is easy ridicule, and it misses the point. Mérimée writes: 'as usual the creature was laughing fit to burst' (1998: 42). In this, as in much else—though eschewing the frame narrative of the novella and, inescapably, many of the details, including the Basque question—the film attempts to be true to the spirit of the original. Carmen's laughter—as in the Lubitsch version, like the Devil's, to whom she is also compared—is partially aimed, like that of her sister in male-directed torment, Sacher-Masoch's *Venus in Furs*, at the order of the universe, where transgression is nature's law (Sacher-Masoch 2000). Mérimée's laughing, tainted beauty reflects in miniature a universe of impermanence, of crime and punishment that mocks the efforts of honourable rational (*payo*) individuals. Taking its cue from the novella, the film opposes Gypsies and *payos*: the latter full of death-dealing honour, the former, in their thieving, anarchic essence at least in harmony with the rhythms of a perverse universe, whose truth is sounded by the mocking laughter of Carmen.

In cultural terms the laughing, devilishly flame-haired Gypsy may be viewed, like Cervantes' 'gitanilla', as an example of Bhabha's 'Mimic (Wo)man' (1994: 85-92), the construction of an other—here an Un-American Gypsy—who is similar to but not the same as the *payo* (the American), an approximation of the *payo* who distorts rather than reassures. As Robert Young (1990) puts it in his summary of the concept: 'thus, the familiar, transported to distant parts, becomes uncannily transformed, the imitation subverts the identity of that which is being represented, and the relation of power, if not altogether reversed, certainly begins to vacillate' (147).

The laughter of Carmen is a form of 'subaltern' speech. Through excess, her laughter—too insistent, too freely available and raucous to seem natural—mimics and parodies the dominant discourse of which it is at once the product and the scourge. It both destroys 'narcissistic authority' and interrogates 'discriminatory knowledge':

Mimicry does not merely destroy narcissistic authority through the repetitious slippage of diference and desire. It is the process of the *fixation* of the colonial as a form of cross-classificatory, discriminatory knowledge within an interdictory discourse, and therefore necessarily raises the question of the *authorization* of colonial representations; a question of authority that goes beyond the subject's lack of priority (castration) to a historical crisis in conceptuality of colonial man as an object of regulatory power, as the subject of racial, cultural, national representation. (Bhabha 1994: 90)

But Carmen's laugh is also Rita Hayworth's, who here, as elsewhere, exemplifies Joan Riviere's notion of the masquerade (1986), and whose femininity in all the many languid poses and sexy pouts of her famous films may be read as a concession to intelligence or power over men, a sexuality and femininity performed in obedience to a social or aesthetic law, whose very artifice is exposed by the mockery of a self-conscious *femme fatale*.

Joan Riviere's notion of the masquerade offers a psychoanalytical contribution to the analysis of femininity. Her account questions whether female identity is an 'essence (preceding the law, preceding any complex), or difference from the masculine— which is then set up as the norm' (Lebeau 2001: 102). Riviere's conclusions derive from analysis of a patient caught between contradictory drives: on the one hand passivity and submissiveness (culturally defined as feminine), and, on the other, strength, confidence and professional achievement (culturally identified as masculine). Riviere's essay (first published in 1929) has been glossed by many subsequent theorists, but in her own original discussion the masquerade represents a patient's form of conciliation with the patriarchal order, an anxiety-induced attempt to make amends for usurpation—in her professional life—of 'masculine' drives. The patient's feminine masquerade aims at reclaiming her castrated identity through surrender of her phallic self:

> The exhibition in public of her intellectual proficiency, which was in itself carried through successfully, signified an exhibition of herself in possession of the father's penis, having castrated him. The display once over, she was seized by horrible dread of the retribution the father would then exact. Obviously it was a step towards propitiating the avenger to endeavor to offer herself to him sexually. (Riviere 1986: 37)

The woman's masquerade as castrated femininity, the desire through over-elaborate femininity to offer reparation and reassurance in the wake of her public exhibition of herself in possession of her father's penis, is clear enough. But consideration of the woman's identity prior to the disguise of femininity is equally important. In one of the most focussed recent discussions of this question Elizabeth Cowie (1997) considers whether, in these circumstances, the woman is phallic (Riviere's view), or only masquerading as such. In the former case, she is not castrated, her masquerade only a disguise of castration; in the latter she is castrated. In either case the woman and the men in her life are caught up in complex forms of representation and fantasy: denying or affirming her phallic identity, swaying between behaviour that threatens or reassures men who are either in dread of difference (and therefore prefer a woman with male attributes), or who welcome it (and therefore are more comfortable with the masquerade of femininity).

The theory of the masquerade has formed the basis of discussion of important essays by Claire Johnston (1975) on *Anne of the Indies* (Jacques Tourneur, 1951), and Tania Modleski (1988: 17-30) and Mary Ann Doane (1991: 40-42) on *Blackmail* (Alfred Hitchcock, 1929). *The Loves of Carmen* is another film that deserves attention from this point of view. As Carmen, Rita Hayworth's destabilized womanliness, sliding between rival identities, highlighted through the double-focussed excess of femininity and the underlying mockery and phallic power that so threatens the men in her life, belongs to the star's projection of a femininity or womanliness at once feared and desired. Hers is a subjectivity that, even in her various screen punishments (e.g. her deaths in *Gilda, The Lady from Shanghai, Carmen*), ultimately resists attempts to control an unmanageable, irrepressible vitality.

Looking at *The Loves of Carmen*, we may now, as reviewers did then, note the defects of a film claiming to retell the story of *Carmen*. But if, instead of lamenting its neglect of Bizet, or its misguided, Hollywoodized *costumbrismo* (localized pseudo-ethnographic realism), or its seemingly perverse casting of Rita Hayworth as a Gypsy, we concentrate instead on the construction of femininity through its choice of one of the industry's most glamorous icons, we may come to view it as a film with unsuspected merit. At the very least, the Rita Hayworth version, with its trace memories of blame and betrayal, of musicals crossed with melodrama and noir, brings to Carmen an internalized history of femininity, of ethnic and national identity, of lip-service to and mockery of a system that seeks to shape as well as to reflect the vivid fantasies of post-war America.

Notes
1. The *People*, 9 January 1949. Unattributed review.
2. The *Daily Mail*, 25 February 1949; The *Evening News*, 24 February 1949; The *Daily Graphic*, 25 February 1949. Unattributed reviews.
3. Production Notes for *Carmen*, 1949. London: Columbia Pictures: 1-3.
4. The *Observer*, 27 February 1949. Unattributed review.

References

Bhabha, Homi K.. 1994. *The Location of Culture*. London: Routledge.

Cowie, Elizabeth. 1997. *Representing the Woman: Cinema and Psychoanalysis*. London: Macmillan.

De La Hoz, Cynthia C.. 2002. 'The Early Years', in Rita Hayworth Biography. On line at: http://members.tripod.com/~claudia79/early.html (consulted 27.3. 2002).

Doane, Mary Ann. 1991. *Femmes Fatales: Feminism, Film Theory, Psychoanalysis*. New York and London: Routledge.

Dyer, Richard. 1978. 'Resistance through Charisma' in Kaplan, E. Ann (ed.) *Women in Film Noir*. London: British Film Institute: 91-99.

Freud, Sigmund. 1977. 'A Special Type of Object Choice Made by Men (Contributions to the Psychology of Love I)' in Richards, Angela and Strachey, James (eds) *On Sexuality: Three Essays on the Theory of Sexuality and Other Works* (tr. James Strachey). *Pelican Freud Library*, vol. 7, Harmondsworth: Penguin: 227-242.

Johnston, Claire. 1975. 'Femininity and the Masquerade: *Anne of the Indies*' in Johnston, Claire and Willemen, Paul (eds) *Jacques Tourneur*. Edinburgh: Edinburgh Film Festival: no pagination.

Lebeau, Vicky. 2001. *Psychoanalysis and Cinema: the Play of Shadows*. London and New York: Wallflower Press.

Mérimée, Prosper. 1998. *Carmen and Other Stories* (ed. and tr. Nicholas Jotcham) Oxford: Oxford University Press.

Modleski, Tania. 1988. *The Women Who Knew Too Much: Hitchcock and Feminist Theory*. London and New York: Methuen.

New York Times. 1970. [Unattributed review] in *New York Times Film Reviews* 3 (1939-1948). New York: New York Times and Arno Press: 2275.

Puig, Manuel. 1975. *La traición de Rita Hayworth*. Buenos Aires: Editorial Sudamericana.

Riviere, Joan. 1986. 'Womanliness as a Masquerade' in Burgin, Victor, Donald, James and Kaplan, Cora (eds) *Formations of Fantasy*. London: Routledge: 35-44.

Sacher-Masoch, Leopold von. 2000. *Venus in Furs* (tr. Joachim Neugroschel). Harmondsworth: Penguin.

Said, Edward. 1978. *Orientalism: Western Conceptions of the Orient*. Harmondsworth: Penguin.

Serrano, Carlos. 1999. *El nacimiento de Carmen: símbolos, mitos y nación*. Madrid: Taurus.

Tambling, Jeremy. 1987. *Opera, Ideology and Film*. Manchester: Manchester University Press.

Wood, Michael. 1975. *America in the Movies: or 'Santa Maria, It Had Slipped my Mind!'*. London: Secker and Warburg.

Young, Robert. 1990. *White Mythologies: Writing History and the West*. London: Routledge.

Screen Politics: Otto Preminger's *Carmen Jones*

Nelly Furman

In the early days of black and white cinema, one finds a surprising number of parodies of Georges Bizet's famous opera, *Carmen*. With his 1954 *Carmen Jones*, Otto Preminger presents the first technicolor version of Bizet's opera. But Preminger's film proposes itself as another kind of parody. Bizet's music serves in this film as a backdrop to Oscar Hammerstein II's lyrics for a thoroughly American story. Filmed with an all-black cast that included well-known stars: Dorothy Dandridge, Harry Belafonte, Diahann Carroll and Pearl Bailey, Otto Preminger's movie tells another black and white story. While its purpose is to showcase the talents of African-American actors and to testify to America's discriminatory social history of the fifties, in so doing it also unwittingly reveals Hollywood's own political paradigms and cultural prejudices. In a most curious manner, Preminger's film, whose aim was to denounce racism in America, becomes itself the blind and unknowing carrier of Mérimée's nineteenth-century racial and social ideology. The purpose of this chapter will be to show how Preminger's film, while purportedly referring back to Bizet's opera, unconsciously projects onto the silver screen one of the most disturbing interpretations of the theme of ethnic difference since Prosper Mérimée's original 1845 short story.

Preminger, Otto: *Carmen Jones*
Dandridge, Dorothy
Race
Opera and film
Hammerstein, Oscar II
American sociopolitical history

In 1954 appeared the first colour version of Bizet's opera, Otto Preminger's *Carmen Jones*. Not a remake of the opera, but more precisely a 'musical' in the Broadway tradition, Preminger's film is decidedly an American story, as the 'Jones' in Carmen's name intimates. While respecting some of the highlights of the musical score of Bizet's opera, Preminger's film proposes itself as another kind of story. No longer located in southern Spain, but in rural Florida, it is the story of an Afro-American soldier who, after killing his sergeant, flees with his beloved Carmen, a worker in a parachute factory, to seek a new life in Chicago. Preminger filmed with an all-black cast that included Dorothy Dandridge as Carmen Jones; Harry Belafonte as Joe; Olga James as Cindy Lou, Joe's sweetheart from back home, (the role of Micaela in Bizet's opera); Pearl Bailey as Frankie and Diahann Carroll as Myrt (Mercedes and Frasquita in Bizet); Brock Peters, as Sergeant Brown; and finally Joe Adams, as a prize fighter named Husky Miller who plays Joe's rival, the equivalent of the toreador Escamillo, in the opera. Although Dorothy Dandridge, Harry Belafonte and Pearl Bailey were popular, highly established singers with very distinctive voices, only Pearl Bailey and Olga James sing in their own voice: the other main roles are dubbed by opera singers. Dorothy Dandridge's part is sung by a young Marilyn Horne and Harry Belafonte's arias by LeVern Hutcherson. Olga James uses her own voice because she was a trained opera singer. The only singing voice that remains culturally identified as Afro-American is that of Pearl Bailey.

With its all-black cast Preminger's *Carmen Jones* not only marks a noticeable moment in film history, but also testifies to the social history of the United States in the fifties. First produced by Billie Rose as a musical on Broadway in 1943, the stage version of *Carmen Jones* was warmly received. In the patriotic fervour of the Second World War, although the American armed forces were still segregated, and would remain so until 1948, the army was seen as a place of social mobility for young black men who could aspire to become flyers. But that was the early forties: eleven years later, as we will see, when Preminger made the film version of the musical play, the message purveyed dramatically changed. The purpose of this piece will be to re-examine the politics of Preminger's *Carmen Jones*, to look beyond the realism, beyond the representational dimension of the film, and by following the interconnected force of its visual and aural narratives attempt to propose a new understanding of its political message.

Carmen Jones begins with a young woman, Cindy Lou, who comes to say goodbye to her fiancé, Joe, a soldier getting ready to go to flying school. But in the cafeteria of the base Joe is enticed by Carmen Jones, one of the factory workers. When later Carmen gets into a fight, the soldier is ordered to escort her to jail. On the way she persuades him to stop at her grandmother's house where they become lovers. He goes to jail: she awaits him. A renowned prizefighter, Husky Miller, and his entourage arrive in town: he sees Carmen Jones looking at him from a balcony and, enthralled, invites her to come to Chicago with her friends. Joe, just released from jail, arrives and gets into a fight with Sergeant Brown, who hits his head against a fountain and dies. Joe and Carmen flee to Chicago. Penniless in a tenement house, Carmen turns to her old friend Frankie for help. Frankie encourages her to become the mistress of the boxer. Joe attempts to attack the boxer at the gym where he practices, and later he goes to the arena where Husky is fighting: there he sees Carmen and drags her into a janitor's closet where he strangles her.

In this film, Bizet's music serves as a backdrop to Oscar Hammerstein's II lyrics. The 'Habanera' becomes 'Dat's Love'; the 'Seguidilla', 'Dere's a Café on the Corner': the Gypsy song that opens the opera's second act becomes Pearl Bailey's show piece 'Beat Out That Rhythm on a Drum'. Finally, the toreador's famous song in its new version resonates with the words 'Stand Up and Fight!'. The choice of Bizet's opera as a vehicle for modern political causes may seem surprising at first. After all, isn't the story a case of fatal attraction? Michel Leiris, for example, perceives Carmen as a *femme fatale* who meets a just retribution:

> Carmencita—who stabs one of her companions in the cigar factory and ridicules the wretch whom she has forced to desert until he kills her; mistress of a matador who dedicates the beast he is about to kill to her, as to a bloodthirsty goddess for whom he must risk death—the lovely Carmencita, before being murdered, is indeed a murderess (Leiris 1963: 54).

On the other hand, in *Opera or the Undoing of Women*, Catherine Clément calls Carmen 'the most feminist, the most stubborn of these dead women', the one who embodies 'the somber and revolutionary proclamation of a woman who chooses to die before a man decides it for her' (Clément 1988: 48, 53). The antithetical interpretations elicited by Bizet's opera are not limited to feminist politics. In Frank Corsaro's 1984 staging for the New York City Opera, for example, the story is set during the Spanish Civil War, and Carmen is portrayed as a freedom fighter who falls in the struggle against fascism. On the other hand, in a similar staging of the opera presented at Pforzheim during the Third Reich, Carmen personified rather the danger awaiting innocent fascist youth who, supposedly, could easily be bewitched by a member of a racial group designated as inferior by the Nazi regime (Malherbe 1951: 305). Because Bizet's *Carmen* focuses on conflict and oppositional structures, it is a ready-made vehicle to represent social and cultural differences, oppositional ideologies, and thus to convey political intent.

Unlike Bizet's opera with its focus on love, Mérimée's original short story has anthropological aspirations. It concerns itself with race, ethnicity, linguistic expression and social issues; *Carmen Jones* thus recalls aspects of the Mérimée story that are muted in Bizet's opera, a point noticed by French film critic Jacques Lourcelles who writes that 'Mais, par-delà le souvenir qu'il conserve inscrit en lui-même de ses diverses origines, [le film] rejoint surtout Mérimée' (Lourcelles 1965: 58). (Beyond the inscribed memory traces of its multiple origins, the film links up most of all with Mérimée). Preminger asserts this link to Mérimée in his autobiography: 'Except for the lyrics, we did not use the text of Hammerstein's revue or the libretto of the original opera by Meilhac and Halévy but went back to the original story by Prosper Mérimée' (Preminger 1977: 133).

While the original *Carmen*, Mérimée's, is without any ambiguity a story about race and ethnicity, Preminger's film, as James Baldwin suggests in his *Notes of A Native Son*, both is, and is not, about race:

> one understands that *Carmen Jones* is controlled by another movie which Hollywood was studiously *not* making. For, while it is amusing to parallel Bizet's amoral Gypsy with a present-day, lower class Negro woman, it is a good deal less amusing to parallel the Bizet violence with the violence of the Negro ghetto. To avoid this [...] it was helpful, first of all, that the script failed to require the services of any white people. This seals the action off, as it were, in a vacuum in which the spectacle of color is divested of its danger. The color itself then becomes a kind of vacuum which each spectator will fill with his own fantasies. (Baldwin 1955: 48)

By casting his movie with all black actors, Preminger, a lifetime member of the National Association for the Advancement of Colored People (NAACP) affirms his commitment to racial equality. According to Bogle (1997: 267-268), 'the script of *Carmen Jones* [...] raised concerns about the response of the African American community to the film', and to make sure that nothing in the film would prove offensive to the black American community, Preminger sent the script to Walter White of the NAACP. Preminger summarized White's opinion in a memo: 'While White indicated that he principally is opposed to an all-Negro show as such, because their fight is for integration as opposed to segregation in any form [...] he likes this particular script very much and has no objection to any part of it' (in Bogle 1997: 268). Preminger proved to the Hollywood establishment that an all-black movie can attract a large audience and make a profit for the studio, while at the same time also lending support to black actors. In a radio interview, Harry Belafonte recalled that *Carmen Jones* marked an important historical moment: 'It was the first all-Negro film that became a great box-office success. It established the fact that pictures with Negro artists, pictures dealing with the folklore of Negro life, were commercially feasible. This was a sign of growth that had occurred in the United States and throughout the world' (Shaw 1960: 140-141). Nonetheless, as Baldwin noted, by excluding any explicit reference to white America of the 1950s and its social context for blacks, wittingly or unwittingly, Preminger erases the specificity of race issues in the story itself. Notions of race, ethnicity, and gender, are then subsumed in the film under class ideology within the Afro-American community.

Notions of social hierarchies or hereditary privileges did not altogether disappear from within modern nations built on republican principles; rather, they seem to have commuted into racial and ethnic rankings. In *Imagined Communities*, Benedict Anderson remarks that

> The dreams of racism actually have their origin in ideologies of *class*, rather than in those of nation: above all in claims to divinity among rulers and to 'blue' or 'white' blood and 'breeding' among aristocracies. No surprise then that the putative sire of modern racism should be, not some petty-bourgeois nationalist, but Joseph Arthur, Comte de Gobineau. Nor that, on the whole, racism and anti-Semitism manifest themselves, not across national boundaries, but within them. In other words, they justify not so much foreign wars as domestic repression and domination (Anderson 1991: 149-150).

In his now infamous *Essai sur l'inégalité des races* published in 1854, Arthur de Gobineau—with whom Mérimée corresponded occasionally—is not as much concerned with the question of supremacy of the Aryan race, although that superiority is implied, as he is with protecting Aryan racial purity from contamination and the threat of degeneration. In such a racial ideology, miscegenation becomes a capital crime precisely because it is viewed as an erosion of the asset that the white race supposedly represents. On May 17, 1954, in a unanimous opinion, the US Supreme Court decided in the case of Brown vs. the Board of Education that the doctrine of 'separate but equal' had no place in the field of public opinion, thus bringing to an end the legal practice of segregation. Robert Jackson, one of the judges on the Supreme Court, prepared a draft of his own concurring opinion that historian David Halberstam calls 'one of the more illuminating documents of the time' (Halberstam 1993: 421) In this draft, Halberstam notes:

> Jackson touched on the most emotional issue of all: blood, or miscegenation, as it came to be called. The mixing of the races, Jackson said, had already far outstripped the speed of the courts, and that 'an increasing part of what is called colored population has as much claim to white as to colored blood' (Halberstam 1993: 422).

When Preminger was filming *Carmen Jones*, the major political issues were segregation, Civil Rights, and discussions of the Cold War.

Film critics and 'carmenologists' have lauded Preminger's *Carmen Jones* for making it possible for black actors to appear in roles from which they had hitherto been excluded, but little else seems to have impressed scholars in terms of the political message of the film. When the film was first shown, the influential film critic of the *New York Times*, Bosley Crowther, described it as 'crowded with more Negro talent than you could catch on a Saturday night at the Harlem Apollo [...] this lot of bamboozling by way of Bizet and Oscar Hammerstein 2d is a sex melodrama with long hair music and a mad conglomeration of bizarre show [...] a crazy mixed-up film' (Crowther 1954: 27). Nor have more recent critics been impressed by the social or political message of the film. In *Opera, Ideology and Film*, for example, Jeremy Tambling declares that:

> In *Carmen Jones* neither black experience nor urban conditions receive an authentic treatment. Instead there is the mythologizing of the dangerous black or mixed race woman, and her ambivalent 'nature', and there is an acceptance of the status quo. The film remains pleasant for all that, and it is arguable that it only replicates, in a different way, the inability of the Bizet to ask important questions: those which would have to do with its failure to ask any questions about the nature of the cigarette factory (Tambling 1987: 31-32).

And Ann Davies in a recent newspaper article argues that

> as the first black Carmen in an all-black cast, Dandridge drew attention to the question of race underlying the story—the Carmen narrative has recycled the ethnically as well as the sexually exotic for the pleasure of bourgeois audiences. But *Carmen Jones* itself does little to confront these issues, since it seems to offer only the 'novelty' of black actors singing jazzed-up opera. (Davies 2002: 19)

In short, while Preminger's film is hailed for its political audacity in casting all black actors, it is criticized for failing to convey any other political message besides simply showing characters tragically caught in the social turmoil of industrial urbanization. But as Susan McClary suggests: 'Nonetheless, there is much to recommend *Carmen Jones* [...] In particular, the experiment of changing the racial dimension of the piece—while finally exceedingly problematic—may encourage us to reconsider Carmen in terms of racial politics and cultural representation' (McClary 1992: 134-135).

Preminger's best known films, *The Court-Martial of Billy Mitchell* (1955), *Anatomy of a Murder* (1959), *Exodus* (1960), *Advise and Consent* (1962) and *The Cardinal* (1963), do not eschew political causes. On the contrary, not only do they illustrate political issues but they take position on those issues as well. Bogle (1997: 265) points out that 'Preminger believed films should address social issues'. It therefore seems all the more surprising that this social consciousness should not apply to *Carmen Jones* as well. Speaking of the film, Preminger is quoted as having said:

> This was really a fantasy, as was *Porgy and Bess* (1959). The all black world shown in these films doesn't exist, at least not in the United States. We used the musical-fantasy quality to convey something of the needs and aspirations of colored people. (in Pratley 1971: 110-111)

From its first image, the arrival by bus of Cindy Lou (Micaela) to the military base, Preminger's visual narrative puts particular emphasis on vehicle of transportation as signifiers of social mobility. Joe's army jeep and the empty freight train on which Carmen Jones jumps to avoid being taken to prison are presented in opposition to Husky Miller's shining green car and the luxurious train that takes him and his entourage to Chicago. The fifties are the years of America's undying love affair with the automobile, and the automobile appears throughout the film as one of the carrier of Preminger's social message. Joe is driving an army jeep when he finds himself at a fork between two roads to Masonville. As indicated by a sign, the new road puts Masonville fifty-four miles away, while the old road, where no motor vehicles are now permitted, is only thirty-two miles from Masonville. In his hurry to deliver his prisoner, Joe opts for the old road. 'I have to see a road that can stop this baby', he tells Carmen Jones who answers, 'You will, baby!'. The jeep does indeed get stuck and has to be abandoned. In the early forties when the military needed new recruits, the army was a road to social mobility for black young men, but clearly, as the visual narrative suggests, a decade later it is no longer the case. Social mobility is now geographical mobility away from the agricultural south towards northern urban centers. Preminger's film recasts in reverse the geographical scale of value operative in Mérimée's novella where a progressively downward slant marks the relationship between the protagonists, and distinguishes the northern French traveller from the bandit, José, who is Basque, and the 'devilish' Carmen of Seville who as a Gypsy is thought to have come from Egypt. In Preminger's film, the industrial north beckons young American blacks. But as the sinister tenement room that shakes with each passing subway indicates, the urban north is no Eldorado.

Preminger's film reworks other elements of the Mérimée story, more particularly its deep and intense misogyny clearly apparent to the reader of the novella, which starts with its opening epigraph attributed to the fifth-century Greek writer Palladas: 'Every woman is as bitter as gall. But she has two good moments: one in bed, the other at her death'. In Mérimée's short story, there are traces of misogyny evident as well in the traveller's retelling of the story, and in José's own confession. Whereas José in the Mérimée story blames Carmen's ethnicity to justify his killing her, in Preminger's film Joe presents his murder as a gesture of anticipatory justice in the name of male bonding: 'Tramp! You ain't never gonna to do that to no man again!' Unlike what happens in the Mérimée's text, in Preminger's film Joe is the only one who articulates a misogynistic stance.

In contrast to Bizet's Carmen, who joins up with Escamillo because she has fallen out of love with José, Carmen Jones refuses Husky Miller's advances repeatedly, and gives in only in the last sequence when she and Joe no longer have any means of survival. This is made perfectly clear by Dorothy Dandridge's superbly wrought interpretation, for which she became the first black performer ever nominated for an Oscar as Best Actress. Carmen Jones becomes Husky Miller's mistress so she can support Joe, with whom she remains in love. Cooped up, hiding from the military police who are looking for him, Joe becomes stir crazy and intensely jealous. In Bizet's opera, Carmen opens the second act by singing and dancing to suggestive Gypsy music. In Preminger's film it is not Carmen Jones but her friend Frankie who sings the exciting 'Beat Out That Rhythm on a Drum', a performance that Bogle characterizes as an 'instance of transcendent fun and high spirits' (Bogle 1988: 50). Thus, in the film, Carmen's persona is split between two characters: the ethnic or racial markings incarnated by Pearl Bailey, and a Carmen Jones that is made to appear more restrained and less exotic than her operatic counterpart. Carmen Jones is shown buying food, cooking, brushing Joe's pants and shoes: in short, she is portrayed as a woman with domestic qualities, sensitive, and generous, who sacrifices herself for her man. Preminger presents us with a Carmen close to being an exemplar of the middle-class values of female domesticity and self-abnegation so celebrated during the Eisenhower era. This is a far cry from Bizet's heroine who accepts death as the price of personal freedom.

Preminger's film thus presents itself as a curious intermingling of opera and musical, high art and folk art. Jeremy Tambling locates the politics of *Carmen Jones* in the cultural contest of high art versus low:

> What the *Carmen Jones* presentation seems to do most interestingly is to question by its status as musical, the position of Carmen as opera [...] *Carmen Jones* will appear a lesser work to those who accept the values of the opera houses: its radicalism, perhaps unintentional, its ability to question those values, to suggest that they are not absolute, but positioned (Tambling 1987: 32-33).

This opposition between opera and musical reflect cultural rankings in step with social hierarchies, and thus their intermingling does indeed, as Tambling suggests, destabilize the accepted notions of high and low art forms. Harry Belafonte explains that

> Because it was to be a black movie [...] and because blacks were still exotic to Europeans—and the movie had to be a financial success in Europe as well—Otto [Preminger] had to find a way to please the Bizet estate, which did not like what Hammerstein had done to the original work. They felt turning Carmen into a folk opera was not servicing the best needs of the opera, so Otto appeased them by hiring two opera singers to dub the main voices (in Bogle 1997: 277).

Whether the dubbing was a commercial necessity or not, the operatic voice and its treatment in Preminger's film seem to carry, as we will see, an additional political message.

In Mérimée's novella pronunciation, language, forms of speech and the sound of somebody's step are audible means of identification. By dubbing well-known black singers with operatic voices, which in the 1950s were culturally marked as high art and hence as white, Preminger presents spectators of the fifties with the unusual sight of black bodies singing with white voices in a strange sort of miscegenation. Joe does not in Preminger's film, as he does in Bizet's opera, stab Carmen: he strangles her in a janitor's closet. Not that Joe is incapable of stabbing: a moment earlier in the film we see him pull a knife on Husky Miller in the gym. If one is to read this cinematographic conclusion, that is to say the strangling of Carmen Jones, as a metaphor for the film, then Carmen Jones dies not only because she has become Husky Miller's, but also because she has fallen prey to the lure of money, and has adopted an urban lifestyle: she has in other words embraced the white values that are inscribed in her voice. By strangling her instead of stabbing her, Joe kills the white woman in her.

Film critics have often noted the class categorization attached to skin colour in both black and white communities. Gary Null notes that

> the role Dandridge plays in *Carmen Jones* and later in *Porgy and Bess* does not essentially depart from the image of the mulatto woman whose white blood makes her beautiful and whose black blood degrades her and who is doomed to die tragically [...] In Hollywood, right up to the present, the beautiful black woman has always been light-skinned and short-lived (Null 1975: 170-171).

Jim Pines provides a similar analysis of the social importance of skin tone:

> Otto Preminger's all-Negro musical *Carmen Jones* (1954) employs the 'qualities' of light and dark complexion in a highly *symbolic* way. It conforms neatly to a recognizable image-pattern. Occupying one end of this motif is the film's protagonists Carmen and Joe (Dorothy Dandridge and Harry Belafonte), whose 'attractiveness' derives much of its vitality from their clear tone or too off-whiteness; while, in contrast, there is the menacingly dark-complexion antagonist Sgt Brown (Brock Peters), a type we all recognize so easily (Pines 1975: 36).

In addition to the perceived hierarchy of skin pigmentation, in the cultural backdrop of the early fifties the voice occupies a significant place in the political fight for civil rights. The famous Afro-American contralto Marian Anderson faced overt racism in the early part of her career. The most highly publicized incident occurred in 1939 when the Daughters of the American Revolution, who owned Constitution Hall in Washington, D.C., barred her from singing there. In protest, the First Lady Eleanor Roosevelt organized on April 9, 1939 on the steps of the Lincoln Memorial, a concert for Marian Anderson that attracted over 75,000 people and millions of listeners over the airwaves. In 1954, when Preminger's film was first shown, Marian Anderson was again in the news as the first Afro-American singer to be engaged by the Metropolitan Opera in New York. On 7 January 1955 she starred as the sorceress Ulrica in the Met's production of Giuseppe Verdi's *Un Ballo in Maschera*.

In Preminger's film the depiction of the segregated army post, the focus on the social relevance of means of transportation, the film's reference to the migration of southern rural blacks to the industrial north, its representation of urban plight and its allusions to shades of blackness, as well as the perceived racial markings of the voice, are all elements that offer an audiovisual commentary on the life of American blacks in the mid-1950s. Because this representation is first of all couched in a musical, and secondly enclosed within the Afro-American community, its political ramifications may appear allusive, if not ambiguous. If, in the history of American race relations and the fight for civil rights, Preminger's *Carmen Jones* has had less political impact than other films of the fifties, such as *Native Son* (Pierre Chenal, 1951), *Cry, the Beloved Country* (Zoltan Korda, 1952), *Something of Value* (Richard Brooks, 1957), *Edge of the City* (Martin Ritt, 1957), and *The Defiant Ones* (Stanley Kramer, 1958), nonetheless it takes its place among those films that have helped bring about social change by breaking with stereotypes and making it possible for spectators to recognize someone very much like themselves in the character portrayed on the silver screen, someone dealing with love, jealousy, fear, poverty, lack of work, and so on. In Null's analysis:

> Audience identification with characters is probably the most important way in which films can influence attitudes and bring about social change. In the fifties, filmmakers attempted to reverse the negative images through which blacks had so long been portrayed and to present 'real' individuals. (Null 1975: 158)

Bogle reminds us that 'Though *Carmen Jones* might strike later generations as having enjoyably dated African American characterizations, it represented a major step forward during the Eisenhower era' (Bogle 1997: 264).

At the start, as well as at the conclusion of the film, a stylized red flame in which a rose is delineated appears on the screen. By appearing twice, this red flame beckons attention. The rose is clearly a visual reference to Carmen Jones, who holds and plays with a red rose when she first enters in the cafeteria scene. The flame could also be associated with Carmen Jones because Husky Miller calls her 'Heat Wave'. But red flames, particularly stylized red flames, are also standard visual icons of western culture. On the one hand the flame symbolizes purification, the inner light, spiritual love, and transcendence; on the other hand, it stands for conflict, rebellion, revolution. The fifties in America are the Eisenhower postwar years characterized by the exacerbated rivalry with the Soviet Union known as the Cold War. At the time when Preminger was making *Carmen Jones*, Senator Joseph McCarthy was at the height of his anticommunist crusade, conducting hearings and accusing many government officials and Hollywood personalities to be, if not communists, at least communist sympathizers. The Hollywood establishment, willingly or unwillingly, lent its support to McCarthy's political crusade. In his autobiography, Preminger recalls the heavy handed censorship of the period:

> The existence of the blacklist embarrassed the studio heads and they persistently denied it, even pretending that they never met at the Waldorf-Astoria to draw it up. I got proof to the contrary when I made a deal with Fox for the distribution of my independent film, *Carmen Jones*. The contract, as usual, gave me complete autonomy, but Fox insisted on one condition: I had to submit the names of everyone I intended to hire, *everyone*, to their legal department, which would have the right to veto without giving any reason. It was not a question of artistic choice. It was the secret blacklist. If your name was on it, you didn't work. For years after it was discredited, McCarthyism remained a blight on the industry. (Preminger 1977: 118)

In such an atmosphere of persecution, liberal political activism could only express itself by subtle means. Thus, the red flame at the beginning and at the end of Preminger's film could be seen as just such a muted visual reminder of workers' struggles for social justice. In this social and filmic context, Husky Miller's song 'Stand Up and Fight!', a popular hit with spectators during the war years, could be heard in the 1950s as another kind of call to arms by the dwellers of urban ghettos.

While it is surely not the best of Preminger's films, nor his most politically powerful, *Carmen Jones* is still a film imbued with political touches that offer today's spectator insights into the life and social choices faced by black Americans during the Eisenhower era. Beyond its representational interest, Preminger's film provides one more example of artistic ingenuity in revealing an ideological stance in opposition to the cultural and political forces in place, and succeeding in avoiding commercial suppression and governmental censorship. Innumerable past and present stage and screen versions of *Carmen* give different inflections to the story, which, in each of its remakes, mirrors the changing concerns and shifting values of societies. Of course, it is precisely because of this process of repetition and change through generations and across media that *Carmen* can be assumed to have attained the status of a myth. Stories that take on mythic status do so precisely because they speak of, and speak to, realities caught in specific time frames. Other films will take up the challenge of presenting new musical versions of the Carmen story. These new musical versions attest to the artistic malleability of the story, and testify to the enduring relevance of the many themes present in Mérimée's short story and Bizet's opera.

References

Anderson, Benedict. 1991. *Imagined Communities*. London: Verso.

Baldwin, James. 1955. *Notes of A Native Son*. Boston: Beacon Press.

Bogle, Donald. 1988. *Blacks in American Films and Televison: An Encyclopedia*. New York: Garland Publishing.

—— 1997. *Dorothy Dandridge: a Biography*. New York: Amistad.

Clément, Catherine. 1988. *Opera, or the Undoing of Women* (tr. Betsy Wing). Minneapolis: University of Minnesota Press.

Crowther, Bosley. 1954. 'Screen in Review: "Carmen Jones"', in *New York Times* (29 October 1954).

Davies, Ann. 2002. 'The Timeless Sex Bomb', in *Times Higher Education Supplement* (22 March 2002).

Halberstam, David. 1993. *The Fifties*. New York: Villard Books.

Leiris, Michael. 1963. *Manhood: a Journey from Childhood into the Fierce Order of Virility*. New York: Grossman.

Lourcelles, Jacques. 1965. *Otto Preminger*. Paris: Seghers.

Malherbe, Henry. 1951. *Carmen*. Paris: Albin Michel.

McClary, Susan. 1992. *Georges Bizet: Carmen*. Cambridge Opera Handbooks. Cambridge: Cambridge University Press.

Mérimée, Prosper. 1989. *Carmen and Other Stories*. Oxford: Oxford University Press.

Null, Gary. 1975. *Black Hollywood. The Negro in Motion Pictures*. Secaucus, NJ: Citadel Press.

Pines, Jim. 1975. *Blacks in Films: A Survey of Racial Themes and Images in the American Film*. London: Studio Vista.

Pratley, Gerald. 1971. *The Cinema of Otto Preminger*. London: A. Zwemmer/ NewYork: A.S. Barnes & Co..

Preminger, Otto. 1977. *Preminger: an Autobiography*. Garden City, NY: Doubleday.

Shaw, Arnold. 1960. *Belafonte: an Unauthorized Biography*. Philadelphia: Chilton.

Tambling, Jeremy. 1987. *Opera, Ideology and Film*. New York: St. Martin's Press.

The Dissonant Refrains of Jean-Luc Godard's *Prénom Carmen*

Amy Herzog

The familiarity of the Carmen story rests upon the circulation of song and narrative within popular culture. The immediate familiarity of the tune unleashes a web of associations extending beyond the realm of the performance or film. Jean-Luc Godard's 1983 film *Prénom Carmen* is, on the surface, one of the least faithful contemporary adaptations of the tale. Godard self-consciously creates a pastiche of elements borrowed from the history of *Carmen*, wound around a loose narrative in which the perennial seductress is transformed into a modern-day terrorist. Yet the exaggerated gestures of Godard's contemporary retelling appear heightened by his irreverence: the music from Bizet's opera surfaces only on the fleeting whistle of a passer-by, having been completely replaced by the strains of a string quartet rehearsing Beethoven. Drawing upon the work of Gilles Deleuze and Félix Guattari, the chapter will suggest that the complex circulations of music, narrative, and popular reference in *Prénom Carmen* function as 'refrains' that move within and across multiple texts. In addition to its co-optation of *Carmen*'s more concrete elements, the structure of the film, built upon the tension between music and image, becomes a refrain in itself. The result is a work that addresses not only the history of the Carmen story, but the very processes through which meaning is constituted.

Beethoven, Ludwig von
Bizet, Georges: *Carmen*
Deleuze, Gilles
Guattari, Félix
Godard, Jean-Luc: *Prénom Carmen*
Music and image

1.

In *A Thousand Plateaus*, Gilles Deleuze and Félix Guattari introduce the notion of the refrain (Deleuze and Guattari 1987: 310-350). Using an amalgam of musical, scientific, and philosophical terminology, they expand the definition of the refrain from its colloquial usage to encompass a highly complex phenomenon. On the most basic level, refrains are fragments of songs, colours, words, or other expressive elements that circulate and repeat through individual articulations. These circulations contain temporal facets, marking with each variation a certain duration; yet they also have an involved relationship to space. The refrain becomes a means of *territorialization*, an utterance that delineates a particular territory through its echoes: a bird's song, for example, is a refrain that marks its domain (312). Refrains can further constitute or create their territory through the act of singing; a child hums a familiar tune to comfort herself when far from home; folk songs have ties to nations, but they can also create mobile territories of people bound by the refrain that they share (311, 347). Refrains may play more specialized functions, defining spaces, actions, and roles. A song shared between lovers affirms their bond. Songs sung by workers solidify their labour through a refrain of solidarity. A lullaby becomes a refrain that encloses mother and child in a shared space of safety and love; it inscribes the territory of 'the child's slumber' (327).

This theorization of the refrain suggests a provocative approach to the question of *Carmen* in film, an approach attuned to the circulations of melody, voice, narrative, and myth that have rendered the tale such a rich subject for continued reinterpretation (see Davies's Introduction to this volume). Tracing *Carmen*'s cinematic refrains becomes an arduous task in the context of this long tradition of reworking. While the strains of Bizet's opera might be the most prominent and identifiable reiterations, one might also point to the characters and plot of *Carmen* as refrains, as well as to the story's thematic echoes: the exoticism of the Spanish setting, the Gypsy as racialized Other, the undercurrents of class, labour and community, the sexual assertiveness of Carmen, and the seeming inevitability of her death.

These varied refrains of *Carmen* each reverberate in a fraught and contentious relationship to space. The 'exotic' Spanish landscape and the nomadic territory of the Gypsy to which Mérimée and Bizet refer are, as many critics have discussed, more accurately located within the space of the French nineteenth-century imaginary. Carmen's character herself functions as the space upon which fantasies of femininity are embodied and rewritten. As these refrains circulate, adapting and evolving to each new setting and retelling, the spaces that they carve out also begin to shift. It is this process of metamorphosis that makes the repetitions of *Carmen* so fascinating and tangled. How, specifically, do the meanings of *Carmen*'s refrains transform with each retelling? Might a radical restructuring of the story result in the marking out of new territories? Or does the core of the refrain persist, its symbolic and semiotic space remaining ever present within each strain?

Jean-Luc Godard's 1983 film *Prénom Carmen* is, on the surface, one of the least faithful contemporary adaptations of the tale. Godard quite self-consciously creates a pastiche of elements borrowed from Mérimée, Bizet, and the history of *Carmen*'s various interpretations. The setting for the film is decidedly modern and designed to invite a direct critique of the gender politics of *Carmen*'s originary versions. The title character is a radical leftist terrorist, a politically driven woman whose goals presumably transcend her personal interests. The characterizations in the film as a whole are stylized and two-dimensional. Drawn with deliberate exaggeration, the collisions and interactions between the key players become, at times, outright farce. While exaggeration and theatricality are central to the operatic form, *Prénom Carmen* seems to focus its attention upon the surface of these representational practices rather than utilizing them to create a new, emotionally convincing account of the Carmen story. The structure of *Prénom Carmen*, as is to be expected in a Godard film, becomes a central component in establishing the meaning and subject of the work. Narrative action is continually interrupted by long, extra-diegetic shots of the ocean and sequences in which a string quartet rehearses Beethoven. These musical interludes can perhaps be seen as Godard's most irreverent move: Beethoven's quartets, along with a pop song by Tom Waits, come to replace Bizet's music altogether, reducing the latter to an occasional whistle heard on the lips of a passer-by.

These factors make *Prénom Carmen* a peculiar subject for a study of the construction of meaning in the larger history of *Carmen* on film. How can questions regarding *Carmen*'s refrains be addressed by a film that intentionally ignores *Carmen*'s primary musical text, its most familiar and predominant chorus? My reasons for taking this approach are three-fold. Firstly, Godard's conscious manipulation of the elements of the *Carmen* oeuvre indicates his awareness of their refrain-like function: meaning circulates through snatches of melody, stereotypical characterizations, and operatic dramatizations.[1] The excessive proliferation of these elements in the film makes their significance all the more apparent. Secondly, the intrusiveness of the structure of *Prénom Carmen* highlights the significance of form, both as a meaning-constituting element and as a refrain that is in itself central to the Carmen story. Finally, Godard's curious use of music works to foreground the larger function of music within the history of *Carmen*. Music lies at the heart of one of the key 'Carmenic' refrains reverberating throughout *Prénom Carmen*: namely the complex, often ambiguous representational framework the story relies upon, and its relationship to the question of difference. Despite Godard's unusual scoring techniques in this film, music and sound provide the very basis for this framework.

The self-conscious intertextuality of *Prénom Carmen*'s larger structure is echoed in the film's narrative. Like many relatively contemporary interpretations of *Carmen* (especially the film versions by Saura, Rosi, and Brook also released in 1983 and 1984), Godard's engages in a critical reappraisal of both Mérimée's novella and Bizet's opera. Transposed to modern-day France, Carmen is now 'Carmen X', part of a group of leftist terrorists. Her uncle, Jeannot Godard, played by Godard himself, is a senile and, in Carmen's words, 'washed up' filmmaker. She convinces her uncle to help her friends shoot a documentary film, although, as she later reveals, the film is merely a ruse (capitalizing on the latest 'video craze') for her gang to kidnap a wealthy businessman.

First, however, the gang holds up a bank: it is unclear whether the robbery is undertaken in order to fund the film project or the group's larger political goals, goals that are never even vaguely intimated during the course of the film. Joseph is the rather naïve and over-enthusiastic guard at the bank who, after a cartoonish shoot out scene, ends up rolling about on the floor of the bank with Carmen in a passionate embrace. Their affair flourishes when they escape to Uncle Jeannot's beach house. Yet the relationship begins to unravel when they rejoin the gang in Paris, particularly when the well-educated and somewhat elitist leader, Jacques, refuses to allow Joseph to participate. Joseph's anger and alienation build as Carmen herself begins to reject him. His desperation culminates in a confrontation with Carmen during the filming/kidnapping attempt in a hotel lobby. It is unclear, in the end, whether or not Joseph shoots Carmen, if she shoots herself, or in fact, if she has been shot at all. She is alive, slumped on the floor in the last frames of the film, which closes on an almost redemptive note: 'What is it called', Carmen asks, 'when everything's been lost, but it's daybreak and yet we're still breathing?' A bellboy, attempting to aid her, answers, 'it is called sunrise...'.

Yet these narrative scenes are in fact only one of several major threads that comprise *Prénom Carmen*, each weaving in and out of the other with a slow, deliberate rhythm. Long shots of the ocean and the sounds of crashing waves and seagulls punctuate the film, accompanying each other at times, or appearing separately, paired with other images or sounds. The narrative action frequently and abruptly cuts to scenes of the string quartet. The musicians pause to argue about technique, and rehearse troublesome passages over and over. These interjections have a shifting relationship to the plot. They initially, and primarily, appear to be extra-diegetic, yet they emerge as intertwined with the various layers of the narrative as the film progresses. The sea becomes a reference point for Joseph and Carmen's love after their stay at the beach house. The viola player in the quartet, Claire, appears in later scenes as Joseph's previous love interest, a somewhat removed reworking of Bizet's Micaela character. The string quartet itself is even hired by the filmmaker/terrorists, and provides diegetic accompaniment for the film's climax.

It is critical to note that while these various threads do in fact prove to be interrelated, the end result is not one of synthesis or integration. Just as soon as one element joins another in a moment of harmonious collaboration, they are interrupted, separating into free-floating sonic and visual elements. Image and sound are continually 'mismatched': the sounds of the sea in certain scenes overlap shots of characters speaking, at times replacing the audio of their dialogue entirely. The music played by the quartet, too, accompanies many scenes non-diegetically, serving in some instances to support the action, in others halting abruptly mid-scene, leaving in its place extended stretches of pure silence.

Structurally, this eccentric combination of image and sound foregrounds the conventions, and the arbitrary nature, of their coupling. The characters frequently refer to sound. Uncle Jeannot tells Carmen, 'we should close our eyes, not open them', as he shows her his new 'camera', a portable stereo that he holds to his ear. Joseph, at one point later in the film, refuses to accept Carmen's rejection, protesting, 'that's not you speaking: the sound of the sea was missing'.

It might thus seem as though the core refrains of *Carmen* have been thoroughly dissipated by Godard's radical dismantling of the story and opera and his utilization of both as fodder for a more generalised meditation on the nature of sound and image in film. *Prénom Carmen*'s unconventional format, however, despite its deviations from Mérimée and Bizet, may in fact engage with *Carmen*'s refrain-like mechanisms more directly than more 'accurate' cinematic versions. The concept of the refrain is not limited to the echoes of concrete sounds and images. Beyond the more ephemeral repetitions of narratives, characterizations, and themes, refrains might be more deeply embedded within particular representational strategies. Indeed the absence of *Carmen*'s most familiar and central elements serves to highlight their dynamic and shifting role in *Carmen*'s various manifestations. As Phil Powrie notes, *Prénom Carmen*'s 'significant intertexts [...] conjure up a distant, indeed absent, narrative, so that *Prénom: Carmen* comes into being only as a palimpsestic gesture which structures the original Carmen narrative as loss' (Powrie 1995: 65). The Carmen narrative, as well as Bizet's music, become a missing refrain that haunts *Prénom Carmen*, a refrain that nevertheless works to define the space of the film through absence. Moreover, the fragmentary and stuttering quality of the film's multiple registers and references results in a work whose meaning is created through the mobile collisions and recombinations of its various disparate refrains. Though *Prénom Carmen* thus distinguishes itself from more unified renditions of the narrative, it draws attention to the operations of these circulating elements within the *Carmen* oeuvre as a whole.

The intercutting of the string quartet's rehearsals is consistent with Godard's larger body of work, in which he repeatedly highlights film's materiality and means of production. The bank robbery sequence is exemplary in this regard. The scene opens with Joseph pacing before the bank's entryway, his rifle slung over his shoulder. Beethoven's opus 74 accompanies the scene non-diegetically, until the image abruptly cuts to the Prat Quartet rehearsing the piece.[2] The players break off as one of them remarks that the tone must be 'more mysterious', 'it develops and then it becomes more tragic'. The camera remains trained on the quartet for well over a minute as they begin the passage again before cutting back to Joseph comically and aggressively hustling pedestrians away from the bank. As the terrorists burst through the door, tackling Joseph, the music periodically pauses and resumes in varying intervals. Joseph chases the gang in a hail of bullets while several of the customers huddle in fear on the floor and others go about their business, oblivious to the chaos. The scene then cuts back to the quartet, with one player insisting, 'it must be more violent'. They repeat several bars twice, with increasing 'violence', and again the scene stays with the players for several minutes until they once again break off. 'Act, don't ask', Claire intones, and the image returns to Joseph, stumbling over furniture and fallen customers as he searches for the gang within the hallways of the bank. The music has stopped, yet Claire's monologue continues over the image, which cuts back to her several times as she discusses the concept of destiny. Throughout the remainder of the scene, the strains of the music momentarily resume and halt in varying relationships of contrast and empathy with the image. Joseph engages in an exchange of gunfire with the gang before encountering Carmen X on a staircase. Realizing that both are out of ammunition, they wrestle on the floor for several seconds before fervently groping one another. 'Let's get out of here',

Carmen says as a female custodian calmly mops up a puddle of blood behind them.

The disruptive cutting in this scene, the multiple references to outside texts, and the comedic theatricality are typical of the film as a whole, as well as of Godard's directorial style. Yet these practices, while similar to the strategies invoked in Godard's other films, are deployed in a new context here. More than Brechtian methods of distantiation, the self-referential elements in *Prénom Carmen* echo the larger structural refrains of the Carmen story. Delving into *Carmen*'s history, one might locate certain representational frameworks linking its multiple permutations. Mérimée's novella is narrated by a French archaeologist who recounts and critiques the story told to him by don José, adding a lengthy commentary on the Gypsy language and culture. Though Bizet's opera does away with the novella's double narration, his musical interpretation of the story adds what we might similarly call a self-reflexive meta-commentary. Bizet's initial version of *Carmen* was an *opéra-comique*, a 'lighter' genre that integrated both spoken and sung dialogue. Much like the mediation of the narrator, the distancing effect of the collision between speaking and singing draws attention to the work's formal constructs. *Prénom Carmen* repeatedly searches for 'the moment that comes before naming', a stage prior to language and the symbolic order.[3] Yet it pursues this moment through an overwhelming collage of musical and textual references. This self-conscious interrogation of the processes of symbolization and representation echoes those framing strategies in Mérimée and Bizet at the same time that it pushes the project to a new threshold. As Evlyn Gould argues:

> Though Godard's film does not use Bizet's score, its unique counterposing of dramatic dialogue and quartets complements the diegetic splicing of shots of ocean waves into the action of the narrative and can only be explained by its renewal, for the modern spectator, of the formal effects of Bizet's original comic-opera form. But this form is itself a renewal of Mérimée's fundamentally formal antagonisms cast in what Wayne Koestenbaum has called opera's 'queer marriage' of music and words (Gould 1996: 13-14).

For Gould, the thread between the three works lies in the active role these frameworks force the reader/listener/viewer to engage in, 'an oscillating position between identification and resistance' (113). The overt structure of *Prénom Carmen*, while seemingly an utter departure from *Carmen*'s foundational texts, in fact reflects the formal core of those works at the same time that it asks its audience to reflect upon that tangled web of associations.

While *Prénom Carmen* does reproduce several of *Carmen*'s key frameworks, however, these repetitions must be understood in the context of the film's thematic project, one which does significantly deviate from both Mérimée and Bizet. Godard and screenplay writer Anne-Marie Miéville's adaptation concentrates almost exclusively upon issues of gender and sexuality.[4] This shift in focus has serious implications in the context of *Carmen*'s narrative. Both Carmen X and Joseph are French Caucasians, a move that displaces the racial tensions central to the opera and novella. Though the orientalism of the Spanish setting and the conflicts between the Gypsy workers, the Spanish officers, and the French narrators are removed from *Prénom Carmen*, some corollary signifiers of 'otherness' persist, if in somewhat veiled forms. Maruschka Detmers, the Dutch actress who plays Carmen, has dark features that have been deemed 'exotic' enough to land her roles as diverse as a Hungarian-Jewish freedom fighter in *Hanna's War* (Menahem Golan, 1988) and a Cuban-American in *The Mambo Kings* (Arne Glimcher, 1992). In *Prénom Carmen* Detmers is not racially coded in this way, yet her character does stand in stark visual contrast to the fairer Claire, whose conservative clothing and closed body language further differentiate her from the assertive, frequently unclothed Carmen X. Rather than exploring *Carmen*'s troubling racial politics, this move could be read as leaving those prejudices intact and projecting them onto an equally troubling portrayal of female sexuality. One might conversely, however, question whether relocating *Carmen* to a French setting has a productive potential. While, in this instance, it obscures the issues of race key to the original story, it does return *Carmen* to the French culture that spawned it, the culture that the story and music, in fact, had far more to do with than the phantom of Spain that they imagine. David Wills makes a compelling argument in this vein, regarding the proliferation of Carmen films in 1983-1984 and crises of economics and nationality within the European Community (Wills 1986).

Nevertheless, while issues of race and ethnicity are not explicitly addressed in the film, Godard and Miéville's interrogation of gender is substantial.[5] Carmen X is a mesmerizing and complex character who rarely falls into the role of the fickle-hearted seductress. Though Carmen X's fate in the film is ambiguous, her dialogue and narration throughout provide a direct commentary upon the dichotomy of fate/freedom central to the Carmen story as a whole.[6] The virgin/vamp duality established in Bizet's opera is further displaced, for despite the visual contrast initially established between the two characters, Carmen X and Claire are almost never presented as rivals. Unlike Carmen and Micaela, they take the form of parallel voices existing on primarily distinct narrative registers. Both speak at length, in monologues, about the tension between fate and improvisation, one of the key conflicts that drives the film. In articulating this shared quandary, Claire has more in common with the historian's role in Mérimée's novella than she does with Micaela; she provides a narrator's interpretation of the action that is unfolding. Masculinity, too, is destabilized; Powrie (1995), for example, points to the ways in which Joseph's character operates in a position of ambiguous gender identification, in effect recasting the myth of the *femme fatale* into one of male desire and masochism.

2.

Rather than exploring these representations in further detail, however, I would put these observations aside to locate the problem of gender difference addressed by the film within the larger economy of difference it interrogates. Within *Prénom Carmen* the emphasis on difference and the other is realized most clearly in the conflict established between music and image. Sound, that which film traditionally renders subservient to the image, is brought to the forefront in a direct challenge of this hierarchy. Music is not a metaphor for femininity, nor vice versa. But each does function as a repeating *refrain* of difference, the unfixed domain of the Other. I would argue that this is in fact the refrain most central to the Carmen myth: that of difference in the realm of representation.

The question of repetition and difference lies at the heart of Deleuze and Guattari's interest in the refrain, and their examination of the concept centres on the degree to which individual refrains either minimize difference, or allow it to flourish unresolved. Looking in this way at the specific function that a repetition performs, they isolate several distinct ways in which the refrain can relate to space. It can, as in the examples of the birdsong and folk music, act to territorialize, inscribe, or fix. Carmen's 'Habanera', for example, as McClary has demonstrated, constitutes an incredibly complex ground, one that includes Cuban-style cabaret, bourgeois nineteenth-century notions of the 'exotic', 'feminized', hip-swaggering 'chromatic excesses' (McClary 1991: 57-58), and the ambiguous space between communal performance and personal expression (McClary 1992: 74-77). With each rearticulation of this refrain, in various venues and mediums, this same ground, more often than not, is re-embodied.

Yet there is a certain creative potential, according to Deleuze and Guattari, which can take hold of the refrain and make it a *deterritorializing* force. A refrain may be highly determined and 'grounded', but it will also 'bring "play" to what it composes', opening up into new configurations as it transects the space of which it sings (Deleuze and Guattari 1987: 336). Many versions of *Carmen* thus utilize the 'Habanera' to critically renegotiate questions of community, nationality, gender, and race. Sound and music especially, for Deleuze and Guattari, have a capability to move between divergent spaces and to elicit affective responses. On the one hand, this accounts for music's tendency toward emotional manipulation (348). On the other, sonorous elements have a potential to free themselves from repressive frameworks, to carry us elsewhere. Carried along by the expressive power of the refrain, music can break pre-existing configurations open and create, out of that raw material, new ways of seeing, hearing, and thinking.

I would not argue that *Prénom Carmen* achieves that level of deterritorialization, a highly specific, nearly impossible movement as it is established in *A Thousand Plateaus*. But I would suggest that this idea of a 'creative play' that utilizes the repetitive power of the refrain to open up new layers of space and expression reveals much about the way *Prénom Carmen* figures itself in relation to the larger Carmen myth. The multiple registers in the film, its poly-vocality and abundant intertextual references, confront the audience with the raw elements of the Carmen narrative dissected and laid bare. More than a deconstruction, however, the systematic unhinging of refrains within *Prénom Carmen* marks a struggle toward the creation of something new. The final moments of the film emphasize less a return to the beginning than the birth of a new dawn. Powrie performs a different reading of this scene, finding within it a return to Carmen's origin and the mythical status the film otherwise worked to undo (Powrie 1995: 72). I would agree that the scene is highly ambivalent, working at once to rehearse and pull apart *Carmen*'s mythology. Yet the 'double theatricalisation' Powrie aptly uncovers here, found in the dialogue's direct quotation from Giraudoux's *Électra* and the stage-like *mise en scène*, might also be read as an attempt to rewrite these myths through a self-conscious staging that subverts their combined meanings. Just as Carmen X's ambiguous fate in the last frames leaves open a window of hope, perhaps the intense dialogue between refrains found here might open onto new territories, improvised variations that serve to 'clear the air' by destabilizing the link between quotation and source. As Verena Andermatt Conley writes, the film's 'many quotations undermine the unfolding of the Carmen story. They introduce different tonalities, vibrations and temporalities allowing, paradoxically, voices to lead toward each other, in a movement necessary for an affirmation of life and breathing' (Conley 1990: 73).

The thrust toward the creation of new spaces through the repetition of refrains in *Prénom Carmen*, as I have suggested, reinscribes the film's interrogation of gender difference into a larger formal sphere. Individual characterizations might indeed remain problematically grounded, yet the film takes its greatest creative leaps in a sonic register. The Carmen story is founded upon a self-conscious interest in representation and difference, from Mérimée's complex narrative framing strategy to Bizet's dramatic collision of musical styles and spoken dialogue. I would identify the strains of this kind of framework within *Prénom Carmen* as structural refrains. The territory these refrains circumscribe is that of representation itself, the representation of difference. Wills makes this argument when he writes that the music in *Prénom Carmen* becomes

> that through which the economy of representation is both articulated and disrupted, inasmuch as it provides a difference against which the visual can define itself while at the same time participating with the visual in the same field of possible representations. (Wills 1986: 42)

Sound and music, which are used in formally similar ways in the film, become a refrain for not only the kind of representational frameworks found in Bizet and Mérimée, but also a refrain for that which is continually elided, dominated, and contained through the process of representation (40).

This, I would argue, is the primary motivation for Godard's use of Beethoven's quartets as opposed to Bizet's opera. Unlike the dramatic form of the opera, which utilizes highly coded signifiers for gender and race, the quartets cannot be definitively linked to a particular characters or traits.[7] This is not to say, of course, that Beethoven's music, in its non-narrative and non-theatrical form, is thus free from political implications. It is to say, however, that the music used in *Prénom Carmen* functions entirely differently from that of Bizet's opera. It does not signify directly, but points instead to the very *weight* of signification music is forced to bear in film.

What becomes provocative about the repetition of refrains in this instance is the manner in which each element has become dislocated from any direct representational relationship. Unlike simpler refrain-functions, such as the birdsong that clearly corresponds to the set territory it marks, here the refrain functions as a floating element that frees itself (to varying degrees) from its traditional, fixed associations, and begins to form new meanings and associations as it adheres to and interacts with other elements and refrains. The distinction to be made here is that the refrain is not bound in the one-to-one relationship of a signifier and a signified. Instead it becomes part of a process of endless circulation and transformation. Again, this is not to say that these elements become dehistoricized or depoliticized, utterly removed from their original contexts. Their emotive impact arises, in fact, from the reverberations of those rich historical associations. Yet rather than conceiving of these meanings as fixed, the repetition of each refrain becomes a process of rending these traditional associations apart, associations that are often deeply coloured by binaristic Western conceptions of race, gender, and class. These originary meanings do not disappear, but through the variations of each recurrence, they become open to interrogation and heighten the potential for new associations, combinations, and meanings.

The selection of Beethoven's music, rather than that of any other composer, is particularly significant in this regard.[8] The reception and categorization of Beethoven has been the subject of fierce debate, and has undergone dramatic historical shifts. Beethoven's late string quartets, Godard's primary source in this film, were regarded by many of his contemporaries as dissonant and fragmentary deviations from his earlier work, and Beethoven received a great deal of criticism for abandoning the classical tenets of unity and reason. He was later embraced as the creative progenitor of the Romantic movement, his late string quartets being viewed as intensely private works that experimented with form and expression in radical new ways. Musicologists of the early twentieth century, however, went to great lengths to disavow Beethoven's Romanticism, rooting his work in the eighteenth-century tradition by pointing to the influences of Haydn and Mozart, and to the persistence of classical forms such as the sonata (Solomon 1994). More recently, theorists have addressed both tendencies within Beethoven from a variety of interdisciplinary perspectives. Feminist musicologists have elaborated on the violent movements of his compositions and associations they have accrued in their cultural recyclings (McClary 1991). The late string quartets have also been read through the lenses of semiotics and postmodernism (McClary 2000).

The circulations of both Beethoven's music and the commentary it has generated are salient here in two key ways. First, within Beethoven's later compositions themselves, there is a formal tension between fragmentary, deconstructing references and a movement toward reunification. Responses to these works, through their interrogation of Beethoven's influences and his dissonant, expressive tendencies, throw into question conceptions of originality and creativity in the artistic process. Secondly, criticism of Beethoven, as a perpetual site of contention and re-evaluation, further probes the roles of interpretation, criticism and 'reading' in the experience of works of art. In essence, these debates engage with what we might call the refrain, the resurfacing of themes and influences, the modes of reception they demand from their audiences, their deviations and flights into new territories, or conversely, their synthesis and ultimate return to the same ground.

The history of the reception and recycling of Beethoven might thus be read as partially analogous to that of *Carmen*. A particularly rich point of correlation might be drawn between the complex relationship between dramatic, literary, and musical texts found within both Beethoven and *Carmen*. Leon Botstein argues that shifts in the reception of music in nineteenth-century Vienna led audiences to become increasingly reliant upon secondary texts and guidebooks in their listening practices. The former 'impenetrability' of Beethoven's late quartets gave way to their rediscovery, when they 'assumed special stature as secret, opaque, and visionary objects requiring special extramusical commentary' (Botstein 1994: 93). He further locates the late quartets within nineteenth-century dramatic traditions, hypothesizing that they may 'have been impelled explicitly by so-called extramusical narrative impulses' (100). Christopher Reynolds similarly discusses the nineteenth-century practice of providing textual accompaniment to a musical work, verbal visualizations that were provided either by the composer or an outside interpreter. While textual annotations of music had fallen out of favour by the twentieth century, contemporary filmic interpretations of Beethoven have reinvigorated, for Reynolds, 'a metaphorical way of hearing related to that which flourished in the nineteenth century':

> Indeed film, with its opera-like dependence on music to convey, create, or comment on aspects of the drama, is the most active heir to a metaphorical mode of expression and hearing that once linked composition and criticism [...]. Whether for Berlioz and Wagner or Kubrick and Godard, artistic reuse

of canonical works takes part in defining the reception of those works, no less than more obvious forms of criticism (Reynolds 2000: 163).

The tensions between text and music, composition and criticism that Botstein and Reynolds locate within the late quartets resonates equally with Mérimée's novella, Bizet's *opéra-comique*, and Godard's film. Each of these tensions I would identify as having a refrain-like function. Most significantly, I would point to the tension within the refrain between the mobile expression unleashed by each articulation, and the grounded cultural spaces to which each chorus refers. Echoing Reynolds, I would further argue that the recycling of refrains works not only to transform that space, but also, potentially, to critically interrogate it. While each of the works discussed here might engage with this collage of contradiction differently, with different degrees of resolution, it is difficult to deny that each demands a new mode of seeing and listening.

Schubert's criticism of Beethoven in a diary entry could easily be read as a contemporary response to Godard; he derides the 'eccentricity which joins and confuses the tragic with the comic, the agreeable with the repulsive, heroism with howlings and the holiest with harlequinades, without distinction'.[9] Each permutation of *Carmen* might likewise evoke such dissonant collisions. Yet *Prénom Carmen* seems particularly attuned to the implications of these juxtapositions, and utilizes them in ways that draw attention to their representational strategies. Its jarring structure might not free itself entirely from the ground that Carmen sings. Yet its active engagement with the viewer throughout these various 'oscillations' carries each refrain beyond the realm of mere repetition, toward unrealized territories. 'To improvise is to join with the World, or meld with it' (Deleuze and Guattari 1987: 311).

This reading of *Prénom Carmen* is by no means exhaustive. In particular, it has neglected the emotive contribution of music to the Carmen legacy, and the effects of the relative absence of this component in *Prénom Carmen*. As that aspect of music that has been consistently denigrated as subjective and 'feminine', a tendency central to the history and reception of versions and adaptations of *Carmen*, a study of the politics of difference and sexuality in the music of *Prénom Carmen* must certainly take this into consideration. I raise this point in conclusion not to question the integrity of Godard and Miéville's adaptation, but instead to suggest that *no* version of *Carmen* could ever address the full range of questions, the cacophony of refrains, provoked by the story. There is something to be learned from Godard's approach, yet there are certain elisions in the film as well: most notably the absence of the creative power of the female voice. We gain more when we view *Prénom Carmen* alongside other artistic co-options of the refrain (Geraldine Farrar's inspired vocal and silent adaptations are a particularly poignant example). Individual *Carmen*s cannot be read in isolation; their discursive strategies must be placed in the context of the hundreds of diverse strategies that comprise the Carmen myth as a whole. The power of *Carmen* lies in its function precisely as a refrain, a series of articulations that are always shifting, moving, and incomplete. We can best understand it not by analyzing the positive or negative aspects of each occurrence, but by mapping the implications of its movements as it circulates *between* texts. Often its strains may serve to territorialize and contain, but it always bears at the same time the potential to break free, to move on the notes of that song toward a new creative plane.

Notes

1. Craven (1988) similarly points to 'Godard's refrain technique', though her theorization of the refrain is drawn from literary theory and genre criticism.
2. For an elaboration of the various Beethoven quartets referenced in *Prénom Carmen*, see Sheer (2001: 173, 181-187).
3. See discussions of this aspect of the film by Powrie (1995: 68) and Conley (1990: 69).
4. McClary (1992: 125) notes that most contemporary 'revisionist readings of *Carmen*' similarly devote the majority of their attention to questions of gender.
5. As McClary discusses in '*Carmen* as Perennial Fusion' (in this volume), class is the other primary conflict that Godard examines through his reworking of the Carmen narrative.
6. In this regard, Carmen X might be read alongside Sally Potter's *Thriller* (1979), in which the heroine interrogates and deconstructs her own position as the Mimi character in Puccini's *La Bohème*.
7. See McClary (1992) for a discussion of the representational function of music in opera, especially Chapter 4. Interestingly, McClary also notes that Bizet cites Beethoven as his greatest idol (48). McClary's '*Carmen* as Perennial Fusion' in this volume specifically addresses Bizet's 'German' leanings and their implications in *Prénom Carmen*.
8. Godard has drawn heavily from Beethoven's string quartets throughout his career, especially those from the composer's late period (Opp. 131, 132, 133 and 135), featuring them in several of his films, including *Le Nouveau monde* (1962), *Une Femme mariée* (1964), *Deux ou trois choses que je sais d'elle* (1966) (Sheer 2001).
9. Franz Schubert, diary entry of 16 June 1816 from O. E. Deutsch (ed.), *Schubert: A Documentary Biography* (London, 1946), as quoted by Soloman (1994: 69).

References

Botstein, Leon. 1994. 'The Patrons and Publics of the Quartets: Music, Culture, and Society in Beethoven's Vienna' in Winter, Robert and Martin, Robert (eds) *The Beethoven Quartet Companion*. Berkeley, CA: University of California Press: 77-109.

Conley, Verena A. 1990. 'A Fraying of Voices: Jean-Luc Godard's *Prénom Carmen*' in *L'Esprit Créateur* 30(2): 68-80.

Craven, Alice. 1988. 'Jean-Luc Godard's Refrain and the Question of Genre' in *Discours social/Social Discourse* 1(3): 301-316.

Deleuze, Gilles and Guattari, Félix. 1987. *A Thousand Plateaus: Capitalism and Schizophrenia*. (tr. Brian Massumi). Minneapolis, University of Minneapolis Press.

Gould, Evlyn. 1996. *The Fate of Carmen*. Baltimore: Johns Hopkins University Press.

McClary, Susan. 1991. *Feminine Endings: Music, Gender, and Sexuality*. Minnesota: University of Minnesota Press.

— 1992. *Georges Bizet: Carmen*. Cambridge: Cambridge University Press.

— 2000. *Conventional Wisdom: The Content of Musical Form*. Berkeley CA: University of California Press.

Powrie, Phil. 1995. 'Godard's *Prénom: Carmen* (1984), Masochism, And the Male Gaze' in *Forum for Modern Language Studies* 31(1): 64-73.

Reynolds, Christopher. 2000. 'From Berlioz's Fugitives to Godard's Terrorists: Artistic Responses to Beethoven's Late Quartets' in *Beethoven Forum* 8(1): 147-163.

Sheer, Miriam. 2001. 'The Godard/Beethoven Connection: On the Use of Beethoven's Quartets in Godard's films' in *The Journal of Musicology* 18(1): 170-188.

Solomon, Maynard. 1994. 'Beethoven: Beyond Classicism' in Winter, Robert and Martin, Robert (eds) *The Beethoven Quartet Companion* Berkeley, CA: University of California Press: 59-75.

Wills, David. 1986. 'Carmen: Sound/Effect' in *Cinema Journal* 25 (4): 33-43.

Carlos Saura's *Carmen*:
Hybridity and the Inescapable Cliché

Andrés Lema-Hincapié

Carlos Saura's *Carmen* (1983) is posited in this chapter as a hybrid work that attempts to challenge Carmen as cliché but fails. After discussing hybridity as a cultural concept, the chapter argues that Saura does not simply retell the story but offers it as a form of intertexuality with both Bizet's opera—in the juxtaposition of flamenco music with the opera score—and Mérimée's novella as Andalusian travelogue. In this way, too, Saura transfers the story out of its traditionally rural Andalusian setting, so that his version offers us a context of contemporary Madrid. But the tendency of the story to cliché—thus petrifying both Carmen and her context—acts here as a force that ultimately constrains both Saura as director and Antonio Gades as choreographer. Nonetheless, Carmen is not totally lost to the force of the stereotype, and the chapter concludes with examples of Saura's attempt to critique the cliché as a sort of last, desperate stand against it.

Andalusia
Cliché
Hybridity
Intertextuality
National Identity (Spanish)
Saura, Carlos: *Carmen*

Carlos Saura's film *Carmen* (1983) is a child of uncertain parentage. Rather than deliver a straight adaptation, the filmmaker has created a fusion of elements from diverse cultural traditions: the Romantic, from Mérimée's novella; the musical, from Bizet's comic opera; and the flamenco, with its voluptuous song, dance and Gypsy resonances. This fusion is both the film's genius and its downfall. Saura appropriates these disparate and derivative components and sets them in unexpected coordinates—cinematic, choreographic, and diegetic—achieving a richness and a dissonance that did not exist before. This allows the filmmaker a fuller palette of languages and milieux: those of the cinema, of Antonio Gades, one of the great figures in Spanish dancing and flamenco, and of 'the fictional content of a narrative world' (Brooker 1999: 169). Though the setting is purposely ambiguous, the story probably unfolds in the Madrid of the 1980s. It moves along two interweaving narrative threads: one thread documents the rehearsals of a ballet company that is adapting Bizet's opera for the stage; the second follows the lives of certain of the dancers.

The confluence of the elements that the various traditions provide, and of the specific features of Saura's cinematic art, give the film its hybrid character. This hybridization redefines, in a less than flattering manner, the myth of Carmen. The film's critical impetus, though timid, comes from its self-conscious treatment of Carmen's character as cliché. In fact, the entire film can be seen as a study of the concepts of hybridization and cliché at work.

Although Néstor García Canclini describes hybridization as a mix of 'lo culto, lo popular y lo masivo' (the learned, the popular, and the mass-consumed) (García Canclini 1990: 15), this narrow definition is inadequate to the study of Saura's film. For hybridization is also the result of relocating pre-existing elements within new co-ordinates. In this sense we are following Tiphaine Samoyault, for whom the hybrid reshapes (*'déforme'*) by various means such as substitution, inversion, and collage (Samoyault 2001: 177-178). For Samoyault the hybrid's use in art is a response to the already known ('déjà connu')—which here takes on the meaning of the cliché. The culturally fecund hybrid, dedicated 'à reconfigurer les éléments du monde' (to reconfiguring the elements of the world) opposes the repetitive and regressive nature of the cultural representations, that is, the cliché, replacing them with 'le bouleversement infiniment plus dérangeant du nouveau ou du renouveau' (the infinitely more bothersome unsettling of the new or renewed) (185-186).

Charles Stewart's article 'Syncretism and Its Synonyms: Reflections on Cultural Mixture' is especially pertinent to the concept of hybridization. According to Stewart, many cultural theorists and anthropologists have used *syncretism, hybridization, creolization, synthesis,* and *mestizaje* (despite these concepts' less than virtuous colonialist pasts) to debunk the notion of culture as something 'too stable, bounded, and homogeneous' (Stewart 1999: 40). According to Stewart, by means of the aforementioned concepts we become aware that culture is essentially a mixture, and that this mixture occurs within a frame of reference that is at once social, political, and historical (57). At this point I depart from Stewart, who sees hybridization as a function of interrelated cultures. The concept could be better explained, in terms both more neutral and more precise, as a mixture that is more *intra-* than *inter*cultural, thereby underscoring its botanical and zoological origins. How, then, is hybridization, as an intracultural phenomenon, expressed in Saura's *Carmen*?

From the opening frame of the movie, we are in hybrid situations. There is, first of all, an intersecting of arts. Saura's camera records the song and dance of flamenco with a documentary intention that is at once cinematic and photographic. We can hear echoes of the director's artistic beginnings, for Carlos Saura was a professional photographer before he began his studies at the Instituto de Investigaciones y Experiencias Cinematográficas (IIEC), in 1955. Moreover, photography and the documentary were his first interests before he dedicated himself to narrative filmmaking. Indeed, the government of Cuenca province in Spain entrusted the young Saura with the task of creating a documentary film to promote the region's industry. Entitled *Cuenca,* it appeared in 1957. This is pertinent and useful, because in Saura's *Carmen* the perspectives of both photographer and documentarian are palpable. Without reaching for more complex interpretation, we can say that Saura's *Carmen* is among other things a documentary about the tense relations in the city between the traditionally rustic flamenco and the urbane, sophisticated ballet. From this same viewpoint, Yann Lardeau has written that '*Carmen* de Saura est un documentaire, portant sur les pas, les rythmes, les figures de danse, la performance des danseurs' (Saura's *Carmen* is a documentary about the steps, the rhythms, the dance figures, and the performance of the dancers) (Lardeau 1983: 38).

However, Saura introduces new perspectives that neither the literary work of Mérimée nor the musical work of Bizet has provided, and because of this it surpasses the merely documentary. Katherine S. Kovacs claims, 'Saura does not intend to rewrite the story in any way. His changes are stylistic rather than substantive' (Kovacs 1990: 107). But she errs. So does Eugene Stein when, forgetting the short story by Mérimée, he contents himself with saying that 'Carlos Saura has refashioned the Bizet opera and the tale of the doomed Gipsy to a Spanish flamenco dance company' (Stein 1984: 111). Apparently, both Kovacs and Stein ignore the conspicuous absence of the erudite foreigner travelling through Andalusia, who is intrigued by the world of the Gypsies and who chronicles the tragic fate of the Basque military officer José Lizarrabengoa. Even though Mérimée's is a Romantic novella, it is worth remembering that his work closes with several pages that come close to the realm of social science:

> L'Espagne est un des pays où se trouvent aujourd'hui, en plus grand nombre encore, ces nomades dispersés dans toute l'Europe, et connus sous les noms de *Bohémiens, Gitanos, Gypsies, Zigeuner*, etc. (Mérimée 1967: 403)

> (Spain is one of the countries where today one can find quite a large number of those nomads dispersed throughout all of Europe, known as *Bohémiens, Gitanos, Gypsies, Zigeuner*, etc.).

Through the fatal love between José and Carmen, Mérimée portrays several things: José's military world and his difficult relationship with his mother; his socially acceptable relationship with Micaela, his betrothed; and the illicit nature of Carmen's 'bohéminée' existence, that of a 'sorcière infâme' or 'démon' (evil sorcerer or demon) conscious of its impending doom. Saura goes beyond this.

In Bizet's *Carmen*,[1] the theme of José's mother and his fiancée is essential to the core of the story, since his ill-fated passion for Carmen destroys his family ties as well as his betrothal to Micaela. In Act 3, Scene 5, Micaela prophesies that he will break his bond with his sick mother:

> Écoute moi, je t'en prie,
> Ta mère te tend les bras,
> Cette chaîne qui te lie,
> José, tu la briseras.

> (Listen to me, I beg you,
> Your mother holds her arms out to you,
> This chain that binds you,
> José, you will break

Saura, though, does something different. He departs from his two forerunners, the literary and the musical, in a way that is more than merely stylistic. His intent is documentary. By recording with his camera the passes, the subtle movements of the dancers' bodies and hands, he also captures the institutionalization of flamenco in Madrid, the location of Antonio's study. Whereas in Mérimée and then in Bizet flamenco is a rural phenomenon of a marginalized people, now, in Saura, it sweeps through the nation's capital. The world of Saura's *Carmen* sets aside the precise geography of Mérimée and of Bizet, Andalusia, and likewise the marginality of the Gypsies and their nomadic life. Saura wants to show that *Carmen* has become a myth of the city, that somehow any Spanish city is also the *Andalucía flamenca.* Here it is enough to recall the scene in which Antonio and his guitarist Paco de Lucía, in search of the ideal actress for the Carmen role, attend the dance class at dancer María Magdalena's flamenco academy. But because of the immense interest in flamenco, the academy is so packed with students that there is scarcely room to stand. The citywide interest in flamenco knows no age limit: even three small children are thrilled to be in attendance.[2]

Kovacs refers to the film's 'inter-art traffic' and its 'multimedia arts that fuse drama, spectacle, music, and dance' (Kovacs 1990: 106). This is hybridization. Yet Kovacs fails to mention another equally relevant fusion, that of a literary work on two planes of existence. Operating on one plane is the short story by Mérimée; on the other, the diegetic intersection of the dancers' rehearsal, that is, fiction, with the emotional life of those same dancers beyond the stage, which is reality. In the film, the first explicit reference to Mérimée and Bizet comes in an abrupt manner, during small talk between Antonio and Paco de Lucía. Antonio expresses his dissatisfaction over the failed search for a suitable dancer to play Carmen. Then the conversation cuts off violently with the opening credits and soundtrack of music from the opera. It is the first explicit reminder of the film production's thematic relationship with Mérimée's novella and Bizet's opera. The credits roll over a background of vintage engravings by Gustave Doré, accompanied, naturally, by Bizet's music. Later this harmonious fusing of novella, opera, film, and graphic art will turn increasingly discordant. As Marvin D'Lugo notes (D'Lugo 1991: 203), Saura will respect the work of Mérimée but will conflict with Bizet. This conflict between art forms anticipates the cultural and human conflict that is the story of Carmen.

A clear-cut instance of 'artistic agression' occurs as Paco de Lucía accompanies on his guitar the flamenco *cante jondo* of an accomplished *cantaora*. Antonio disparages this music as inferior to the cultivated strains of Bizet, and drowns it out with a harsh, over-loud tape recording from the opera. For Antonio, the flamenco is perhaps *too* popular, lacking the artistic values of 'high culture' that Bizet's music represents. And so, with a blatant gesture of disrespect, he imposes Bizet's music over that of Paco de Lucía and the *cantaora*. But the guitarist's reply could not be more fascinating. Instead of rising to the bait, Paco de Lucía demonstrates the receptivity and adaptability of flamenco in the face of Antonio's slight. Paco de Lucía can, with his guitar, make a flamenco variation on the operatic music of Bizet, giving us an spontaneous demonstration of how the popular can be more malleable and fluid than the homogeneous, static purity of 'high' art. In the words of Charles Stewart, flamenco is readily 'porous', 'overlapping' (Stewart 1999: 41, 44), that is, disposed to becoming a hybrid. Here, perhaps, Saura idealizes the capacity of popular culture to adapt itself to new conditions.[3]

Some French-speaking critics have lamented Saura's lack of originality in his mimetic approach to the opera of Bizet. However, they miss his portrayal of the tensions that arise between classical music—and classical culture in general—and popular music (and also, quite possibly, popular culture). Lardeau makes no secret of his position, suggesting, in frustration that '*Carmen* de Saura est peut-être un bon document de télévision' (Saura's *Carmen* is perhaps a good television document), but that it is hard not to suspect that really it was made to avoid the challenge of a full film version of Bizet's opera (Lardeau 1983: 38).[4] But in fact Saura's continual references to Bizet show that the fusion, or hybridization, of the multifarious cultural representations in play is no peaceful thing. For Carmen is a myth that tries to bond the popular world of the flamenco—including the marginal life of the Gypsies—with the European elitist musical tradition. Although Evlyn Gould errs perhaps in her overly daring extrapolations, her notions are useful in understanding how she has seen the cultural tensions in Saura's *Carmen*. She speaks of the 'tense juxtapositions' between the European and flamenco artistic traditions, between the cinematic narrative and the dance, between the voice offscreen and the voice onscreen. She goes on to conclude:

> In keeping with the bohemian quality of its models, Saura's *Carmen* moves oppositionally between the pressures of two cultural systems and two mental landscapes, one private or psychic, the other public or social. (Gould 1996: 154)

Gould sees in Saura's film an 'unsettling confrontation' (152) with the narrative presented by Mérimée. But this is not the case, because whenever Antonio needs to better understand Carmen as a character, or to give the appropriate instructions to his actor-dancers, he refers not to the libretto of Bizet's opera but to the lines by Mérimée. According to D'Lugo (1991: 203), this preference for the novella by Mérimée is indisputably confirmed by declarations from Saura himself. For Saura, Mérimée's accurate depiction of customs demonstrates a broad and canny understanding of Spain. In his diegetic preference for Mérimée, then, we see a hybridization by substitution, to use the terminology of Samoyault. There is, however, a principal element in the novella by Mérimée that Saura does not consider, that is, the perspective of the erudite foreigner, moralist, and moralizer visiting Spain. During the night in the hostel, the erudite Frenchman warns José of the impending arrival of the soldiers who come to arrest him. Antonio, the foreigner's guide, has informed the soldiers of José's whereabouts in the hopes of getting the bounty on José's head. And with this warning the foreigner gives his farewell:

Pour prix du service que je vous ai rendu, promettez-moi, don José, de ne soupçonner personne, de ne pas songer à la vengeance. Tenez, voilà des cigarres pour votre route; bon voyage! Et je lui tendis la main. (Mérimée 1967: 355-356)

(To repay me the service I have just given you, promise me, don José, both not to suspect anyone and not to think of revenge. Take these cigars for your journey and have a good trip! And I offered him my hand).

Although the perspective of the erudite foreigner is not so clear in Saura's *Carmen,* this perspective has become a commonplace, or cliché, within Spain itself. Saura has not liberated himself from this outside perspective, although he has been explicitly conscious of the cliché's stifling effect. Carmen and her myth, along with all the reverberations that she carries with her, still continue to be useful beyond the borders of Spain, as a simplistic key for the interpretation of all things Spanish. The myth of Carmen fossilizes in cliché. It is suggestive, and also terrifying, to think that the myth of Carmen ceases to be a dynamic cultural blend and turns into the mould of a static representation, resistant to all change. That which in its origins could have been fluid is now a crystalized synthesis.

We can think of the terms *cliché, stereotype,* and *commonplace* as synonyms, for they all translate the awareness of reality and of the use of a certain class of ideas about things. In his *Topics* (I, 100a 20), Aristotle (1967: 1) spoke of *topoi* and also of *endoxoi,* that is, of ideas easily accepted via popular opinion, which appear to admit no contradiction and which serve as premises in rhetorical syllogisms. Chaïm Perelman and Lucia Olbrechts-Tyteca, in their *Traité de l'argumentation: la nouvelle rhétorique,* pinpoint the contemporary meaning of the commonplace. The commonplace loses the argumentative value that it had in Aristotle and becomes cliché. Both authors write that 'les lieux communs se caractérisent de nos jours par (leur) banalité' (Perelman and Olbrechts-Tyteca 1970: 113) (Nowadays, commonplaces are characterized by their banality). And later: 'La formule cliché n'a de valeur que comme moyen facile, trop facile parfois, de communion avec les auditeurs' (223) (The only value of a cliché formula is to be an easy means, too easy sometimes, of communion among listeners). Several dictionaries, such as the *Trésor de la langue française* and the *Dictionnaire alphabétique et analogique de la langue française,* note under the entry for *cliché* that the banality of the cliché stems from its mechanical, automatic repetition, and that it is comprehended as a stereotype because of the blurring that it causes on the *'singularités'*. The abstract representation of the commonplace does not allow us to see the concrete thing in all its astonishing detail. The actual origins of the term *cliché* lie in printers' jargon, where it refers to a series of words so often used together that they are set as a single slug, or piece of type. A cliché is uttered so repeatedly that its success lies in avoiding the particular detours, the differences with respect to an 'archetypal' original. In Samoyault's terms, the cliché can be understood as an overly facile representation, one in which there is no risk of difference (Samoyault 2001: 185).

In the cliché, three polemics are in play. The first is the polemic, of medieval origins, about the referential value of abstract representations (class terms) and singular things; the second polemic deals with authentic and inauthentic cultural representations; and the third, with the difference between *ignava ratio* (lazy reason), which is drawn from popular opinion, and critical reason—enlightened, watchful, and awake. Critical reason always demands that the representations be justified.

In the myth of Carmen there is a dance (flamenco), a geography (Andalusia), a rite (the bullfight) and a human group (the Gypsies). The four elements have illustrious antecedents in Spanish cinematography and, more broadly, in the culture of Spain. Their recurrence without criticism has even produced what critics have called *'españoladas'*—the popular assumption that Spain is a land of toreadors, castanets, and lugubrious songs played on gut-string guitars. In Saura's film the geography is elsewhere, but the flamenco, the bulls, and the Gypsies have their place. It sounds paradoxical that the sensual, orientalized *andaluz* as a cliché—the myth of Carmen included—is offered in order to please the foreigner (in the figure of the tourist), but that at the same time this commonplace cannot claim a Spanish pedigree. The story of the lovely and indomitable Gypsy Carmen, considered one of the few modern myths (along with those of Faust and don Juan), has its origins, for the 'high' culture of Europe, in works by non-Spanish authors.[5] D'Lugo emphasizes the theme of the foreign viewpoint that is imposed on Spain through the Carmen myth:

> The essential point of Saura's archeological recouping of the sources of the Carmen myths is a very contemporary one: Spaniards, having come under the spell of the foreign, imposter impressions of Spain, find themselves seduced by this falsification of their own cultural past. (D'Lugo 1991: 203)

The Romantic image of the Spanish geography, beginning with the decade of the 1830s in Europe, and infesting Spain itself, circulates with Victor Hugo, Théophile Gautier, and Mérimée himself. Carmen is one of the human prototypes of this geography. Frédéric Deval has expressed this adroitly:

> c'est le Romantisme qui va donner naissance à des 'modèles intermédiaires' entre le Flamenco tel qu'il se vit en Andalousie, et sa perception ailleurs. Ce sont ces 'modèles intermédiaires' (Carmen, le torero, le Gitan, l'œil de braise) qui vont servir de relais à l'attirance, cette attirance que ne cesse d'éprouver l'Occident. (Deval 1989: 12)

> (Romanticism gave birth to models which served as intermediaries between authentic Andalusian flamenco and the way it was perceived abroad. Such intermediaries for the continuing attraction of the West to all things Spanish were Carmen, the bullfighter, the Gypsy, the eye of fire).

Deval further notes that the Romantic view fosters a simplistic image of this culturally and geographically complex land, so that by the end of the nineteenth century, the identification of Spain with Andalusia was complete; and that this specious identification remains anchored in 'la profondeur dans l'imaginaire français' (23) (the depths of the French imaginary). The cliché, the commonplace, or the stereotype is expressed in the equation that reduces Spain to Andalusia, and where Andalusia is equivalent to flamenco and the Gypsies.

A large part of Spanish cinema has shown both a fascination with and a struggle against the stereotypical elements that resound throughout the myth of Carmen. For example, in *Bienvenido, Mr. Marshall* (Welcome Mr. Marshall, 1952) by Luis García Berlanga, the Andalusian theme (music, dance, and dress) appears as an imposture of the entire Castilian people. The pretence is necessary in order to please the distinguished guests, the Americans, whom they hope will provide aid with the Marshall Plan. In this way, what is Andalusian expresses itself internally, as a cultural resource for a community that can find no other values that it might recognize as its own. And externally, this community, which is in fact Castilian, perceives all that is Andalusian as a bridge with the world beyond Spain, in this case, the world of the American visitor. What is Andalusian is represented as a Spanish 'product', used by the Castilians and consumable by those who are not Spaniards. By means of humour, that which is Andalusian has in Berlanga's movie already become a cliché, that is, a commonplace that is now automatized and empty of any authentic cultural meaning. If the townspeople alienate themselves temporarily in an external, artificial cliché, they do it knowing that this cliché does not provide them the genuine representation of their own identity. However, even without any authentic existential content, the cliché is useful as an instrumental decoration. The schoolteacher of Villar del Río, the Castilian town of the film, details the distinct aspects of Andalusian dress thus: 'El sombrero, chaquetilla, la camisa y el fajón, / La peineta, florecilla, los volantes, pañolón'. (Hat, shirt, jacket, sash, / comb, flower, ruffles, scarf).

In the same way as in *La muerte de un ciclista* (Death of a Cyclist, 1955), by Juan Antonio Bardem, and in *Cet obscur objet du désir* (*That Obscure Object of Desire*, 1977), by Luis Buñuel, in Saura's *Carmen* the Andalusian theme reappears in the guise of a performance suitable for fatuous American tourists. None of the three directors, however, has dared dismantle this stereotype within the Andalusian theme. The dancer Carmen, before joining Antonio's ballet company, and Buñuel's Conchita both make a living performing Sevillana dances on a small stage. In the film by Bardem, the Americans who plan to do business with Jorge are guests of honour to a flamenco performance by Andalusian *cantaores*. Here the cliché is conveniently integrated within the narrative tension, since the joy of the private spectacle contrasts with the anguish on the faces of Juan, María José, Miguel, and Rafael. However, Bardem does not manage to develop the disharmony between the individual dramas of his characters on the one hand and the Andalusian fiesta on the other. All of this plainly belongs to the logic of self-seeking servility: with false humility they wine and dine the foreigner, hoping that he will soon leave his money in the hands of the locals. This perspective is common to the films of the four Spanish directors: García Berlanga, Bardem, Buñuel, and Saura.

So what still exists of Romantic cliché in Saura's *Carmen*? Although Deval argues that Saura tries to make flamenco classical ('classiciser') in order to give it a European respectability as a form of high culture, the critic has also perceived that in Saura's film the stereotypes reach the point of vulgarity (Deval 1989: 47–48). Philippon adds that the film sinks into cliché by promoting a superconventional and machista image of Spain, one that is anachronistic and inappropriate to this crucial time of the country's Europeanization. And Philippon asks:

Le flamenco implique-t-il nécessairement ces personnages de garces allumeuses ou jalouses, et d'hommes sombres prêts à sortir le couteau à la moindre peccadille? (Philippon 1983: 62)

(Does Flamenco always imply those characters who are jealous little sluts, or sombre men ready to take out their knives at the least peccadillo?).

For D'Lugo, the music of Bizet becomes a trap from which Antonio cannot extricate himself. Thus, D'Lugo also feels that Bizet transmits cultural cues and contents that still impede transcendence of the stereotype (D'Lugo 1991: 203; 207). Finally, Robin W. Fiddian and Peter W. Evans argue that Saura's film bows to Mérimée's novella and Bizet's opera as 'the film's images of authority' (Fiddian and Evans 1988: 87).

Saura merely replicates the image of José, without any alteration, in a mould of idealistic sentimentality, and replicates the image of Carmen in the mould of a temperamental sensuality; seductive, lying, and absolutely free. And this preservation of the cliché is even more radical since it goes beyond the ballet rehearsals: the myth of Carmen reaches through the mirrored walls of the dance studio to the very lives of the characters. The cliché controls the life of Antonio and determines the unfettered, domineering, and supremely self-confident gestures of the flesh-and-blood Carmen. The scene in his apartment, particularly in the bedroom, shows that, for Carmen, Antonio is merely another José.

Carlos Saura has limited himself to repeating the essential characteristics of the personalities in play within the myth. Saura falls into the stereotype of having maintained the timelessly consistent traits of his characters. His Carmen, like her predecessors, embodies force of character and the absolute freedom to love, and in doing so resorts easily to caprice and lies. And Saura's Antonio/José, also like his predecessors, lives in a state of alienation and dependency created by the heteronomy of love. Saura even copies, simplistically and without thematizing, the zoological images found in Mérimée. Mérimée's animals analogically illustrate ethical issues. Two in particular serve Antonio in unveiling the real identity of Carmen: the wolf and the cat. When he meets Carmen for the first time, in María Magdalena's dance class, Antonio contents himself with appropriating the words of Mérimée. Here is part of the erudite foreigner's first description of Carmen:

C'était une beauté étrange et sauvage, une figure qui étonnait d'abord, mais qu'on ne pouvait pas oublier. Ses yeux surtout avaient une expression à la fois voluptueuse et farouche que je n'ai trouvé depuis à aucun regard humain. Œil de bohémien, œil de loup, c'est un dicton espagnol qui dénote une bonne observation. Si vous n'avez pas le temps d'aller au Jardin des Plantes pour étudier le regard d'un loup, considérez votre chat quand il guette un moineau. (Mérimée 1967: 360)

(She had a strange and wild beauty, a face that surprises at first, that one cannot forget. Her eyes had above all an expression both voluptuous and savage, which I never found later on in any other human gaze. Gipsy eye, wolf eye—this Spanish saying refers to a person's good powers of observation. If you do not have time to go to the Jardin des Plantes to study a wolf's gaze, just look at your cat as it stalks a sparrow) [6]

These zoological images insist on the relationship between predator (he who desires) and its prey (the object of desire). In this regard, Nelly Furman's comments about Bizet's *Carmen* serve also for Mérimée's *Carmen* and for Saura's:

for José, desire is always triggered by someone else, determined by another, inscribed therefore in a mimetic system [...] For Carmen, however, it is not the lover—he is not a mirror for her own image—but the freedom to love that matters, to love without constraints. Her object of desire is desire itself, not simply to be desired, but herself to be desiring. (Furman 1988: 175–176)

Saura laments the inescapable cliché while never imagining that it is within his power to destroy it. He remains a prisoner in it, and therefore, his criticism is still timid. There is in the film an awareness of the cliché but no liberation from it at all. D'Lugo says as much, referring to Antonio: 'The artist's inability to separate his own life and consciousness from that of the Bizet opera is key to one of the film's central themes: the susceptibility of Spaniards to the imposture of their own culture (D'Lugo 1997: 41). There are, however, a few important moments of criticism attacking the cliché, in the form of a restrained, playful mocking. But it is an infantile parody without any real force. The ridiculing of the cliché in Saura's *Carmen* comes when the troupe of dancers combines its traditional music with a comedic representation of the *fiesta brava,* and a Carmen/Laura del Sol, dressed up as an Andalusian girl, plays with a buffoon in bullfighter's garb. This feeble parodic protest against the cliché continues later in the film, in the mock-clumsy movements of the dancers as they execute the *paso doble.* This *paso doble* is the prelude to the separation of the two groups: some will go with the bullfighter in his suit of lights, who leads the group loyal to the traditional music and dance; the others align with Antonio and his 'high' culture of classical ballet. The bullfighter, no longer comical, represents Mérimée's Lucas and Bizet's Escamillo. And Carmen, like her predecessors, goes not with Antonio/José but with the torero and his faction. The human drama of love between Antonio and Carmen is expressed in this conflict between popular dance and music on the one hand, and the classical forms on the other. Thus, the weak parody of the *paso doble* is subsumed in the return of the cliché, which once again imposes itself, more stubborn than ever.

The clichés or commonplaces that reveal only the superficiality of the imposture—the 'inauthenticity', to use Heidegger's word—also seem to pertain to the deep structures of the personalities of the protagonists. The following illustration is useful. Antonio is alone before the mirror, painfully aware that his conquest of the mind and body of Carmen is a mirage. And, in a moment of hyper-reflection (for it is at once mental, verbal, and speculative), Antonio recreates with his words the spectral image of his ideal Carmen, dressed to the nines in Andalusian splendor. The words take human shape, and the seductive and defiant apparition appears magically from the quicksilver of the mirror. It is the cliché of Carmen, the Andalusian woman—and the music of Bizet anticipates and accompanies the apparition. Antonio/José thinks aloud: 'Y ahora ella... con el abanico, la peineta, la flor, la mantilla... Con todo. El tópico. ¿Qué más da? ¿Qué más da?' (And now there she is... with her fan, her comb, her flower, her mantilla... With everything. The old cliché. What does it matter? What does it matter?).

Kovacs is right to point out the weakness and limitations of 'the conservative impulse of parody' against the stereotypes in the myth of Carmen as presented by Saura. Ultimately, Saura does not succeed in opening new avenues of thought about Spanish traditions. Kovacs goes on to say:

> [Saura's *Carmen*] is yet another stylized encoding of the notion of woman as foreign, mysterious, dangerous, of woman as underdeveloped terrain waiting to be explored. These are the psychological mechanisms, the mental set of Antonio, of Saura, and of the other Spaniards of their generation who, ten years after the death of Franco, have not yet completely overcome the lure of Carmen and stylized representation. (Kovacs 1990: 111–112)

Saura perceives from time to time the cliché of the myth and manages to be aware of it and of the counterfeit values that it expresses. Taking the film as a cultural hybridization, we find elements of earlier, different traditions repeating themselves. But Saura never succeeds in going beyond the commonplace, never manages to dismantle it or to demonstrate its inadequacy when confronted with the reality of actual men and women living in a Spain that is no longer the Spain of the Romantics. Instead of promoting a mistrust of the myth of Carmen, Saura gets buried in the fascination that it produces. As Perelman and Olbrechts-Tyteca would say, even when Saura takes a 'recul au niveau de la pensée' (Perelman and Olbrechts-Tyteca 1970: 233) (a mental step back), he lacks the greater boldness to propose a true representation contrary to the myth. Saura continues a prisoner of the myth of Carmen: *mythos* here becomes *endoxos*, the popular truth, uncritically taken as fact. So is it ever possible to escape the cliché? Or can it be that the commonplace, like any general idea accepted without scrutiny, is hard-wired into us? Achievable or not, it is ever the artist's task to try to find a way to spurn the easy image for the real one.

Notes

1. D'Lugo tells us that in 1981 Saura rejected the proposition by French producer Gaumont to make, 'with a maximum of fidelity to the original text', a cinematic version of the Bizet's opera (D'Lugo 1991: 202).
2. María Magdalena's school is not in Seville. Still, its geographical place remains unknown. Paco de Lucía announces a trip to Seville, and Antonio asks him to look there for a dancer for the role of Carmen. Did the two go to Andalusia together? This question only has an oblique answer: their destination is not limited to Andalusia, which suggests that Carmen could be found anywhere in Spain.
3. As Joan Ramon Resina points out, Carlos Saura 'no lleva razón en una confrontación de lo popular español con lo culto europeo. Lo popular, como tal, es mucho más reiterativo e inercial que las fórmulas disciplinadas, mucho más diversas y evolutivas' (is wrong when he confronts the Spanish popular with the European cultivated. The popular formula, as such, is more repetitive and full of inertia than more disciplined formulae, which are more diverse and evolutive). Personal Interview. 14.12.2001.
4. Alain Philippon, another critic of the *Cahiers du Cinéma*, summarizes Saura's intention as the 'réappropriation' (reappropriation) of the myth of Carmen, in the sense that it works to 'réhispaniser à mort *cette* Carmen' (rehispanize to death *this* Carmen). But is Philippon not falling into the nostalgic trap of wanting to find Bizet or Mérimée, pristine and untouched, within the film by Saura? Regardless, Philippon does not merely speak of 'paresse' (laziness) in order to judge this film—and Lardeau has already spoken of 'paresse'. Philippon even uses the expression 'malhonnêteté' (dishonesty) in the conclusion of his devastating critique. This critique finds mere cliché in the idea of the stage and of the *mise en scène*, in the poverty of the soundtrack, and in the abusive confusion of planes (reality vs. fiction). Philippon closes his remarks with these words: 'Quant au filmage de la danse, si Saura y témoigne d'un relatif savoir-filmer, il fait l'impasse sur le travail réel de tout choréographe sur un plateau (les danseurs sont bons dès les premiers essais)'(62) (With regards to the dance scenes, if Saura shows some filming know-how, he doesn't

get the point when recording the actual stage work of a choreographer. The dancers are good from their first rehearsals).

5. This affirmation merits a nuanced clarification, since, according to Maurice Portier, Prosper Mérimée knew *La gitanilla* of the *Novelas ejemplares* by Miguel de Cervantes. There is no doubt that he borrowed aspects from Cervantes in his portrayal of the Gypsy world (Portier 1967: 341).

6. Some pages later in the novella, Carmen thinks of herself as a wolf, and José is for her a dog and, often, her *'canari'* (canary). (Mérimée 1967: 380). In this way she justifies herself to José for not engaging in a stable relationship: 'Chien et loup ne font pas longtemps bon ménage' (379) (The dog and the wolf cannot live under the same roof for long).

References

Aristotle. 1967. *Topiques* (tr. Jacques Brunschwig). Paris: Les Belles Lettres.

Brooker, Peter. 1999. *Cultural Theory: A Glossary*. London: Arnold.

Deval, Frédéric. 1989. *Le flamenco et ses valeurs*. Paris: Auvier.

D'Lugo, Marvin. 1991. *The Films of Carlos Saura: The Practice of Seeing*. Princeton, NJ: Princeton University Press.

— . 1997. *Guide to the Cinema of Spain*. Westport, CT: Greenwood Press.

Fiddian, Robin W. and Evans, Peter W. 1988. *Challenges to Authority: Fiction and Film in Contemporary Spain*. London: Tamesis.

Furman, Nelly. 1988. 'The Languages of Love in *Carmen*' in Groos, Arthur and Parker, Roger (eds) *Reading Opera*. Princeton, NJ: Princeton University Press (1988): 168–183.

García Canclini, Néstor. 1990. *Culturas híbridas: estrategias para entrar y salir de la modernidad*. México: Grijalbo.

Gould, Evlyn. 1996. *The Fate of Carmen*. Baltimore: Johns Hopkins University Press.

Imbs, Paul (ed.). 1977. *Trésor de la langue française* vol. 5. Paris: Centre National de la Recherche Scientifique.

Kovacs, Katherine Singer. 1990. 'Parody as "Countersong" in Saura and Godard' in *Quarterly Review of Film and Video* 12: 105–124.

Lardeau, Yann. 1983. 'Le désir à la chaîne' in *Cahiers du Cinéma* 348/349: 37–38.

Mérimée, Prosper. 1967. *Carmen* in *Romans et nouvelles* vol. 2. Paris: Garnier Frères: 337–409.

Perelman, Chaïm and Olbrechts-Tyteca, Lucia. 1970. *Traité de l'argumentation: La nouvelle rhétorique*. Bruxelles: Institut de Sociologie de l'Université Libre de Bruxelles.

Philippon, A. 1983. '*Carmen* de Carlos Saura (Espagne 1983) avec Antonio Gades, Laura del Sol, Paco de Lucía', in *Cahiers du cinéma* 352: 62.

Portier, Maurice. 1967. 'Introduction' in Mérimée, Prosper, *Romans et nouvelles* vol. 2. Paris: Garnier Frères: 339–344.

Samoyault, Tiphaine. 2001. *L'art et l'hybride*. Saint-Denis: Presses Universitaires de Vincennes.

Stein, Eugene. 1984. 'Carmen', in *Films in Review* 25(2): 111.

Stewart, Charles. 1999. 'Syncretism and Its Synonyms: Reflexions on Cultural Mixture' in *Diacritics* 29(3): 40–62.

Cinematic *Carmen* and the 'Oeil Noir'

Jeremy Tambling

In the 'Toreador' song, Escamillo reminds himself that an 'oeil noir' is looking down on the Toreador while he battles: the eye—human's or bull's—makes him subject to the Lacanian gaze, and is a key for thinking of Rosi's film of *Carmen* (1984). This inherently technologizes looking, itself so much a thematic feature of Bizet's opera, implicit in almost every line of the text: the camera becomes the 'oeil noir' that encapsulates the male gaze but also induces male paranoia. The chapter then turns to the film *Mongkok Carmen* (aka *As Tears Go By,* 1988) to suggest that the seductiveness of the woman cannot quite compete with a violence in the male which destroys the self and other, and which has its own feminine aspect, and, through reference to the orientalizing aspects of Argentine literature and tango, and to Rita Hayworth, goes on to claim that no Carmen, however affirming, has the power to be other than subordinate within a culture of violence. Ultimately Carmen rather than don José is betrayed.

Kar-wai, Wong: *Mongkok Carmen*
Habaneras
Lacan, Jacques
Mamoulian, Rouben: *Blood and Sand*
Puig, Manuel: *Betrayed By Rita Hayworth*
Rosi, Francesco: *Carmen*
Tango

1. The power of the eye
To begin with two quotations, first with the chorus for the most famous of all opera tunes:

> Et songe bien, oui, songe bien en combattant,
> Qu'un oeil noir te regarde
> Et que l'amour t'attend.

(To translate: think carefully, yes think while fighting, that a black eye looks at you and that love waits for you). Not 'two dark eyes' as many translations of the libretto render Escamillo's words, but *one* eye.

The reference to Mérimée's *Carmen* is helped by Naomi Segal (1988: 47-49) who shows how the single eye overlooks the novel. García, Carmen's husband, is one-eyed, and Segal connects that to the 'oedipal loathsomeness of the legitimate rival'. As don José leads Carmen to prison, 'she slipped her mantilla over her head, leaving only one of her large eyes visible, and followed my men, quiet as a lamb'. When she involves José in deceiving the Englishman, 'the blinds were half-open, and I could see her large black eye watching me'. And after José has stabbed her: 'I can still see her large black eye staring at me, then it clouded over and closed'. The woman is made grotesque. Naomi Segal gets from the single eye three meanings: in the husband, castration—or perhaps the castration fear—and then the sense of the evil eye, and, as having genital significance, that it is 'the black gulf to the tempted hero, the pool in which Narcissus finds death'.

The second quotation runs:

> There is no trace anywhere of a good eye, of an eye that blesses. What can this mean except that the eye carries with it the fatal function of being in itself endowed [...] with a power to separate. But this power to separate goes much further than distinct vision. The powers that are attributed to it, of drying up the milk of an animal on which it falls [...] of bringing with it disease or misfortune—where can we better picture this power than in *invidia*?
>
> *Invidia* comes from *videre*. The most exemplary *invidia* [...] is the one I found long ago in Augustine, in which he sums up his entire fate, namely that of the little child seeing his brother at his mother's breast, looking at him *amare conspectu*, with a bitter look, which seems to tear him to pieces and has on himself the effect of a poison.
>
> In order to understand what *invidia* is in its function as gaze it must not be confused with jealousy. What the small child, or whoever, *envies* is not at all necessarily what he might want [...] Everyone knows that envy is usually aroused by the possession of goods which would be of no use to the person who is envious of them, and about the true nature of which he does not have the least idea.
>
> Such is true envy—the envy that makes the subject pale before the image of a completeness closed upon itself, before the idea that the *petit a*, the separated *a* from which he is hanging, may be for another the possession that gives satisfaction, *Befriedigung* [...]
>
> The evil eye is the *fascinum*, it is that which has the effect of arresting movement, and literally, of killing life. At the moment the subject stops [...] he is mortified. The anti-life, anti-movement function of this terminal point is the *fascinum*, and it is precisely one of the dimensions in which the power of the gaze is exercised directly. (Lacan 1977: 115-116; 118)

If you felt that the eye that was watching you while you attacked the bull was the evil eye, that would be the power of castration. Mérimée's anti-feminism works that way; the woman's eye destroys the power of the man. Bizet's text is more ambivalent. The *oeil noir* looks at you, but love waits for you. It is not possible to say that the eye is evil; it is rather like Derrida's *pharmakon*, medicine and poison at the same time (Derrida 1981: 63-171).

Rosi's film of *Carmen* begins with the bullfight, and the wounded bull in profile looking at Escamillo, so that the 'oeil noir' is not simply Carmen's, but the bull's. Just before it is stabbed, there is a shot of Escamillo's two eyes looking at the camera. When Escamillo puts on his outfit to the prelude music of Act 4, there is a sudden cut to the bull, seen looking, one eye clearly focused. If we are thinking about being looked at, there are also the eyes looking down voyeuristically, as Zuniga looks at the women through his binoculars while they are splashing in the water. The camera shows the male gaze in action, but it also shows the close-up that he sees. This gaze is part of the scopic drive, it is men looking at women, and may suggest the power of the cinematic camera, the power of film, constructing women as subject, so that the film builds into its own narrative awareness of the character of film, and of opera. The camera may also be regarded as the evil eye, as Zuniga's look at the women who are splashing and singing is also envy of their jouissance, envy coming from the officer in uniform. But then the *oeil noir* is also the thing that looks back at you, it is the Lacanian gaze, that interrupts the subject's sense of the self; it looks back, it sees you, or it doesn't see you.[1] By dazzling the subject, as in Rosi's film, Carmen dazzles Escamillo as he sings his all-important words which put the subject on guard; by the use of a mirror that throws back the light into his eyes, the subject becomes the stain.

If we take the eye that looks on negatively, that will produce male paranoia, a defining emotion within film noir. Paranoia, which is perhaps encouraged in the words telling the toreador to watch out— 'Toreador en garde'—strikes out at the other in the field of vision, identifying that other with the woman, and with the evil eye. Paranoia lines up with patriarchy: the eye of envy is elsewhere than in the woman. The desire to name the other as the feminine Orient or the Oriental may relate to this fear, and may be behind fear of the other, the 'Oriental' woman, which would bring colonialism, patriarchy and paranoia into alignment. And Spain has been the Orient since Victor Hugo, in the Preface to his poems *Les Orientales* (1829) :

Il résulte de tout cela que l'Orient, soit comme image, soit comme pensée, est devenu, pour les intelligences autant que pour les imaginations, une sorte de préoccupation générale à laquelle l'auteur de ce livre a obéi peut-être à son insu. Les couleurs orientales sont venues comme d'elles-mêmes empreindre toutes ses pensées, toutes ses rêveries; et ses rêveries et ses pensées se sont trouvées tour à tour, et presque sans l'avoir voulu, hébraiques, turques, grecques, persanes, arabes, espagnoles même, car l'Espagne c'est encore l'Orient; l'Espagne est à demi africaine, l'Afrique est à demi asiatique. (Hugo 1970: 1829)

(The Orient, either as an image or an idea, has become, both for the mind and for the imagination, a kind of general preoccupation to which the author of this book may have unwittingly succumbed. Oriental colours have appeared as though by themselves to mark all his ideas and all his daydreams, and his thoughts, nearly without his intending it, have been in turn Hebrew, Turkish, Greek, Persian, Arab, even Spanish, for Spain is still the Orient, Spain is half Africa, Africa is half Asiatic). (Lacombe 2001: 195)

Spain became the Orient for French culture, with Hugo and Mérimée, and has remained the Orient for North America. Is it that for Bizet's *Carmen*? What about the eye that looks in that text, which Escamillo knows is watching? The eye looks, and the camera constructs what is to be looked at, active and separating.

2. *Carmen*, violence and betrayal

If Spain was seen as oriental and exoticized, so that women in it would become doubly marginal in relation to males themselves not empowered (the point applies to both don José and Escamillo), what implications would this have for violence and feelings of envy? Does the structure of oppression produce the knifing of Carmen as inevitable? And can the dispossessed figure—seen as marginal, and as feminine, and colonized claim any space for herself? I would like to illuminate these questions by comparison, which will invoke not just Spain but Spain's former colonies in Latin America. It will lead up to discussion of the *habanera*, making the first half of this paper, as the tango will make up the second.

But Argentina and the tango could also be reached from another source: from Hong Kong and Wong Kar-wai. Upstream of *Happy Together* (1997), set in Argentina, is another film, Wong Kar-wai's first, giving no space to Orientalism, and carrying the Chinese title *Mongkok Carmen*, though to Anglophone audiences it is *As Tears Go By* (1988). Perhaps its lack of concession to Europe appears in that it uses nothing out of Bizet's *Carmen*, though its associations add to a reading of it. The title is an apparent oxymoron, for Mongkok is one of the poorest and most densely populated areas of Hong Kong, furthest away from Western opera, and its influences. It stars Andy Lau (Brother Wah) and Jacky Cheung (Fly) as two working-class gangsters, where the older, Wah, feels a responsibility for the wholly inadequate Fly. They are engaged in a protection racket which might be compared with the smuggling in *Carmen* Act 3, and which puts them quite outside the law; both men are shot by the end of the film. Maggie Cheung (playing Ah Ngor), acts the part of a cousin to Wah,

(Andy Lau), and meets him at the beginning of the film when she arrives from one of Hong Kong's outlying islands, Lantau, to come to stay at his flat in order to see a doctor. She has a gag, or bandage over her nose and mouth to keep her from taking in the Hong Kong air: she is breathless to start with, as though consumptive, like an operatic heroine, Violetta or Mimi. The word 'breathless' points, first, to a visual gag that relates the film to Godard's *À bout de souffle*, which is evoked in the text. Andy Lau is divided between his growing relationship with Maggie Cheung, and his loyalty towards Fly, and the film is studded with scenes of violence that marginalize the woman and polarize the film between Lantau island, where she lives and works in a hotel, and Kowloon. The woman is quite unfazed by the violence of her cousin, and watches him with no possessive eye, experiencing his violence when she suggests that he is 'lovelorn' in relation to a girlfriend he has at the beginning whom he treats pretty roughly. Half way through the film, she has enticed him over to Lantau, in a sequence which is backed by the music 'Take my breath away'.[2] He attempts to go back the first time by ferry to Kowloon, but she calls him on his pager and makes him return. 'Take my breath away' refers to her breathlessness, now cured, and it aligns sexual desire with death; so that there is a choice of deaths offered in the film: death in Mongkok, death in relation to the woman. Wah comes twice, but she can make no impression upon the life he lives in Kowloon. The title *Mongkok Carmen* could refer to the enchantment of the violence of the life in Kowloon. On one reading, that excludes the woman, Maggie Cheung, who can be no Carmen, more like a Micaela, but on another, the film is like *Carmen* in that it implies that the seductiveness of the woman cannot quite compete with a seductive male violence which destroys the self and other, and which has its own feminine aspect.

As there is a fascination with violence in *Carmen*, so there is, deeply, in Wong Kar-wai, who won the Cannes Palme d'or with *Happy Together*, his film about two Chinese gay men in Buenos Aires, initially called *The Buenos Aires Affair*. The film, which reworks many of the images of *Mongkok Carmen*, illustrates a keen relation to Argentine fiction (the writings of Borges, Cortázar, Puig). I shall refer to these through Manuel Puig's *Betrayed By Rita Hayworth*. Here, Herminia, embittered by provincial life and embittering herself because of her lack of romance, complains about conditions of life in small-town Argentina in 1948: 'you can't even listen to the radio here, except for the tango stations which can afford powerful antennas and so educate the public on how the ruffian knifed the maid next door' (Puig 1971: 201).

It is the Carmen plot. Earlier in *Betrayed by Rita Hayworth*, two young women, who work as maids, discuss their employer, Mr Berto, and one asks '"What did he get away with?"' Answer: '"With being killed by a jealous husband"' (Puig 1971: 20). He has had a reputation with women, it seems, and has sidestepped punishment. It is also part of the cultural expectations of the *Carmen* world. But that is not where the title of the novel locates betrayal.

Rita Hayworth (1918-1987), real name Margarita Carmen Cansino, relates the *oeil noir* to film noir, Nino Frank's term of 1946, the moment when *Gilda* came out.[3] Hayworth's parents were Spanish; her singing and dancing in Latin American style eroticized and exoticized her for North American consumption (see also Peter Evans' essay in this volume). In 1941 she starred as the Spanish doña Sol, opposite Tyrone Power in *Blood and Sand*, a Hollywood film about Spain directed by Rouben Mamoulian, who had had a career directing operas in the 1920s (*Carmen* in 1923), including the original *Porgy and Bess*.[4] The relevance of *Blood and Sand* will become clear in a moment. Hayworth's last film of the 1940s, complete with flamenco dancing, was *The Loves of Carmen*. It was directed by Charles Vidor, and she played opposite Glenn Ford. It was the team responsible for *Gilda* which was set in Buenos Aires (as Hitchcock's *Notorious* (1946) was set in Rio). The Latin American locales fitted film noir.[5] *Blood and Sand* is discussed in *Betrayed by Rita Hayworth*. She plays a betraying woman in it, but the title is a double genitive: it is the betrayal of Rita Hayworth. Rita Hayworth has been betrayed, as much as she betrays (Kerr 1987: 27-30). For she is both made North American, and must act as Hollywood's version of Spain. She is betrayed by Hollywood's Orientalism, both towards her personally as Hispanic, associated with Mexico, and towards Spain. Sexually, she is betrayed by her films since she must become the betraying woman in them. The woman who thinks she is betraying, in film noir, is already betrayed by an ideology which creates the myth of the *femme fatale*, a term belonging to the history of cinema, its first citation in the Oxford English Dictionary being 1912.[6] The knifing of Carmen at the end is an example of the betrayal of Rita Hayworth. You can compare *Betrayed by Rita Hayworth* with another title: Catherine Clément's *Opera, or the Undoing of Women*.

Blood and Sand,[8] a film which stands behind Rosi's *Il momento della verità* (1964), itself an inspiration for his *Carmen*, was a remake of a 1922 Rudolph Valentino film, which was directed by Fred Niblo for Paramount, with Nita Naldi playing doña Sol. Both are American versions or translations of the novel by Vicente Blasco Ibánez (1867-1928), *Sangre y Arena* (1908). Gallardo, the matador, takes foolish chances, both with bulls and women, and his death is 'one foolish chance too many' (Magnarelli 1985: 142).[7] He only thinks he has been betrayed by doña Sol. In the film, Juan Gallardo, who has risen from being a street urchin, becomes Spain's greatest matador. He is married to the faithful Carmen (Linda Darnell), a character associated with the colour white, but, as is the case with *Mongkok Carmen*, she cannot save him. But, unlike *Mongkok Carmen*, this is not because of a delight in male violence, but because he falls in love with the high-class doña Sol (Hayworth). She is first seen in the chapel while he prays before entering the ring (note the equivalent prayer in the prelude to Act 4 of Rosi's *Carmen*). Sitting watching Juan in the bullring, dressed in red, like Rosi's Carmen in Act 4, one character (Curro) says, 'If this is death in the afternoon [a reference to Hemingway's book, published in 1932] she is death in the evening'. Betrayed by her as she turns to the new rising star, Manolo de Palma (Anthony Quinn), he is gored and killed in the bullring. As he prays in the chapel before he dies, Carmen is in the shadows. Unlike the remake, the Valentino film had him nursed after being gored in the bullring, and brought back to health by his faithful wife.

One effect of *Blood and Sand* is to suggest, through the name Carmen, that the character of 'Carmen' from Mérimée and Bizet needs pluralizing: she is not a single identity, but the woman divided within patriarchal culture. No Carmen, however affirming, has power to be other than subordinate within a culture of violence. Hence Puig's word 'betrayal'. Positioning Hayworth as the *femme fatale* makes her gaze at the bullfight vampirish, that of the evil eye. Such a reading, however, disallows the question of the woman's fascination, which implies that she is not wholly in power. A moment from *Gilda* is quoted in Manuel Puig's *The Buenos Aires Affair*, two novels after *Betrayed by Rita Hayworth*. It is when she is 'dazzling in her gauze negligée but profoundly disturbed since she has just discovered that her husband's new bodyguard is none other than the man she ever loved in her life and by whom she was abandoned; she talks trying to hide it all' (Puig 1976: 211). Two betrayals are implied—betrayal by the man she loved, and betrayal of herself in speech. The dazzling appearance and the psychic disturbance she feels show a woman whose body—the object that is brought under scrutiny by the cinematic eye—and whose thinking are not in alignment; another form of betrayal.

In *Betrayed by Rita Hayworth*, the young boy Toto who has seen *Blood and Sand* with his parents reflects:

> Dad liked it when she did 'toro, toro' to Tyrone Power, him kneeling and her with a transparent dress that you could see her bra through she came right up close to him to play toro, but she was laughing at him, and in the end she leaves him. And sometimes she looks wicked, she's a pretty actress but she's always betraying somebody. (Puig 1971: 63)

Toto's language is his parents': she's always betraying somebody. The actress becomes identified with her betraying role. Looking wicked is inseparable from being pretty and this becomes a matter of ideology; but it is also noticeable that Toto's recall of the film action makes single identity impossible in the question which is the bull and which the bullfighter. The masculinity of the bullfight and masculine violence contains something else in it, a sense that this masculinity includes something feminine within it neither wholly exclusionary of Carmen, nor inclusive of her.

Blood and Sand makes *Gilda* a continuation of Carmen material, since in this film, Rita Hayworth plays the only woman present, between two men, her husband (Bullen, George Macready) and Johnny Farrell (Glenn Ford) whose relationship with each other is mutually misogynistic and, while potentially violent, bordering on the homoerotic, as though, for Farrell, homosexuality responded to the *femme fatale*. Both Farrell and Gilda have been bought by Bullen; the parallels in their relationship are pointed out by Gilda. (So, in Rosi's *Carmen*, Escamillo is accompanied by middle-class people who 'won' him, and who presumably include a doña Sol amongst them). The evil eye is Bullen's; he uses a jalousie window to spy out what is going on in his casino. Clicking shut this window marks his presence. Gilda's seductiveness as the displaced American in Buenos Aires (Buenos Aires as a prison) is a reaction to the impossibility of breaking through this male cartel; her method is to sing and dance. She is heard singing in the middle of the night, to herself and to the black men's attendant, 'Put the Blame on Mame', looking relaxed and accompanying herself on the guitar, which is a moment of identification with Latin-American culture. Fitting the silencing of women that film noir involves, and apparently against her will, her voice was dubbed by

Anita Ellis for her song 'Amado mío', a song sung in a nightclub in Montevideo, in Latin-American style. 'Put the Blame on Mame' (the song by Doris Fisher and Allan Roberts, the choreography by Jack Cole) is performed at the end in a black satin gown, while peeling off long black gloves. The song, bits of which have been heard on two occasions, and is never heard right through, as though it was inexhaustible, puts the blame for every economic, man-made and natural disaster that has happened in the United States on the woman; the two songs in their order thus indicate the supremacy of North American over Latin American culture, so that 'Amado mío' becomes, incidentally, another example of cultural betrayal; aligning Hayworth with the US rather than Spanish culture. Later she is seen singing and dancing, and Richard Dyer points out that no other *femme fatale* in film noir dances (1998: 120). It is for herself as well as for the spectator; it gives her space. Just so, Carmen when she sings the 'Seguidilla' and is told that she must not speak to José, says 'Je ne te parle pas...je chante pour moi-même, et je pense...il n'est pas défendu de penser' (I'm not speaking to you...I'm singing for me, and thinking...it's not forbidden to think). The woman's song and dance in the case of *Carmen* grants her a place; in the case of *Gilda* it makes the woman resist the position into which she is fixed, and draws her towards the genre of the musical.

3. Affirming the Other: the 'Habanera'

Mérimée's *Carmen* is quasi-anthropological. The narrator, a French savant, trying to find out the truth about Spain as a picturesque other country is led on to find out the truth about Carmen: and learns how she has destroyed the life of don José who makes a confession to him of his past life in a letter—that nineteenth-century novel form which anticipates the flashback. In these ways, the novella anticipates film noir, which Christine Gledhill (1998: 27-32) argues is characterized by three things: an investigative drive, the male flash-back, like Glenn Ford's in *Gilda*, and the impossibility of knowing the dangerous woman. When the narrator meets Carmen in Andalusia, he is not sure whether she is Moorish or Jewish. She then claims to be a Gypsy (Mérimée 1977: 44). In chapter 4, after reading don José's confession as to why he killed Carmen, another narrator, who speaks as the author Mérimée, and as an 'Orientalist' (86), as if rounding off the narrative which has been supplied by the *savant*, gives an account of the Gypsies. Islamic North Africa, Jewish, Gypsy and Spanish cultures are indiscriminately oriental to the French culture that writes them. The Carmen-film that Hayworth starred in was from Mérimée's novella, rather than Bizet's *Carmen*—this has been the case with many of the adaptations of *Carmen* for the screen. So Rita Hayworth is betrayed by the establishment of the figure of Carmen as a model for the Hollywood star.

Bizet's *Carmen* came from no firsthand knowledge of Spain, and only limited access to authentic Spanish songs. If *Carmen* defines Spain it does so from imitative sources. This makes the work ambiguous; Carmen is the object of Orientalist reverie, her sexuality the dream of the European male. Bizet adds to Mérimée a bullfight and toreador: Escamillo. This is Orientalizing: but two points should be added. Bizet said of the 'Toreador' song, 'so they want shit? [l'ordure]? All right, I'll give them shit' (quoted in Curtiss 1974: 390). (I shall return to this comment). Also, after the unsuccessful first night, he said that 'these bourgeois have not understood a word of the work I have written for them' (392). Camille DuLocle, who commissioned the opera, disliked the music saying it came from 'Cochin China' (Dean 1965: 113). Bizet's Orientalism was not bourgeois Orientalism, and the mode of Mérimée's *Carmen*, by which she is the object of male discovery, as in a detective text, is reversed. She presents herself at the beginning in the 'Habanera', in words which Bizet wrote himself:

> L'amour est un oiseau rebelle
> que nul ne peut apprivoiser,
> et c'est bien en vain qu'on l'appelle,
> s'il lui convient de refuser.
> Rien n'y fait, menace ou prière,
> l'un parle bien, l'autre se tait;
> est c'est l'autre que je préfère:
> il n'a rien dit, mais il me plaît.

> L'amour est enfant de bohème.
> il n'a jamais connu de loi:
> si tu ne m'aimes pas, je t'aime,
> Mais si je t'aime, prends garde à toi!

> L'oiseau que tu croyais surprendre
> battit de l'aile et s'envola–
> l'amour est loin, tu peux l'attendre;
> tu ne l'attends plus, il est là!
> Tout autour de toi, vite, vite,
> il vient, s'en va, puis il revient–

> tu crois le tenir, il t'évite,
> tu crois l'éviter, il te tient.

(Love is a rebellious bird
that no one can tame,
and it's quite useless to call him
if it suits him to refuse.
Nothing moves him, neither threat nor plea,
one man speaks freely, the other keeps mum;
and it's the other one I prefer:
he's said nothing, but I like him.

Love is a Gypsy child,
he has never heard of law.
If you don't love me, I love you;
if I love you, look out for yourself!

The bird you thought to catch unawares
beats its wings and away it flew—
love's far away, and you can wait for it:
you wait for it no longer—and there it is.

All around you, quickly, quickly,
it comes, it goes, then it returns—
you think you can hold it, it evades you,
you think to evade it, it holds you fast).

The words double identities: love and Carmen are neither the same, nor the same gender, but they are not separate either. Love is a bohemian, and Bohemia is where Gypsies were supposed to have come from. Love as destabilizing is associated with that which, repressed, must take other, violent forms. If Carmen is Jewish, that may recall the point that Luther had said Jews should be treated like Gypsies; and that Jews and Arabs alike had been repressed out of Spanish existence, forced to reappear in other forms, in the very moment when the Gypsy emerged. If love is bohemian, that is not so much affirmatory of rebellion as implying that love is displaced, not where you think it is, and it is other from what you think it is wherever you are, a symptom of something repressed within political life.

Yet the evocation of the bohemian appropriates it for middle-class existence; 'Bohemian' life became part of Parisian discourse in the 1830s, as a way of evoking the rural Gypsy way of life within the city in a desire to appropriate the Gypsy lifestyle for bourgeois life. In a related, Orientalist discourse, the Gypsy became the object of study.[9] A history of nineteenth-century music, certainly of opera, could be written which saw it as the history of writing Gypsy music. But Bizet's Carmen is more than a stage Gypsy. The music sung is not quasi-Spanish as an Orientalist music, but comes from the place that

Spain had colonized: Cuba. The *habanera*, a Cuban dance, 'Negro music' (Dean 1965: 228) comes from Havana. In Bizet's 'Habanera', it is a question of the colonized body (that of the woman, the Gypsy, the working-class figure, the prostitute: Carmen is all these) which asserts itself, in music from the colonies.

The *habanera* is not operatic but cabaret music, taken from Sebastian de Yradier (1809-1865) who had spent time in Cuba and wrote as *habaneras* songs such as 'La paloma' (1859) and 'El arreglito ou la Promesse de mariage'. Bizet works from the second of these, giving it new words, two verses, in the minor, and the refrain in the key of D major. Those Nietzschean formulations, 'Truth is a woman' and 'Music is a woman' (quoted Tambling 1996: 44) which relate to Carmen, and her critique of phallocentric possessiveness, and Nietzsche's critique of the ascetic ideal, recall Nietzsche's words in French in *Der Fall Wagner*, 'Il faut méditerraniser la musique' (music must be Mediterreanized) (Nietzsche 2000: 615)—making it Southern, or North African. They are a reminder that black music is within what Carmen sings.

In *Music in Cuba*, Alejo Carpentier discovers the work of such a composer as Esteban Salas y Castro (1725-1803) and suggests that he might have been an example of a black composer writing European music (2001: 106-118). He brings don Esteban Salas into his novel *The Kingdom of this World*, at a crisis moment for revolution and for music, where the exiled French from Santo Domingo (Haiti), arrive in Spanish-held Cuba after the revolt in Haiti by the blacks there in 1791. The French give themselves over to a carnival spirit, including 'a great pastoral ball—a fashion now outmoded in Paris' where

> the palm-frond dressing rooms were scenes of pleasant encounters while some baritone husband, carried away by his role, was immobilized on the stage by the bravura aria of Monsigny's *Le Déserteur*. For the first time Santiago de Cuba heard the music of *passepieds* and *contredanses*. The last powdered wigs of the century, worn by the daughters of the colonists, swayed in time to the music of swift minuets that were forerunners of the waltz. (Carpentier 1967: 63)

Opera (Monsigny) gives opportunity for other pleasantnesses. Santiago de Cuba recalls Spain's patron saint, Saint James and Santiago de Compostela, but Saint James to the black slaves such as Ti Noël becomes identified with the African god of war, Ougoun Fai (65-66). European culture is meaningful because overladen with something else. The implication of the revolutionary moment is that these French dances are now to be translated by the energies of black

Cuban composers, for example into the nineteenth century *habanera*, just as the waltz will become a Latin American dance. In his chapter, 'Introduction to the *Contradanza*', Carpentier links the contradance to an African expression of 'the battle of the sexes with the ensuing attack and flight, union and separation', saying that

> the French *contradanza* was adopted [after 1791] with surprising swiftness, staying on the island and transforming itself into a Cuban *contradanza*, cultivated by all the creole composers of the nineteenth century, even becoming Cuba's first musical genre to be triumphantly exported [...]. From the 2/4 *contradanza* came the *danza*, the *habanera* and the *danzón*, with its ensuing more or less hybrid offshoots. (Carpentier 2001: 147)

In 1881, Cuba's colonial bourgeois society said *habanera* music was

> of African origin. The music of these dances embodies the concupiscence and sensuality that characterizes the unruly natives of passionate Africa. The essence of African character is to be found in them. Further, the rhythms of the *danza* and *danzon* [both related to the contradanse] are very similar to those of the tangos that the sons of uncultured Africa dance in our streets. (Martínez Fure 1991: 32)[10]

The *habanera* becomes an instance of what Carpentier's Preface to *The Kingdom of this World* calls 'the marvellous in the real' ('*lo real maravilloso*') (1967: Prologue). And so is Bizet's—Carmen's—'Habanera'.

When Carmen calls love a rebellious bird, she describes music—for the name Carmen implies the *femme fatale* and music too. Looking around as she sings, she throws a flower at don José; her version of firing a bullet. The Toreador warns himself, 'Toreador, en garde!', recalling 'prends garde à toi' in the 'Habanera'. As tauromachy requires one life, either that of the bull or the man, so does love. Fighting the bull has an erotic charge, as Michel Leiris suggests, and the erotic is not the source of wholeness, such as of classical beauty, but splits such a beauty, bringing it into contact with that which is antagonistic to it. Leiris quotes from Baudelaire on beauty, and suggests that in the bullfight, beauty comes about 'not simply by the joining of opposite elements, but by their very antagonism, by the altogether active way in which the one tends to erupt in the other, making its mark like a wound, like devastation' (Leiris 1993: 21-40). That antagonism Carpentier found in the contradance. The toreador's tune orientalizes in trivializing the bullfight which it has, perhaps, brought on to give Victor Hugo's 'local colour', and it fails to meet such a sense of beauty, since it fits the major key; it has no disharmonies, unlike the (feminine) chromaticisms within the 'Habanera'. The Toreador song does not fit convulsive beauty. It is kitsch, but then Bizet thought of it as such. Though Blasco Ibáñez, in *Blood and Sand*, discusses the bullfight as the product of eighteenth-century Spain, at the moment when Spain had retreated from its position of dominance, so that it seems like a reaction to loss of power (Blasco Ibáñez 1958: 207-211), in Leiris, the bullfight shows the destabilizing power of the erotic; the fault-lines that run through it which make it impossible to think of it in terms of the harmonic. Leiris says that 'not only the Apollo-Dionysos opposition, but everything Nietzsche says of music in *The Birth of Tragedy* is applicable to the bullfight' (1993: 30). So, *The Birth of Tragedy out of the Spirit of Music* is *The Birth of Tragedy out of the Spirit of the Bullfight* and the bullfight and music are equated. And while the toreador's tune is kitsch, that is also destabilized, or betrayed. While you are fighting, or singing, you are being looked at. An *oeil noir* is an eye too many or too few, and it points to the non-harmonious, or to the wound or to devastation.

4. From *Habanera* to Heartbreak Tango
Dictionaries of dance link the *habanera* with the Argentine tango: both African forms overlaid on European, specifically Spanish music. Developing an argument from the *habanera* to the tango enables another, Argentinian, perspective on the Carmen narrative. To discuss the tango is the project of the second half of this paper. It is tightly written, integrated music, the opposite of jazz, with its improvisations. In Bizet's *Carmen* the woman sings and dances the 'Habanera' alone as an expression of otherness. There is a break-up of heterosexual doublings, man/woman, but these have in any case, gone in Mérimée's *Carmen*, in a text where the ultimate symbol of masculinity, the bull, has been associated with the woman. Gender, it seems, cannot be thought of in binary terms: a space created for polymorphous relationships, or for the 'other' to be recodified, in a different mode. How, then, does the tango, in comparison to the *habanera*, construct gender and gender-relationships, considering that *Betrayed by Rita Hayworth* argues that it enables a culture where men knifed women? From 1869, when statistics were first kept, to 1914, three million European immigrants—mostly male, Italian and Spanish principally—arrived in Buenos Aires, constructing a new *porteño* (port) society where they competed with the existing *criollo* society.

They came to work in the hinterland, but many stayed in Buenos Aires. There were too few women for these men. The tango, an urban dance, originated, according to Borges, in the brothels of Buenos Aires in the 1880s: that is, with these new immigrant males (Borges 2001: 394). It is contemporary with *Carmen*, and like Carmen's 'Habanera', it is the dance of the colonized body. Brothel music, it was danced by men waiting their turn and according to Borges, it was too disgusting in its sexual implications for women to participate in. It had, like the *habanera*, Afro-Caribbean roots, associated with the *milonga*—a festive dance (an Afro-Brazilian word).

For Borges, the nineteenth-century tango shows men interacting so that 'a fight becomes a celebration' (2001: 396). The old tango transmits 'joy of combat' (397), and evokes a memory:

> We read in one of Oscar Wilde's dialogues that music reveals a personal past which, until then, each of us was unaware of, moving us to lament misfortunes we never suffered and wrongs we did not commit. For myself, I confess that I cannot hear 'El Marme' or 'Don Juan' without remembering in detail an apocryphal past, simultaneously stoic and orgiastic, in which I have challenged and fought, in the end to fall silently, in an obscure knife fight. Perhaps this is the tango's mission, to give Argentines the belief in a brave past, in having met the demands of honour and bravery. (397)

The knife fight recalls Escamillo and José's duel in Act 3 of *Carmen*. Borges's paragraph may be compared with a poem he wrote called 'The Tango', which uses the medieval 'Ubi sunt' tradition as a lament for the old *compadritos*; saying that 'those dead men live on in the tango':

> They are in the music, in the strings
> Of an obstinate and elaborate guitar
> Which weaves a fiesta and the innocence
> Of courage into a fortuitous milonga.
>
> The yellow carousel of horse and lion
> Whirls in the hollow while I hear the echo
> Of those tangos of Arolas and Greco
> I watched danced on the pavement
>
> Of an instant that today stands out alone,
> Without before or after, against oblivion,
> And has the taste of everything lost,
> Everything lost and recovered.
>
> There is nostalgia in every chord:
> The other patio and the half-seen vine.

(The South, behind suspicious walls
Keeps a knife and a guitar).

This burst of sound, the tango, this
Wantonness defies the routine years:
Made of time and dust, man lasts
Less long than the libidinous melody

Which is only time. The tango spawns a turbid
Unreal past in certain measure true:
An impossible recollection of having died
Fighting, on some corner of a suburb (Borges 1968: 160-161) .

As Carpentier found a different sense of time in Afro-Cuban
music, so does Borges. Music constructs for him, as if in a form of
Nachträglichkeit, deferred reaction, another past by which masculinity
is vindicated. (This is different from the Wagnerian motif, which sets
up memory as something determinate). The tango allows in
involuntary memory.

The argument reappears in Borges's story 'Man on Pink
Corner' (1998: 47-53), in *A Universal History of Infamy* (of 1935), set
in the poorest parts of Buenos Aires (Palermo). The narrator, an older
man now, speaks to another whom he calls Borges. The date of the
events recalled, then, may be presumed to be that of the 1880s. The
narrator tells Borges of his neighbourhood with its rough bar and
brothel, where the men were tangoing, 'we boys were dancing, "most
like bein" in a dream' when in walks Francisco Real, who knocks him
over and challenges Rosendo Juárez to a knife-fight. Lujanera, the
beautiful prostitute, urges Rosendo to fight but he refuses and
disappears, throwing away his knife. The tango starts again and
Francisco Real goes out with Lujanera, 'cheek to cheek, like in the
drunken dizziness of the tango, like they were drowning in the tango'
(Borges 1998: 49) and it is to be presumed that the narrator follows
them and kills Francisco Real for the insult offered him. The man
staggers back to the bar and dies; his body is thrown into the river
before the police can arrive. The violin strikes up the 'Habanera', and
the narrator possesses Lujanera for the night. The first half of the
name Lujanera means 'luxurious', there seems a pun on *habanera*,
and it makes *Carmen* one of this text's intertexts. The narrator has
vindicated the honour of the neighbourhood.

The text creates the Borges who listens and the I who tells, and
who leaves out the detail that he is the murderer. The narrating voice
is of a masculinity which has asserted territorial rights. The tango and
the *habanera* work to establish such a masculinity, and I take that

point back to *Carmen*. The slang used by Borges, describing the *guapo* (the tough guy) and the *compadrito* (the godfather) is a form of what he calls the baroque. Masculinity here is baroque in style, if the baroque is, as Borges says, 'that style that deliberately exhausts [...] its own possibilities and that borders on self-caricature' (Borges 1998: 4). Support for this view comes from the writer José Tallon who is quoted by Ernesto Sábato in his work on the tango, for saying that the *compadritos*

> were excessive in every way, especially as regards attire and adornment [...] They followed the fashion of the well-to-do and they dressed and embellished themselves with feminine narcissism, blatantly sexual and suspicious. [...] Their typical gait, the swaying of the hips, was caused by the high heels; they made it rather fussy, if not effeminate. From a distance they smelled like the whorehouse, like mental degeneration, hereditary alcoholism, and erotomania. (in Woscoboinik 1998: 89).[11]

This is baroque masculinity, which is caricatural in contesting the feminization implied in being a man in postcolonial Argentina.

In 'The History of the Tango', masculinity is associated with being penetrated by a knife. In Julio Cortázar's short story 'Return Trip Tango', the returned husband of Matilde, who has been replaced by another husband, ends up so penetrated (Cortázar 1983: 60-77). He comes back, like the return of the repressed, to find his wife who has married bigamously, and he watches outside her house, like don José haunting Carmen. Her present husband has gone away on a business trip; the first husband secures entry to the house by making love to the servant, and when he goes in to his wife, she stabs him, in a reversal of *Carmen*. Bizet's opera has a fight in each act. In Act 1, it is an offstage and then onstage fight between two women—Carmen and another factory-worker. In Act 2, don José fights Morales, who also wants to possess Carmen. In Act 3, José and Escamillo fight for the same reason, with the words 'mettez-vous en garde', and Escamillo makes a direct reference to the bullfighting; so that the game he plays with don José—for he is not fighting seriously—is again like teasing the bull. In Act 4, José stabs Carmen over the background of the bull-fight. Though she has sung 'prends garde à toi', not till the end do the man and woman fight each other, where Carmen, is, unlike Violetta or Mimi, whose deaths happen to them, what Clément says, 'the sombre and revolutionary proclamation of a woman who chooses to die before a man decides it for her' (1988: 53).

Some conclusions may be drawn from the violence in Bizet's *Carmen*, and from *Blood and Sand* and *Gilda* and *Mongkok Carmen*:

that fighting masculinizes women, or feminizes men if they take it seriously. Singing may be a form of feminine aggression against men (José hardly has a solo save of a very conventional kind) but it is hardly possible, in considering the bullfight, to think of violence gendering the subject in a single way. The bull is erotic as much as the woman may be, and when Borges speaks of his memory of being stabbed, this is not necessarily a form of feminization; it is part of a dream of masculinity; Borges: Carmen: Carmen the bull.

5. (Re)turns of betrayal

Bizet's *Carmen* would not lead to the betrayal of Rita Hayworth; but it partakes of the orientalism that is her betrayal. Each of Puig's first four novels—*Betrayed by Rita Hayworth, Heartbreak Tango, The Buenos Aires Story* and *Kiss of the Spider Woman*—shows postcolonial subjects held by the ideology of, and so betrayed by, Hollywood film. The first two show it happening in provincial Argentina; the others in Buenos Aires. *Heartbreak Tango* shows the tragedy of men who would like to be don Juans, and women whose emotional lives are formed by the serial romances of popular magazines. Their fate is to be described by the lyrics of the tango which itself has become betrayed into nostalgia. The old tango gave, Borges says, 'the hard and blind religion of courage, of being ready to kill and to die' (2001: 403). The tango lyrics of the twentieth century soften and betray that; for, as Marta Savigliano (1995) says, the tango was cleaned up by being sent to Paris, commodified and presented as the exotic, taken over by a newer form of Orientalism. The betrayal of Rita Hayworth and the betrayal of the tango are analogous, and the tango now causes heartbreak when, in its commodified form, it excludes those who would dance it. The migrant's dance, the expression of the body in colonialism, was re-exported from the European centre, a doubly colonized dance now, which became an expression of melancholy. The postcolonial history of Argentina is, for Ernesto Sábato, one of 'resentment and sadness' and he adds that 'the tango is often accompanied by desperation, rancour, threats and sarcasm' (quoted by Bacarisse 1988: 37, 240). The tango becomes 'a sad thought that can be danced' as tango writer Enrique Santos Discépolo (1901-1951) called it (Castro 1990: 89). It is the opposite of Carmen. Or, as Sábato (quoted by Savigliano) puts it:

> It was not [sex] that the lonely man of Buenos Aires was worried about; nor what his nostalgic and even frequently cruel songs evoked. It was precisely

the contrary: nostalgia for love and communion, the longing for a woman, and not the presence of an instrument of his lust. 'In my life I had many, many *minas*, but never a woman'. [Tango lyric: Mina is the wife in *Betrayed By Rita Hayworth*.] Tango expresses an erotic resentment and a tortuous manifestation of the inferiority complex of the argentino [is a reminder of postcolonialism] since sex is one of the primary shapes of power. Machismo is a very peculiar phenomenon of the *porteños* [...] The porteño feels obliged to behave as a male to the second or third power [...] The guy carefully observes his behavior in front of others and he feels judged and potentially ridiculed by his male peers. (Savigliano 1995: 45)

Savigliano argues that the tango makes class problems appear as sexual: 'tangos are male confessions of weakness in terms of sex and class, but the class issues are interpreted as a sex problem' (62). Puig supplements that by concentrating on the history of women in relation to that crisis of masculinity. Gladys D'Onofrio, the woman in *The Buenos Aires Story*, even has only a single eye, since the other was lost when she was attacked and raped. Her eye makes her a memory of Mérimée's Carmen, but it is not associated with the veiled woman, source of auratic power, save that Gladys thinks of herself in a love-situation for which, in an imaginary dream for the Paris based magazine *Elle*, she wants the glamorous Hitchcockian title 'The Buenos Aires Affair' to be the title. Further, the text emphasizes what is lacking in the missing eye. It is also what the woman emphasizes, turning the sign of her loss into the marker, for future relationships, of being both the victim and the fascinating woman with the dark glasses. It is the continuation of the betrayal of Rita Hayworth.

Carmen offers the chance of seeing the woman, however, as not caught in a love-situation dictated to by popular romance, but outside it, keeping an independence for which two images might be the *habanera* and/or the tango step, the first for its independence of a dominant colonial or patriarchal narrative; the second, stripped of its melancholic associations, because it seems to offer in its extraordinary dance steps, and its revaluation of gender which still includes the need for a partner, an alternative form of narrative, one moving differently. Carmen can dance the first, but the second partakes of the history of the century after Bizet's opera, and shows signs of having been under a continuing and increasing domination, bearing down especially on countries that have been through forms of colonialism, and on the men and women in them, and on the way gender is positioned within them. It may however still be possible to think of the tango as providing a utopian image of resistance and difference, and keeping its potential 'other' valencies. In that it corresponds to something different and affirmative and other in Bizet's *Carmen*.

Notes

1. This refers to the tin can that Lacan writes about, and the fisherman who said to him, 'You see that can? Do you see it? Well, it doesn't see you' (Lacan 1977: 95). The can is the stain that interrupts vision, and that in looking back or not looking back, interrupts the subject's sense of itself, makes it a stain.
2. Composed in 1986 by G. Morodor and T. Whitlock; the singer was Emma Bunton.
3. For information on Hayworth, see Morella and Epstein (1983).
4. On film noir and Hayworth see Dyer (1998).
5. See James Naremore (1998: 229-233), who discusses the representation of Latin America in film noir.
6. See Allen 1983 (vii-x), who connects the phrase with the rise of feminism. See also pp. 186-187 for a discussion of 'vamp', first used in 1902 (OED, 1911) in relation to Theda Bara.
7. Magnarelli gives excellent support for this view.
8. On this film, see Milne (1970: 128-134).
9. See Seigel (1986: 3-30) and Clark (1973: 33-34).
10. Compare Martínez Fure (1991: 118) for the link with the '*contradanza*', which he takes as the same as the *habanera*; the glossary (315) speaks of the *contradanza habanera*.
11. The narrative of the story is impossible to follow from its account here.

References

Allen, Virginia M. 1983. *The Femme Fatale: Erotic Icon*. Troy, NY: Whitston Publishing Co..

Bacarisse, Pamela. 1988. *The Necessary Dream: A Study of the Novels of Manuel Puig*. Totowa, NJ: Barnes and Noble.

Blasco Ibáñez, Vicente. 1958. *Blood and Sand* (tr. Frances Partridge). New York: Frederick Ungar.

Borges, Jorge Luis. 1968. *A Personal Anthology* (ed. and tr. Anthony Kerrigan) London: Jonathan Cape.

— 1998. *Collected Fictions* (tr. Andrew Hurley). Harmondsworth: Penguin.

— 2001. *The Total Library (Non-Fiction 1922-1986).* (ed. Eliot Weinberger; trs Esther Allen, Suzanne J. Levine and Eliot Weinberger). Harmondsworth: Penguin.

Carpentier, Alejo. 1967. *The Kingdom of this World* (tr. Harriet de Onís). London: Andre Deutsch.

— 2001. *Music in Cuba* (ed. Timothy Brennan; tr. Alan West-Durán). Minneapolis: University of Minnesota Press.

Castro, Donald S.. 1990. *The Argentine Tango as Social History, 1880-1955*. San Francisco: Mellen Research University Press.

Clark, Timothy James. 1973. *Image of the People: Gustave Courbet and the 1848 Revolution*. London: Thames and Hudson.

Clément, Catherine. 1988. *Opera, or the Undoing of Women* (tr. Betsy Wing). Minneapolis: University of Minnesota Press.

Cortázar, Julio. 1983. *We Love Glenda So Much and Other Stories* (tr. Gregory Rabassa). New York: Knopf.

Curtiss, Mina. 1974. *Bizet and his World.* New York: Vienna House.

Derrida, Jacques. 1981. *Dissemination* (tr. Barbara Johnson). Chicago: University of Chicago Press.

Dean, Winton. 1965. *Georges Bizet: His Life and Work.* London: J.M. Dent.

Dyer, Richard. 1998. 'Resistance Through Charisma: Rita Hayworth and Gilda' in Kaplan (ed.) (1998): 115-122.

Gledhill, Christine. 1998. '*Klute* 1: A Contemporary Film Noir and Feminist Criticism' in Kaplan (ed.) (1998): 20-34

Hugo, Victor. 1970. *Oeuvres complètes* (ed. Jean Massin) vol. 3. Paris: Le Club Francais du Livre.

Kaplan, E. Ann (ed.). 1998. *Women in* Film noir. 2nd ed. London: British Film Institute.

Kerr, Lucille. 1987. *Suspended Fictions: Reading Novels by Manuel Puig.* Urbana: University of Illinois Press.

Lacan, Jacques. 1977. *The Four Fundamental Concepts of Psychoanalysis* (tr. Alan Sheridan). Harmondsworth: Penguin.

Lacombe, Hervé. 2001. *The Keys to French Opera in the Nineteenth Century* (tr. Edward Scheider). Berkeley: University of California Press.

Leiris, Michel. 1993. 'The Bullfight as Mirror' (tr. Ann Smock) in *October* 63: 21-40

Magnarelli, Sharon. 1985. *The Lost Rib: Female Characters in the Spanish-American Novel.* Lewisburg: Associated University Presses.

Martínez Fure, Rogelio. 'Tambor' in Peter Manuel (ed.) *Essays on Cuban Music: North American and Cuban Perspectives.* New York: University Press of America: 25-47.

Mérimée, Prosper. *Carmen* (tr. and intr. Walter F. C. Ade). New York: Barron.

Milne, Tom. 1970. *Rouben Mamoulian.* Bloomington: Indiana University Press.

Morella, Joe and Epstein, Edward Z. 1983. *Rita: The Life of Rita Hayworth.* New York: Delacorte Press.

Naremore, James. 1998. *More than Night:* Film noir *in its Contexts* Berkeley: University of California Press.

Nietzsche, Friedrich. 'The Case of Wagner: Turinese Letter of May 1888' in Walter Kaufmann (ed.) *Basic Writings of Nietzsche* (tr. Kaufmann). New York: The Modern Library: 609-648.

Puig, Manuel. 1971. *Betrayed By Rita Hayworth* (tr. Suzanne Levine). New York: Vintage Books.

— 1976. *The Buenos Aires Affair* (tr. Suzanne Levine). London: Faber.

Savigliano, Marta. 1995. *Tango and the Political Economy of Passion.* Boulder: Westview Press.

Segal, Naomi. 1998. *Narcissus and Echo: Women in the French Récit.* Manchester: Manchester University Press.

Seigel, Jerrold. 1986. *Bohemian Paris: Culture, Politics and the Boundaries of Bourgeois Life, 1830-1930.* Harmondsworth: Penguin.

Tambling, Jeremy. 1996. *Opera and the Culture of Fascism.* Oxford: Oxford University Press.

— 2002. *Wong Kar-wai: Happy Together.* Hong Kong: Hong Kong University Press.

Woscoboinik, Julio. 1998. *The Secret of Borges: A Psychoanalytic Inquiry into his Work* (tr. Dora Carlisky Pozzi). New York: University Press of America.

The Turbulent Movement of Forms: Rosi's Postmodern *Carmen*

Mary P. Wood

Francesco Rosi's reputation as film director had been built on his hard-hitting political investigations of the 1960s and 1970s, his technical expertise in creating cinematic set-pieces with hundreds of extras, and the beauty of his images. This chapter examines Rosi's *Carmen* in terms of his visual style, with emphasis on framing, cinematography, figures, landscape and space, elaborating the ways in which the film's *mise en scène* dovetails with—or counters—Rosi's previously avowed aims as auteur. It also places this discussion in the context of the film's production, in order to explore the tensions between the universalizing tendencies of mass entertainment, the demands of the quality film, and the individual artistic impulse of the director.

Gaumont
Landscape
Mise en scène
Neo-baroque
Popular entertainment vs. high art
Realism
Rosi, Francesco: *Carmen*

Francesco Rosi's *Carmen* was released in 1984 and has now spent over seventeen years in circulation, tempting successive generations to invest in the video and now the DVD. My aims in this chapter are to put Rosi's version of Carmen into a context, and to suggest some of the reasons for the convergence of interests between studio and director and, following on from this context, to discuss some of Rosi's artistic choices in making the film. That is, to explore the tension in a film between the universalizing tendency of mass entertainment and the desire of a director to signal his own, personal interpretation, whilst still appealing to a non-specialist audience.

Rosi's *Carmen* is a Franco-Italian co-production, produced by Gaumont. Gaumont has been an important force in the European film industries growing from a family firm to an international operation practising vertical integration on a modern industrial model by combining production, distribution and exhibition. As such it is a good illustration of what David Harvey (1990: 147) terms 'flexible accumulation', the defining characteristic of postmodern, globalized economies: new ways of providing financial services and information have made it possible to open up new markets and to achieve 'greatly intensified rates of commercial, technological, and organizational innovation'. By the 1970s, Gaumont, for example, had moved from the production of 'family' cinema to more 'auteurist' art cinema projects, combining, under the direction of Daniel Toscan du Plantier, art and commerce. It had formerly avoided art cinema but for various reasons, including the growth of higher education worldwide, increased prosperity and demographic factors, this niche market is now a large one in global terms. This policy was both a strategy to fight the US majors, and an acknowledgement of changed audiences and patterns of leisure.

Until 1984, Gaumont was a considerable force in the industry. Gaumont Italia made its appearance in the Italian industry in the 1978-79 season under the direction of Renzo Rossellini. In 1982 it was commended for producing twelve films of cultural significance. It was also said unkindly of it that it was an elephants' graveyard, producing glossy films by quality, but ageing, directors. From an initial slate of three productions, it grew to thirty by 1983 when its enormous deficit led to the collapse of the company, the sacking of Rossellini, and difficulties in the French parent company. Its exhibition sector, which had always been profitable, was sold off to Cannon in order to limit the Italian company's liabilities.[1] Culturally, therefore, Gaumont had a considerable impact in the 1970s and 1980s in favouring the production of prestige, art cinema projects which then had wide, international theatrical release and television exposure. Its directors included Rohmer, Bresson, Bergman, Fellini, and Rosi himself (who had already made two films with Gaumont, *Christ Stopped at Eboli* (1979) and *Three Brothers* (1981)). However, as Renzo Rossellini admitted when he was sacked, only one of the fourteen films on his 1983 *listino* of thirty films made money. Rosi's was exceptional in its success and was rumoured to have saved the bacon of Gaumont France.

By the early 1980s, Gaumont had clearly taken several factors into account in evolving its production policy. Firstly, that the cinema audience had changed. By the 1970s, various Italian film industry surveys had conclusively shown that cinema was no longer mass entertainment. That role had been overtaken by television. Those who went to the cinema were generally better educated and middle to upper-middle class in social origin, so that we can see that an opera film, which at first sight might seem to be an élite art form, could have mass appeal to the contemporary, international cinema audience.[2]

Secondly, the cost of all but the most modest film was now such that its costs could not be amortized on the home market alone. A film of any ambition had to aim at a pan-European or preferably a world market. Bizet's *Carmen* is already a classic, and already international in that it is sung in French and set in Spain, and forms part of the repertory of opera houses worldwide. Gaumont was used to operating on an international level through co-productions, the advantages being that easy access to two or more markets (and government subventions) could spread the costs.

Thirdly, one of the interesting cultural phenomena of the 1980s was the growth of interest in all forms of opera. Italy did, of course, have much success in exporting opera films in the silent film period, and in the 1940s, but opera films now constitute a definable genre of their own. It would have been an important consideration when putting together the production package of this *Carmen* that it was a classic opera, and therefore not likely to go out of fashion, or be a passing fancy.[3] This gives Rosi's film what the film business calls 'legs'. That is, opera films are successful financially on their first runs and have a virtually infinite shelf life amongst 'opera buffs', in the same way that classic vinyl or CD recordings have. Paradoxically, television has been the catalyst here by showing complete, unabridged opera performances, and by using opera as background music for television commercials. By the 1980s it was noticed that opera audiences were getting younger and bigger and, being visually (or at least televisually) literate, were able to appreciate the constantly changing spectacle and emotional charge of opera (Allsop 1989). On a more basic level, *Carmen* could be said to contain its potential share of sex and violence, then as now a staple of mass cinema entertainment. Moreover, the 'legs' phenomenon is assisted by the vertical integration which has taken place in the media industries since the 1970s, and which is a feature of postmodern, globalized business. Film production companies are often only a part of the interests of a parent company which may also have television, or music recording interests, and large companies have to amortize their costs by continually exploiting the possibilities of new technologies.

Rosi's film was a co-production of Gaumont France and its music wing, Opéra Film Produzione. It has lasted for almost twenty years on celluloid, then on the shelves of the video shop and frequently re-released: in the racks of music shops on vinyl and CD; on videodisk; and, more recently, on DVD (with twenty different language subtitle options). The audio and the visual aspects of filmed opera allow a double exploitation of the film as product and the music as product (Toscan du Plantier 1987: 14). In summary, therefore, a 1980s Gaumont production had to be a prestige, artistic production, with international appeal, aimed at an educated, 'quality' audience, who would pay higher ticket prices, and buy the video.[4]

Although his reputation is based on his political films, such as *Salvatore Giuliano* (1961), *Le mani sulla città* (*Hands Over the City*) (1963) and *Cadaveri eccellenti* (*Illustrious Corpses*) (1976), the choice of Francesco Rosi to deliver such a production was not illogical. He was born in Naples in 1922 and got his start in film working as assistant director to Luchino Visconti on one of the classic films of neorealism, *La terra trema* (1946). Before his début in 1958 he worked across the spectrum of Italian popular and art cinema. His own career has been in the art, and then 'quality', film sector of the industry and his work has been categorized as political, realist and visually complex. At this point in his career, Rosi's films had generally been successful at the box office and, importantly, had also been acclaimed critically. His films treated important subjects and were discussed in newspaper and journal articles. Moreover, as a political filmmaker, Rosi was concerned to make his conclusions about the political mysteries he investigated very clear. It is this clarity of film language which facilitated his move into mainstream, quality cinema.

In secondary texts surrounding his work, Rosi constantly foregrounds himself as the prime creative force behind his films by his meticulous researching into the background of his stories and his enormous visual and organizational flair. This is allied to a desire to discover truths, usually explored through the use of the investigative format, so that facts, truths, meanings are often suggested in several ways at once, through the dialogue, sound and visuals—a useful ability in adapting an opera to the screen. In addition, from the 1950s onwards, his *mise en scène* has included set piece sequences mobilizing hundreds of extras and complex choreography and camera movements. His gradual move, from the 1970s onwards, into the 'quality' sector of the industry meant that Rosi could therefore deliver the sort of product Gaumont required.[5] He could handle the five-million pound sterling budget, foreign locations and international stars, and the level of organization needed to work with many extras and eight hundred costumes. He could express himself in an accessible film language.

In considering Rosi's *Carmen*, two interlinked aspects of his film language are important—firstly, his strategies to make the 'story' of the opera clear and understandable to his international, educated and mass audience, and secondly, how a deeper level of complexity and interpretation is suggested. Although both strategies involve a stress on directorial presence in the text, the first represents a closing off of areas of possible meanings, whilst the second permits a range of hypotheses to be made. Rosi's first artistic choice was his usual one of using of the conventions of realism to suggest the authenticity of his view of his story world. Rosi grounds the action in the geographical reality of southern Spain and in locations which enable a creative use of framing and camera work. This strategy also provides economical and simple ways of varying the *mise en scène* during the songs and orchestral interludes. Most of the film was shot in Ronda, which not only has the oldest fixed bullring in Spain, but is also divided into two, having an upper and lower town. This allowed Rosi to shoot in several planes and is one of his prime tools both to vary the visuals during the songs, and to connote other levels of meaning. In addition, by using the properties of the zoom lens and the possibilities of the rack-focus, Rosi is able to move the sphere of action from the foreground to the background and vice versa, for example, as the soldiers of the guard approach the town walls, the camera rack-focuses to reveal the Gypsy encampment, bringing the wagons in the foreground into focus, in one of which Micaela awakes as the troupe's trumpets sound.

In creating a plausible and comprehensible representation of nineteenth-century Spain, Rosi uses another realist strategy in the full use of offscreen sound which reinforces the impression of action happening around the frame and models space by indicating volume. In the town, the noises of crowds, voices, shouts from the bullring, draw attention to the social use of space. In the countryside, the use of the noise of birds is used to connote different territories and the boundaries between them. Town birds are used in the shots of Carmen bathing; hawks calling in the gorge indicate wildness and the volume of the scene by the reverberation of the sound from the rocks.[6]

Rosi's primary interpretative strategy, the search for realism of location was underpinned by his sense that Carmen's world and don José's are radically different, and that the difference is one of class. When I interviewed Rosi in 1996, I took the opportunity to ask him about *Carmen*, because at first sight it seemed somewhat atypical. He told me that, in defining the look of the film, his researches led him to Gustave Doré's illustrations of a little known travel book of Baron Davillier. Rosi is convinced that he found the very places which Doré had sketched, such as the quarry in the mountains above Ronda which was the smugglers' hideout, and the old Roman road which Mérimée describes as the smugglers' trail. Rosi told me that this was the only project in which a producer, Daniel Toscan du Plantier, had suggested

to him, rather than his usual method of working on a screenplay and
then persuading a producer to arrange the finance to film it (Wood
1998: 290). He agreed to do it on condition that he could work in his
usual way, in interpreting the work. Rosi saw the nub of the work as
the clash of the bourgeois world—with its unwritten rules, its
exploitation, its masking of its own operations—with Carmen's world,
dominated by emotion, the erotic, and by a certain anarchic spirit.
Rosi's interpretation of *Carmen* stems from these ideas. His aim was to
give visual expression to the conflict between the instinctive and
irrational and the attempt to use reason to dominate instinct (Mori
1982).

The impression of realism extends to the choice of extras, who
embody their ethnic and class positions, grounding the narrative in a
social reality. The casting of the principals mainly reflects the iron
necessities of the marketplace, but the stars are also essential in making
the story comprehensible and here cultural and gender clichés are
brought into play. The two male leads are played by established opera
stars, Plácido Domingo and Ruggero Raimondi, who have world-wide
reputations and will therefore sell records. Domingo's participation
may be essential commercially, but his stature (literally) and his
presence generate some plausibility to the mutual desire between him
and Carmen. Jeremy Tambling suggests (1978: 17) that the cinematic
close-up emphasizes Domingo's miscasting in terms of age and looks,
but it can be argued that these provide a metaphor for the rigidity of
don José's world view and guiding principles, motivating the challenge
which he represents to Carmen. Escamillo is a star in his field, as is
Raimondi, and only he is permitted the challenging stare-to-camera of
the opening sequence. Rosi and his producers chose the American
soprano, Julia Migenes-Johnson, for her physical appearance and
performance, and because she could draw on her varied career, singing
opera and review, operetta and theatre and television. She fitted with
Rosi's conception of Carmen's character, combining 'intelligence and
independence, eroticism and sensuality' (Wood 1998: 293). Migenes-
Johnson could dance, and Rosi saw dance as integral to the cultural
expression of both Gypsies and Andalusians to the extent that it
constitutes an additional level of language (Bertolotti 1984). It is also
used so as not to 'exhaust' the image during song. That is, the dances
create an internal dynamic to the image by motivating the use of the
long take, following the movement of figures in space.

Visual beauty and the ability to use the full extent of cinematic
language also enable Rosi to add a second level of complexity. Part of

this strategy results in a noticeable number of diagonal compositions, where the spectator's eye is drawn into the scene via a strong orthogonal emphasis. Diagonal compositions allow the eye to move into the frame, whilst figure movement moves out of it.

It is interesting that the use of diagonal compositions has been associated with both Baroque and with Constructivist art. These movements can be seen to be a reaction against previous artistic norms of harmony and balance between emotion and reason, imagination and reality and to express a certain spiritual disquiet. Baroque art in particular has been seen as a reaction to Renaissance ideals of harmony and to the austerity of the Counter Reformation (Huyghe 1961: 329). The turbulent movement of forms, their richness and abundance, were harnessed to the stirring of emotions and aimed at increasing awareness. Baroque art aimed to create atmosphere by using images 'more forceful and arresting than reality itself' and mainly associated with the manipulation of space (Venturi 1961: 220). Baroque art employs asymmetry to help resolve the contradictions of realistic content with richness and excess of form. Diagonal, asymmetrical compositions are able to suggest a plausible world by drawing the eye into their depth of field, and at the same time draw attention to themselves as constructed. In Rosi's film, visual richness and asymmetry complement the display of excessive emotions (desire, passion, betrayal, hatred) and the disruptive force of a woman who refuses to live by the rules of bourgeois society.

Huyghe also mentions (1961: 334) the Baroque penchant for pageants and festivities and that these were conceived architecturally as the interaction of crowds and buildings around public space. In this connection it is interesting to note Maravall's contention (1986: 125) that the buildings and social spaces of the baroque period were organized in response to the need for the containment of an unreliable populace. Crowds in Rosi's films are made visible by their containment within social spaces; the size and noise of the crowds indicates their potential for violence and disruption. The theatricality of the events and conflicts played out in these containing spaces enable, as Buci-Glucksmann has suggested (1994: 60), something invisible to be made visible. The life and death struggles played out in the bullring, for example, allow power relationships usually masked by the cult of the star performer to become clear.

The Baroque therefore comes to represent the tension between power and order, and revolt and disorder. Internal conflicts are externalized. According to Bryan Turner (1988: 38), the tension marks a moment of historical change when a very hierarchical status system is challenged by the pressure of bourgeois individualism. At this stage the pressure towards a new social stratification is unable to be contained and results in an excessive display by the threatened power system. The scene where Carmen is arrested, bound, and dragged through the streets is a visual representation of the operation of coercive power, both on Carmen, and on the townspeople who look on, but are contained within the streets.

The pictorial qualities of the composition and framing of the film's action are thus able to facilitate both emotional and social readings of the action. Omar Calabrese's exploration of definitions of the neo-Baroque suggests reasons for the prevalence of conflict and disruption in Rosi's *Carmen*. Calabrese (1992: 25) defines as neo-baroque the rejection of judgments strongly ordered towards stably ordered correspondences, and a pre-disposition towards 'those categories that powerfully "excite" the ordering of the system, that destabilize part of the system by creating turbulence and fluctuations within it'. In this respect the neo-Baroque in Italy is an expression of the postmodern undermining of the grand metanarratives. By foregrounding disruption and excess, value is given to other versions of social organization. Thus don José's world is characterized visually by rigidity and order. The military occupy a tall building whose windows look over the town in symmetrical rows; the soldiers on horseback are depicted in orderly lines as they control the town; and the architectural paradigm selected for the interior courtyard of the barracks is that of classical columns and a colonnade around a rectangular space. The tobacco factory is of plain, rectangular form with symmetrical rows of windows. Its interior is characterized by symmetrical colonnades and coffered ceilings, linking it visually to the rational world of the exercise of military or commercial power. In contrast, the town below is a jumble of streets and houses which rhymes with the seeming chaos of the women at work alongside their babies, singing and chattering. Carmen's world is visually associated with fluidity of movement within space, with turbulence and rejection of order, whether represented by the military or the bosses. Don José's world is one of social order and the imposition of a closely knit system of rules.

This opposition is the organizing principle of the film at a fundamental level. On the one hand, the conventions of cinematic realism (authenticity of Spanish location, decor, sound, morphology and gesture of the actors, use of camera movement within the long take) seek to impose a unified interpretation of story events; this is paralleled by Rosi's insistence, within the secondary text of articles and interviews, on his fidelity to the intentions of Mérimée and Bizet.[7] On the other hand, opera is, by definition, not a realist dramatic form (the characters sing and dance instead of speak). Some critics found the juxtaposition of realism and artifice jarring, but in fact they coexist within the text as expressions of tension between two organizing systems.[8] Rosi's cinema is, as I have suggested, also typified by a flamboyant drawing of attention to the visuals, a demonstration of virtuosity that Calabrese sees as a quintessentially neo-Baroque, or postmodern feature. Virtuosity is a 'total flight from central organizing principles', destroying ideas of harmony and order (Calabrese 1992: 40-41). Thus Rosi's virtuosity in *Carmen* expresses a tension between the attraction of a stable, ordered, patriarchal system, and the attraction of other modes of existence.

Virtuosity is another artistic strategy in making the story comprehensible, using excessive visual beauty to heighten the emotional impact of the music for an audience who, as I have suggested earlier, had been schooled by television to competence in 'reading' emotions. These instances of heightened reality, linked to architectural space, constitute moments of excess, defined by Kristin Thompson (1981: 288) as moments where 'the physicality of the image goes beyond the narrative structures of unity in a film', so that the audience is made aware of an intention external to the film's diegesis, that of the filmmaker/director. These moments correspond to Barthes's 'third meaning' or 'the obtuse meaning', a site of emotion, of 'an emotion-value, an evaluation' (Barthes 1977: 12-19). The scenes of the bullring of Ronda, the romantic and gothic grandeur of the scenery in the hills, the romantic night-time scenes in the Gypsy encampment outside the walls, are arenas where life and death struggles are played out. The emotional content forcefully suggests hypotheses for making sense of the action.

In an article aptly entitled 'Carmen Cojones', Julia Migenes-Johnson is reported as typifying Carmen as 'what our age needs, and women want. Carmen is dirty' (Fernández 1984).[9] The singer likens the conflict between Carmen and don José to that of the bull and the toreador, with Carmen as the fighter. Rosi has always stressed that he was faithful to Bizet's score in not portraying Carmen as a whore. However, his Carmen is socially rather than racially different, and only able to operate in the sphere assigned to her. Within that sphere she stresses her desire for personal autonomy, which clashes with the exercise of male power. This gives the film an added ideological dimension, finding a resonance not only with the political emergence of women during the 1970s, but also with the contemporary entry of Spain into modernity. Sex is politicized.

The love scene between Carmen and don José lasts about fifteen minutes and runs the gamut of sexual passion from seduction, falling in love, eroticism, disappointment, fights, passion, romance, irony, teasing, cruelty. Don José is visually constrained by sharp-angled frames at the decisive moment when he decides to return to barracks. Carmen is seductively objectified on the bed by the camera. The eroticism of Migenes-Johnson's performance is a deliberate choice, given that don José's aria expresses desire, stressing the roles of scent, perfume, sight, glance. It's also interesting that the two-shots are asymmetrical, featuring two empty chairs in the rest of the room, into which Carmen dances, moving out from don José and back to tease him. Her autonomy is indicated spatially by her ability to move around the space of the bedroom, whilst don José's movements are severely circumscribed. His desire is expressed as shorter movements which constantly return to proximity with Carmen. So, whilst the narrative stresses the social differences between the two characters, performance cues emphasize sexual charge, sexual chemistry and the nature of the two, different manifestations of sexual desire. Here we have the paradox that Carmen is represented as ignorant, superstitious, a Gypsy, but is very aware of the realities of how power is exercised in her world. Don José is educated, but is ignorant and has no inner resources when he steps outside the conduct expected of his world. Rosi saw him as a weak man, but in the patriarchal sense that he is not strong enough to dominate the woman (Wood 1998: 293).

However, the sexual conflict also reveals all the tensions which are so evident in his later films, contributing to their general lack of popularity. That is, whilst his political agenda still has a left-wing validity, his gender ideology is problematic.[10] The film shows a level of ambiguity about the exercise of female power. Tambling suggests (1987: 37-38) that Rosi's film appears to present a coherent reading of Carmen as victim rather than vamp and that his intermittent use of naturalism demystifies the heroine so that the contradictions between her freedom to love and her social and sexual oppression by men becomes visible. Whilst Rosi himself insists that his Carmen was to be "'like every other woman'", rather than a *femme fatale*, he also states that his aim was to express her Gypsy marginality, her demanding nature and erotic charge (Bertolotti 1984: 18). It is the latter part of the equation which finds its expression in the film as the display of hypersexuality. Her figure is objectified by the camera which follows the movements of her breasts and hips, or the arching of her back as she lies on the bed in the tavern with her skirts around her waist. She is both attractive to women in her challenge to male power, and to men in her promises of sexual pleasure. However, the excessiveness of this representation of Carmen's sexuality both emphasizes her as an individual case, and indicates the strength of the feeling of danger represented by her challenge. Carmen is a Gypsy only in the sense that those popular paintings of Gypsies in a state of undress, staring provocatively at the spectator, generally are; Gypsy figures are used to suggest an alluring, essential femininity, free of social constraints, and available for the purchaser.[11]

Rosi's use of architectural space therefore corresponds to Lefebvre's notion (1991: 34) that space is the product of spatial relations and can therefore work 'as a tool for the analysis of society' so that power relationships can be suggested through the evocation of architectural space. I have indicated how character, class and motivation have been suggested through performance in architectural space, showing difference that is, marking off one character from another, one class or group from another. Space and place gain significance not just by how they are evoked visually, but through the physical gestures and movements of people within them (Lefebvre 1991: 200). Here Foucault's notion of the heterotopia is useful. Foucault defined a heterotopia as an enclosed society, populated by those whose behaviour or condition deviates from the cultural norm. Heterotopic sites are not freely accessible. Entry is via compulsion (the prison, the cemetery) or ritual (the Masons, the mafia). In *Discipline and Punish* (Foucault 1977) he examined these heterotopias as part of modern society's systems of disciplinary power and social control, suggesting that institutions are the places where the technologies of power are most visible. In *Carmen*, the heterotopias are those of the military, sport, and criminality. Carmen represents the disruption which enables access to these closed, intimidatory, spaces. The characters who lead us into these closed worlds are their typical representatives, the brigadier and the bullfighter.

The orchestral preludes provide examples of how these ideas find their expression in the film. Classically, the first ten minutes of a film set in place all the narrative hooks to interest the audience and prevent them from getting up and demanding their money back. Rosi himself says that he wanted the preludes to function as establishing shots, setting scene and location. The editing is fairly fast compared to Rosi's other recent films and there is a certain amount of stereotype and cliché in operation, also the display of virtuosity of camera work. Colour and composition create a heightened realism, a heightened visual beauty that draws attention to itself. Rosi achieves this by a stress on symbolic spaces and social ritual. Rosi makes the bullfight and the presence of the church central to his film. The first image is of the ritualized conflict of man and bull. Close-ups refuse the wider view and fill our screen with the enormous testicles of the uncastrated bull, and the tight trousers of the toreador. What is at stake is sexual power, male dominance. Escamillo is the star who dominates the arena, and who interpellates the audience with his challenging stare at the 'moment of truth'. The bullfight symbolizes male power at work; the female spectators admire and approve. Don José and Escamillo both live by this power, both are fighters by profession. Carmen is disruptive because she too is a fighter and, as such, threatens the established codes of southern society. By the proximity of the religious procession, the Church is indicated as complicit in this domination, the orderly procession of the masked penitents representing the arcane rituals involved in maintaining it. By contrast, the ethereal, golden beauty of the statue of the Madonna and the strangeness of the behaviour of the women who appear to be actively bargaining with her, indicate the feminine principle as something unassimilable within the Church's system.

The scene where don José's sweetheart, Micaela, brings a message from his mother also demonstrates Rosi's particular interpretation, and signals his own virtuosity as a filmmaker. Here the long take functions not just to explicate the singing and to vary the *mise en scène*. Character glance in onscreen and at offscreen space cues the construction of a realistic space. The light intensity, white walls, architecture and so on signal this as Spain, the South, a mythic space. Camera angle and framing also set up the themes of power and control, restraint and release. Women in the opening sequence have been decorative bystanders at the bullfight, passive observers of male games. We have seen the townswomen and gypsies coralled into the tobacco factory; here we see the danger that male force represents for Micaela. The soldiers surround her, constraining her physically, and she has to burst away from them in flight.

The camera angles, use of architectural planes, framing and depth of field also emphasize the power of the military and their position of surveillance, beyond the indications of the libretto,[12] and emphasized by the extraordinary extreme long shot from the crane's nest over the town. In a jutting triangular space the tiny figure of Micaela is visible surrounded by soldiers, the rest of the frame occupied by the jumble of roofs and the crane. Rosi uses this trope, which is that of the panopticon, in many of his films. Foucault writes about prisons being designed so that the prison population (the prison heterotopia) can be under surveillance at every moment. Those in the barracks are shown to be in a commanding position physically and able to observe everything which happens in the town below. In this film we have a visual representation of the panopticon suggesting an all-powerful control of society. It thus makes plain the ideology of those who use it. In this connection it is interesting that Carmen, although ostensibly a free spirit, is first identified as she washes and splashes in the water trough via the objectifying gaze of Morales, the officer 'controlling' the town through his binoculars from the barracks. The trope of the panopticon links patriarchal, military and political power.

In conclusion, I would like to suggest that, in *Carmen*, the needs of the production company, Gaumont, coincided happily with the interests of the director, Francesco Rosi. The resulting film is a postmodern product, combining interesting performances, attractive actors, beautiful scenery, beautifully shot interiors and exteriors, natural sound, plenty of movement and pace, a good story clearly presented. At the same time, both within the film itself, and in the secondary text of articles and interviews, it is signalled as a spectacle which can be appreciated at several levels. The film makes visual the tensions between the desire for stability and order, and the attractions of ambiguity, disorder and turbulence which are very much part of a postmodern experience of life in the latter part of the twentieth century. Rosi tells his audience, implicitly and explicitly, that this is a personal interpretation, and, thus interpellated, we the audience therefore watch out for signs of interpretation in a very postmodern way. However, the theatricality, asymmetricality and intensity of late twentieth-century Baroque are an indication both of inequalities in social power and status, and of the difficulty in evolving valid ways of being to replace ones recently discredited.

Notes

1. These cinemas were what was left of the State Eci circuits, whose private sale in the early 1960s provoked a huge scandal (Rossi 1985). On the demise of Cannon, these cinemas were equally as swiftly purchased by Berlusconi's Fininvest and renamed Cinema 5.

2. The findings and statistics of a Doxa enquiry into these issues were published in issues 37-40 of *Giornale dello Spettacolo*, October-November 1982.
3. The average life of an Italian film was two years at this time and most made 90% of their returns in the first year after release (Ferraù 1984).
4. Its audience appeal in France was such that it played, without protests, at an enhanced ticket price of 40 French Francs as opposed to the usual first run price of 33 French Francs (*Giornale dello Spettacolo* 1984).
5. I have defined 'Quality cinema' elsewhere as 'characterized by technical expertise, set pieces of showy *mise en scène*, complex narratives, serious ideas, and the personal signature and commitment of one person, the director/author' (Wood 2000).
6. I am indebted to Amy Herzog for crystallizing this idea, which arose from her paper on *Prénom Carmen*, delivered at the Carmen Conference, 2002 (and see her essay in this volume).
7. For example, Rosi demonstrates his work of research and preparation by explaining his choice to set the film in 1875, the date that Bizet's opera was first performed, in Kezich 1983. His knowledge of other, earlier versions, both operatic and cinematic, and his three years of preparation work are also stressed in Pancaldi 1984.
8. Michel Chion (1984) in particular wrote of the 'choc lorsqu'après un premier bain de réalisme, résonne en français le premier chœur "Sur la place"' (the shock when, after the [film's] first dose of realism, the chorus 'In the square' rings out in French).
9. The photograph in the centre of this article is captioned, 'Migenes-Johnson at home: no hormones for house cleaning'!
11. Rosi characterizes Southern European society as one where men have the upper hand and women have a subordinate position, and that because he is interested in depicting how power is exercised, this is how he represents women (Wood 1985). Women are represented as marginal to the exercise of public power, but the films lack 'instructions' to examine and contest gender power relations, which is in itself significant.
10. Mario Martone's 1995 film, *L'amore molesto* (*Wounded Love*) uses these popular genre paintings to resonant and ironic effect. The heroine, Delia, is trying to find the facts behind her mother's drowning and her journeys across Naples are accompanied by flashbacks to a problematic, 1950s girlhood, when her father, jealous of any autonomous action of her mother, regularly beat and constrained her. Her father is a painter, churning out copies of paintings of Gypsies for which Delia's mother is the model.
12. 'Reprenons notre passe-temps et regardons passer les gens, / sur la place, chacun passe, / chacun vient, chacun va.' ([Let's] get back to killing time by watching people come and go. Here and there across the square people come and people go).

References
Allsop, D. 1989. 'The New Culture Club' in *Options* (October): 24-26.
Barthes, Roland. 1977. *Image-Music-Text* (tr. Stephen Heath). London: Fontana.
Bertolotti, Franco. 1984. 'Rosi: la mia Carmen' in *Avvenire* (11 May): 18.
Buci-Glucksmann, Christine. 1994. *Baroque Reason: The Aesthetics of Modernity* (tr. Patrick Camiller). London: Sage.
Calabrese, Omar. 1992. *Neo-Baroque: A Sign of the Times* (tr. Charles Lambert). Princeton, NJ: Princeton University Press.
Chion, Michel. 1984. '*Carmen*' in *Cahiers du Cinéma* 358: 51.
Fernández, Enrique. 1984. 'Carmen Cojones' in *Voice* (25 September): 67.
Ferraù, Alessandro. 1984. 'Vita breve per il film italiano' in *Giornale dello Spettacolo* (14 April): 14.

Foucault, Michel. 1977. *Discipline and Punish* (tr. Alan Sheridan). London: Allen Lane.

Giornale dello Spettacolo. 1984. 'Taccuino parigino' (30 March): 5.

Harvey, David. 1990. *The Condition of Postmodernity: An Enquiry into the Origins of Cultural Change*. Malden, MA and Oxford: Blackwell.

Huyghe, René. 1961. 'Art Forms and Society' in Huyghe, René (ed.) *Larousse Encyclopedia of Renaissance and Baroque Art*. London: Paul Hamlyn: 329-340.

Kezich, Tullio. 1983. 'Sarà libera, come un musical' in *La Repubblica* (3 February).

Maravall, José Antonio. 1986. *Culture of the Baroque*. Manchester: Manchester University Press.

Mori, Anna Maria. 1983. 'Una zingara eccellente' in *La Repubblica* (8 September).

Pancaldi, Augusto. 1984. 'Questa è la vera Carmen!' in *L'Unità* (15 March).

Rossi, Umberto. 1985. 'Arrivano i nostri: Cannon compra Gaumont Italia' in *Cinemasessanta* 1(161): 23-24.

Tambling, Jeremy. 1987. *Opera, Ideology and Film*. Manchester: Manchester University Press.

Thompson, Kristin. 1981. *Eisenstein's 'Ivan the Terrible': A Neoformalist Analysis*. Princeton, NJ: Princeton University Press.

Toscan du Plantier, Daniel. 1987. 'La politique des producteurs', in *Cahiers du Cinéma* 395/396: 14-18.

Turner, Bryan S.. 1988. *Status*. Milton Keynes: Open University Press.

Venturi, Lionello. 1961, 'Realism and the First Classical and Baroque Trends' in René Huyghe (ed.) *Larousse Encyclopedia of Renaissance and Baroque Art*. London: Paul Hamlyn: 219-223.

Wood, Mary. 1985. Unpublished interview with Francesco Rosi (28 July).

— 1998. 'Francesco Rosi: Heightened Realism' in John Boorman & Walter Donohue (eds) *Projections 8*. London: Faber and Faber: 272-295.

— 2000. 'Cultural Space as Political Metaphor: The Case of the European "Quality" Film'. On line at: http://www.mediasalles.it/crl_wood.htm (consulted 31.12.2003).

Carmen as Perennial Fusion:
From Habanera to Hip-Hop

Susan McClary

Bizet's opera *Carmen* depended on a fusion between high art and what he termed music of 'ill repute'. As Carmen ascended the cultural ladder, it lost the taint of its hybrid origins: today's listeners hear the passages that first scandalized Parisian audiences simply as classical music. Thus, productions that fuse Carmen with the latest music of ill repute can claim greater fidelity to Bizet's vision than more worshipful renditions. This chapter examines films that rework the opera's tunes by means of still-scandalous forms of popular music, arguing that the ambivalence between high and low artistic styles which lies at the heart of the opera replays itself in Preminger's *Carmen Jones*, Godard's *Prénom Carmen* and one of the most recent versions, the MTV *Carmen: a Hip-hopera* (starring Beyoncé Knowles of the group Destiny's Child).

Bizet, Georges: *Carmen*, reworkings of
Carmen: A Hip-hopera
Godard, Jean-Luc: *Prénom Carmen*
Hammerstein, Oscar: *Carmen Jones*
Hip-hop
Preminger, Otto: *Carmen Jones*

'I am German by conviction, heart and soul, but I sometimes get lost in artistic houses of ill repute'. With these words, Georges Bizet, the composer of the opera *Carmen*, confessed to his incurable addiction to slumming—an addiction that drew him on a regular basis to the red-light districts of Paris, to the night spots where he first encountered the music of Gypsies, to the cabarets where he first heard Sébastián Yradier's Afro-Cuban song 'El Arreglito', which became Bizet's most famous tune, the 'Habanera'. Before Bizet latched onto Mérimée's novella as a potential subject for an opera, he had managed to compartmentalize his two sides: he wrote symphonies and respectable music-dramas by day, indulged in his taste for brothels by night. The scandal—and also the genius—of *Carmen* lies in Bizet's decision to bring those mutually exclusive worlds, his Jekyll-and-Hyde polarities, together on the stage of the Opéra-Comique. Opera hasn't been the same since.

The last decade has witnessed a flood of films that translate into the terms of teenage, high-school culture stories from Shakespeare and Jane Austen. Whether, like *O* (Tim Blake Nelson, 2001), they attempt to retain the seriousness of their prototype or, like *Clueless* (Amy Heckerling, 1995), they revel in the secularization of the update, such movies always pride themselves on the slight naughtiness of their endeavours. So do the productions by Peter Sellars, who has set Mozart operas variously in the Trump Towers or the mean streets of Harlem or greasy-spoon diners.

We might be inclined to position the myriad film versions of *Carmen* among these, except that *Carmen* started off as a fusion between high and low forms of entertainment: a *vade mecum* extended by Bizet to accompany him (at least vicariously) into the seedy dives otherwise avoided by the middle-class patrons of operas. Consequently, the modern productions that strive worshipfully to replicate Bizet's original, that fetishize the entire score as transcendent art, betray his original impulse much more profoundly than those that merrily inject into it whatever counts at the moment as sleazy. It actually proves difficult to compete with Bizet at this game. At best, productions can aspire to approach—though they never can match— his sublime degree of naughtiness. Indeed, most of them pull their punches instead of pushing through to their ultimate conclusions the transgressions, pleasures, and dilemmas posed so provocatively by Bizet already in 1875.

He paid the price, of course. To his first audiences and critics, Bizet had simply defiled the operatic stage. He died three months after the premiere at age 37, still in a state of disgrace with only his closest friends standing by him. Even his erstwhile mentor, Charles Gounod, viewed him with utter contempt after the scandal of *Carmen*. If the accolades of major representatives of German high culture such as Brahms and Nietzsche vindicated Bizet shortly after his death, it was in part because they tended to see French culture *tout court* as pure titillation: 'Oh, those Parisians! What *will* they think of next?!'.

What crime precisely did Bizet commit? Before he wrote *Carmen*, Bizet's double life—his split roles of respectable bourgeois composer and aficionado of disreputable night spots—was only a problem for his wife (later to serve as a model for Proust's Duchesse de Guermantes). And a formidable problem it apparently was, for Geneviève Bizet and the Halévy family destroyed many of the letters and diary entries dating from the time Bizet was composing the opera. But as soon as Bizet proposed his project, it also became a problem for the management of the Opéra-Comique, which did everything it could to dissuade Bizet from his plans.

From the vantage point of the Opéra-Comique's staff, the difficulty lay primarily in Bizet's decision to write an opera based on Mérimée's still-infamous novella, complete with the on-stage stabbing of the lead character to celebrate closure. To be sure, this kind of violence, especially against women, had never yet occurred in opera; nor had sexuality this explicit appeared since the long forgotten early years of commercial opera in seventeenth-century Venice. But the most severe wound inflicted by Bizet on operatic propriety was musical: he brought onto that august stage not merely characters who behave in unseemly ways but also the songs and dances he had picked up like a virus during his escapades.

More than that, he enacted the confrontation between the cultivated tradition we now call 'classical music' and the tidal wave of urban popular music that threatened to overflow the slums and contaminate the more élite elements of Parisian life. (We should recall that *Carmen* appeared a mere four years after the bloodbath of the Commune). In his essay 'Mass Culture as Woman', Andreas Huyssen (1986) analyzes how late nineteenth-century purists conflated such cultural practices with aggressive women, clambering immigrants, and class rebellion; he traces how the modernist trends towards abstraction and asceticism emerge in part as a reaction formation against this ostensible rubbish that nonetheless appealed far more directly to the senses than anything available in the concert hall or art museum. Bizet drags not only don José but also the unsuspecting audience into the artistic houses of ill-repute. And although he appears to kill off his purveyor of popular entertainments as a last-ditch effort to reimpose hierarchical normality, anyone who has ever seen *Carmen* knows that her music wins, hands down.

Only a couple of decades later, this paranoid fantasy concerning the defeat of impotent high art in the face of vigorous (if vulgar) new forms becomes the centre of debates over the future of cultural expression. Film, photography, and sound recording raise substantially the anxieties associated with art in the age of mechanical reproduction, as Walter Benjamin called it, and the space between traditional media and those that rely on the new technologies became the principal aesthetic battlefield of the twentieth century—a battlefield on which the well-being of our very souls got fought out (or so Theodor Adorno claimed). But Bizet already had staged that armed conflict, making *Carmen* a dress rehearsal for the dominant cultural tensions of the last hundred years. If film has throughout its history found the cross-over opportunities offered by this opera irresistible, that was, as Carmen herself might say, already in the cards Bizet had dealt.

The hybridity of Bizet's *Carmen* allows it to operate in many unpredictable ways within the cultural hierarchy, very much like Mérimée's character who smuggles goods back and forth through dangerously porous borders. On the one hand, its official pedigree as high art grants it license to pull onto screen activities that might otherwise appear intolerable. When Cecil B. DeMille bought Geraldine Farrar for his silent production of 1915, he could not convey her voice, which had made her a reigning diva at the Metropolitan Opera. But with her prestigious presence, he could stage cat fights in which women rip each other's blouses to shreds and in which the lead actress gleefully participates in a lethal bar room brawl. Even the parody of DeMille by Charlie Chaplin, in which he plays a particularly hapless Darn Hosiery, continues to shock with its degree of physical violence; in fact, the periodic incursions of The Little Tramp into this treacherous plot make the casual mutilations and homicides of the opera stand out in even greater relief. Both DeMille and Chaplin could bank, however, on a mass audience's associations of *Carmen* with élite culture. That Seal of Approval even sanctions a 1991 Covent-Garden production (released by the BBC),[1] in which Maria Ewing ends up impaled on a meat hook—a decision by director Núria Espert that radically raises the stakes beyond the now quaint knife stabbing of the original, and that would provoke the convening of a Senate hearing if it were to appear in the context of a rap video. So long as classical music thunders away in the background, anything goes.

In such productions, Bizet's music is positioned for strategic purposes as elevated, its own internal divisions glossed over for the sake of the cultural prestige it lends to other projects. Put differently, even *Carmen*'s 'Habanera' qualifies as coming from what Bizet affectionately labels as his 'German' side. It's all opera, it's all good. Now sit back and enjoy the mayhem.

On the other hand, the exotic music calculated to evoke Spain remains the indisputable draw for élite and mass audiences alike. It is no accident that more homogeneous operas rarely appear in latter-day fusions or even that don José's pathos-ridden 'Flower Song' (the opera's 'German' moment *par excellence*) falls inevitably to the cutting-room floor in *Carmen* pot-pourris and adaptations. The pop-music side of Bizet's Janus-faced proclivities reaches out and grabs listeners, even as it flatters them that they too can appreciate high art.

We should recall, however, that Bizet dabbled in two kinds of pop styling in *Carmen*. One that associated with the sentimental maidens and jocular heroes native to Opéra-Comique he himself regarded as rubbish. Concerning the 'Toreador Song' (for which the score directs the singer to perform 'fatuously'), Bizet said: 'So they want trash? All right; I'll give them trash'. To adapt the saying, nobody ever went broke underestimating public taste, and never have calculations proved more accurate than Bizet's. But Escamillo fits, along with Micaela, into a middle-brow category that also includes all the stereotypical ingenues and pompous dignitaries of Gilbert and Sullivan. As to the second kind, however, Bizet identified profoundly with his more explosive ingredient—the sounds he drew from the houses of ill repute, the songs and dances performed by Carmen herself. It was, in fact, his determination to bring this unabashedly sexual music and its implicit social realism onto the operatic stage that plunged him into scandal. He realized in advance the risk he was taking yet insisted all the more stubbornly on highlighting this taboo element as institutional opposition to it mounted.

The *Carmen* films that most interest me are the ones inspired by Bizet's inclusion of disreputable music in his opera, the ones that ground their adaptations in similarly transgressive moves or that grapple with tensions between incompatible registers of musical expression. In this category I would include Carlos Saura's flamenco version, which confronts Bizet's mock-up Gypsy music with actual Spanish musicians who strive to convert the 'Seguidilla' into danceable rhythms. Peter Brooks' austere, minimalist *Carmen* sometimes sustains itself with nothing more than the 'Habanera' vamp played by solo timpani, which suffices to conjure up the character and her affiliation with the brothel. Because I have already written in detail about both these versions, I will not pursue them further at this time.

I want to use the rest of this essay to address three of the most serious attempts at translating Bizet into radically different cultural contexts: Oscar Hammerstein's *Carmen Jones* (1943-1944), MTV's hip-hopera *Carmen* (2001) and Jean-Luc Godard's *Prénom Carmen* (1983). Each of these interferes radically with Bizet's version of the story and his music, but each takes its cue from his self-confessed ambivalence between high and low culture. Neither Hammerstein nor the producers of the hip-hopera can boast the bi-musicality that allowed Bizet to play both sides of the cultural divide with comparable power, and Godard—who elsewhere proves himself a connoisseur of popular music—chooses in his setting of *Carmen* mostly to reverse the terms of Bizet's hierarchy. Despite their obvious differences, all three films reject the impulse to reify the opera and attempt, rather, to emulate Bizet's determination to fuse canonic prestige with shockingly inappropriate materials.

Oscar Hammerstein II happened on the idea of an updated *Carmen* in the wake of *Porgy and Bess* (1934), George Gershwin's successful infusion of the operatic genre with stories and musical types drawn from black culture. Taking Bizet's own hybrid score as his point of departure, Hammerstein transferred the opera's plot to the Southern part of the United States and adapted its musical numbers with the aim of matching them with the impulses of African-American popular musics and performers. When Otto Preminger made Hammerstein's Broadway hit into a film in 1954, he signed on an utterly brilliant cast that included Harry Belafonte, Pearl Bailey, Diahann Carroll, and Dorothy Dandridge. Although Bailey could handle her musical numbers herself, Dandridge (as Carmen) had to lip-synch to performances sung by Metropolitan opera star Marilyn Horne.

A somewhat uneven mixture of success and miscalculations, *Carmen Jones* sacrifices the racial tensions of Bizet and Mérimée with the decision to make all the characters, including Joe, black. Relationships between men from Navarre and women from Andalusia might have passed muster with American audiences not clear on the distinction, but the same audiences that prided themselves in their liberal acceptance of Bizet's opera not would have tolerated the miscegenation inherent in the original plot when transposed into the explosive terms of American racial politics. Moreover, Hammerstein pulls Carmen back considerably from the outlaw status she had always enjoyed. Sexy, hot-tempered, and occasionally promiscuous—yes; but scarcely the leader of a band of smugglers. She's actually rather a nice girl, who means well for Joe—takes him home to meet grandma, bakes a peach cobbler for him—but who finally cannot bear being cooped up with him as he hides from the law.

And we can tell all this by her vocal sound. Oddly enough, given the celebrated depth and richness of Marilyn Horne's mezzo-soprano voice, her performances for this Carmen have a light, flute-like quality. She even fluffs the ornamental passages in her 'Seguidilla' ('Dere's a café on de cor- - - - - - - -ner'), so as not to appear virtuosic. All of these decisions cause her to sound like an ordinary woman rather than someone with the vocal power to ensnare men with the sonic signifiers of feminine evil.

But the scene that justifies Hammerstein's adaptation and that comes close to duplicating Bizet's fusion of incongruous musical types is Pearl Bailey's song-and-dance number in Billy Pastor's juke-joint, 'Beat Out Dat Rhythm on a Drum.' Only here does a cast member get to bring along the idiom that had made her famous. For all its incongruities—including jazz dancers simulating an abstract jitterbug to Bizet's pseudo-flamenco (the same stuff Saura's Spanish musicians claim they can't dance to)—Bailey pulls this number off with extraordinary charisma and colloquial authenticity. Indeed, the success of this number makes one long for a black version of that would give Carmen the voice of Bessie Smith, and Belafonte the sound of a gospel stylist—thus maintaining the divide between cultural registers but locating them all within the diverse musics of African Americans.

MTV's hip-hopera *Carmen*, directed by black filmmaker Robert Townsend, relies much more heavily on *Carmen Jones* than on Bizet or Mérimée. Its plot parallels Hammerstein's, in that Carmen does not belong to an outlaw gang, and its inspiration to base the adaptation around a transgressive music also mimics its Broadway-musical predecessor. References to Bizet's score occur only occasionally: Carmen enters the screen accompanied by the inevitable 'Habanera' vamp, for instance, and the rapid-fire cutting between Stephen James Taylor's underscore and Casey Lee's rap concert in the final scene simulate the discontinuities that make Bizet's finale ratchet up its tensions so unbearably. For the most part, however, the performances make use of original numbers composed in the rap idiom by Kip Collins.

As in *Carmen Jones*, the decision to eliminate the élite side of Bizet's dichotomy flattens out some of the antagonistic components of Bizet's opera. Like its Broadway predecessor, the hip-hopera features only black actors, with no trace of the racial tensions that drive the original; moreover, all of the characters express themselves through rap, thus eradicating even the contrast between lyrical song and pop song that obtained in Hammerstein. Strangely enough, the woman chosen to play the part of Carmen Brown—Beyoncé Knowles of Destiny's Child—is an accomplished, virtuoso singer, and she has difficulty bending her particular talents to spoken delivery. Mehki Phifer (her José, here named Derek) has proven himself elsewhere an effective actor for television and film, but he seems to be uncomfortable here either rapping or singing. By contrast, the professional rapper in the cast, Mos Def, steals the show. Just as I would want to see a *Carmen Jones* with Bessie Smith's voice, so I wonder why MTV did not turn to a powerful, pungent female rapper like Lil' Kim or Missy 'Misdemeanor' Elliott for the part of Carmen or why they didn't try to preserve the cultural divide by having Derek sung by a hip-hop-oriented virtuoso like Usher or R. Kelly.

Be that as it may, the one scene that seeks to play off the energies of Bizet's music is the place in the plot that usually features the 'Seguidilla' but here is set to the instrumental introduction to Bizet's second-act 'Gypsy Song', the number performed by Pearl Bailey in *Carmen Jones*. Why this music rather than the 'Seguidilla'? In part because (as the Spanish musicians in Saura's film point out), Bizet's triple meters don't correspond to the kinds of rhythmic impulses characteristic of either actual flamenco or (in this case) rap. But the 'Gypsy Song' has a percussive beat, and it easily absorbs the extra beat per measure that converts it into rap's inevitable duple; it also allows far more room for the give-and-take, call-and-response debate between Carmen and Derek than would the slinkier 'Seguidilla'. Moreover, Bizet's layered harmonic strategy, in which the first pitch centre simply gives way to another a step lower, resembles not only the flamenco Bizet intended to imitate but also the minimalist procedures of many rap tunes. Kip Collins can thus refer to Bizet (he even retains the solo flute from Bizet's orchestration) and, at the same time, hail hip-hop fans with something that sounds quite familiar.

To my mind, the best moments in the film—the moments where the fusion with rap really pays off—are the prologue and epilogue performed by Da Brat, who knows how to deliver her message powerfully within this idiom. As for Beyoncé Knowles, she offers her own version of Carmen more effectively in her song 'Independent Women', with Destiny's Child, in which she splices in segments of the 'Habanera' and manages to sound properly assertive—which she does not, alas, in the hip-hopera.

In the end, both *Carmen Jones* and Townsend's hip-hopera seem to experience a failure of nerve. Neither allows its Carmen the low voice and rhetorical prowess that makes Bizet's character so irresistible, and neither situates its heroine within the world of organized crime that gives Mérimée's and Bizet's Carmen a position of considerable authority outside her ill-advised affair with José. Both Carmen Jones and Carmen Brown have lives built around clubbing and romance, depriving them of motivation and a sense of moral integrity at the end. They register as little more than party girls whose former boyfriends have become stalkers. In the hip-hopera, it isn't even Derek who murders his Carmen but rather the corrupt police officer (played with serpentine brilliance by Mos Def) who has tracked Derek to his lair. These 'bad girls' turn out to be only misguided good girls, and a potential platform for the genuinely powerful women of rap is squandered, as is the singing talent Beyoncé Knowles might have brought to a different concept of a hip-hop *Carmen*. Still, whatever the discrepancies of their versions from Bizet's opera, Hammerstein's and Townsend's courage at tackling a high-art genre and melding it with the culturally deplored musics of their own time produces insights into the original that outstrip most more faithful renditions.

Jean-Luc Godard, in his *Prénom Carmen* (1983), does not pull his punches, though he avoids completely the racial dimension so central to most other versions. Instead, he inverts the class affiliations of his principals: Carmen (supposedly the niece of 'Godard', a derelict film director) and her bandit friends come from privileged backgrounds, and they repeatedly deride Joseph, the seduced, working-class police officer, for his lack of education. Over the course of the film, the armed robberies and murders committed underwrite the expenses of their movie-making. High art thus collaborates with and even provides the motivation for criminal activity. Bizet's music figures only minimally in Godard's film: a couple of times someone absent-mindedly hums the 'Habanera', a passing allusion to the opera that made the story famous and a useful paradigm for Godard's own purposes. Moreover, except for a song performed by Tom Waits, no popular music appears in the course of the film, a point signalled explicitly in dialogue.

Instead, Godard takes Bizet's 'German' side to an extreme the composer could never have envisioned. In his soundtrack, he utilizes Beethoven's late string quartets—even foregrounding within the visuals the activities of the Prat Quartet rehearsing various movements. Sometimes the cutting between the action, the rehearsals, and the soundtrack seem deliberately arbitrary. But occasionally Godard's adaptation of Mérimée appears to draw on the energies of the string quartets: the yearning melancholy of Beethoven's late style helps underscore the existential angst of the characters, particularly when juxtaposed with footage of the always-restless sea. Godard also insists on the brutality of Beethoven's obsessively goal-oriented music. Near the beginning, the ensemble's coach urges them on to greater violence in their execution, and the players lash out against the female member of the group for her inability to keep up. The most shocking performance of Beethovenian violence occurs, however, in the rape scene in the shower, which makes use of the scherzo from Beethoven's last quartet, Op. 135.

A word about this scherzo. Beethoven's other Late Quartets had sprawled, challenging basic premises of compositional propriety, sprouting additional (often fragmentary) movements, juxtaposing laments with coarse slapstick comedy. When he wrote Op. 135, however, he seemed to have compressed all these experiments back into the four-movement frame of the traditional quartet. Superficially well-behaved, this quartet veers between apparent conformity and moments in which utter lunacy threatens to rupture the surface. The scherzo (literally: joke) occurs as the second movement of the cycle. Almost Haydnesque in its friskiness, the movement pays penance for the incoherences of so much late Beethoven by verging on harmonic paralysis: the principal part of the scherzo sits on little more than a single harmony except for a discombobulated moment in which tonal and rhythmic chaos suddenly erupt—then just as quickly get pushed back under. The trio (or middle) part of the scherzo becomes even jokier, with rapidly ascending violin lines that seem to be trying to escape from reality. The harmonies remain static, though they give way in succession to other similarly static poses. Finally the cello takes up the little turn figure that had always served to launch the violin on its airborne flights. But it gets stuck, as though slipping over and over on a banana peel, while the violin traces in its highest register a maniacally merry tune that mindlessly reiterates, gets derailed, reiterates, and finally dies down in a kind of fade-out. In passages such as this one, Beethoven appears to simulate his own inappropriately raucous laughter that made many of his contemporaries think him mad.

The scene in question makes use of snippets of this quartet throughout. As Joseph enters the hotel room in which Carmen and her co-conspirators are hatching their schemes, fragments of the innocuous opening pop in at incongruous moments. Only the discombobulated passage hints that it might be (but again might not be) a sign of affective trouble for the film. As Joseph's temper flares (he slaps the bellboy, pursues Carmen into the bathroom where she is preparing to shower), the sound of the string quartet rises in volume, its energies now sounding like the underscore of a soundtrack. And as the scherzo hits the passage where it gets stuck and keeps mindlessly thrusting nonetheless, Joseph tries desperately to bring himself to erection, mickey-mousing his masturbatory gestures to the sounds of Beethoven's scherzo. Here the violence of 'classical music' becomes painfully explicit. We should recall that Nietzsche said in praise of Bizet's score, 'This music [...] does not sweat' (1976: 157). But Beethoven's *does* sweat (as does don José's in the opera, for that matter), and that is what Godard's *mise en scène* reveals.

In the next scene, Godard, Carmen, and their cinematography colleagues hire the string quartet we have watched rehearsing to perform live in the background as they execute an actual kidnapping; an elegant restaurant with its up-scale (though violence-saturated) music stands in for the bullring, the art-film makers toying out of boredom with genuine lives, while Joseph—always the uncomprehending outsider—watches from the sidelines and only barely manages to stab Carmen in the midst of all the intellectually motivated slaughter surrounding him.

In most productions of the opera *Carmen*, disorder seems to enter the world by way of the outlaw Gypsies, with José's 'German' medium striving heroically to put everything right again, to reestablish the claims of classical music to occupy the pinnacle of the cultural hierarchy. But Bizet's opera is in part, of course, an exercise in higher-stakes violence, in which a stereotyped Other becomes a mere pretext for blood-letting on an unprecedented scale: it is Bizet who hauls all this disorder onto the stage for his own aesthetic ends. As Godard casts himself in his film as a cynical purveyor of élite culture drawn to crime in part because of a Raskolnikovian sense of his own autonomy from ordinary ethical standards, he lays bare the complicity of high art with questionable ideologies. But Godard implicates not only Bizet in his critique; he draws into his web of references the most revered of cultural treasures, for Beethoven's late quartets rank at the very top of the food-chain of classical music. As Walter Benjamin wrote in his 'Theses on the Philosophy of History': 'There is no document of civilization which is not at the same time a document of barbarism' (Benjamin 1992: 248), and Godard exempts not even Beethoven from his meditation on culture and morality.

At the beginning of my essay, I quoted Bizet's admission of his allegiances to both 'German' high art and music from artistic houses of ill repute. At the very least, filmed versions of his masterpiece have managed to tangle hopelessly these binary oppositions, as *Carmen* comes to stand in some instances for classical music with all its prestige, while in other instances it invites the recasting of the entire project in the terms of disreputable musical genres or even (in

Godard's case) disreputable readings of revered music. Bizet's opera remains alive and vital in part because it so easily relinquishes its status as an artwork of the past and participates in making sense of subsequent moments of cultural history.

'So they want trash? All right; I'll give them trash'. The volatile mix of élitism and trash that is *Carmen* has served as our constant companion as we have negotiated the Great Divide between canonic and mass culture over the course of the last hundred and twenty-five years or so. So long as men fear independent women, so long as those with class or ethnic privilege resist the claims of the disenfranchised, so long as the art world perceives itself as under siege from popular culture, *Carmen* will continue to provide a ready template for articulating the anxieties that assail us. It can never solve those problems. But its performances—especially in the medium of film—can make us recognize the persistence of the fault lines Bizet first presented so forcefully in 1875. In giving us trash wrapped up as high art, Bizet bestowed on us a treasure far greater than he could ever have imagined.

Notes
1. Re-released on DVD by Image Entertainment (1999). ASIN 6305609306.

References
Benjamin, Walter. 1992. *Illuminations* (ed. Hannah Arendt, tr. Harry Zohn). London: Fontana.
Huyssen, Andreas. 1986. 'Mass Culture as Woman: Modernism's Other' in Modleski, Tania (ed.) *Studies in Entertainment: Critical Approaches to Mass Culture.* Bloomington: Indiana University Press: 188-207.
Nietzsche, Friedrich. 1976. *The Birth of Tragedy and The Case of Wagner* (tr. Walter Kaufman). New York: Vintage Books.

List of Contributors

Gillian Anderson is an orchestral conductor specializing in American music and music for film. She has restored and conducted 32 of the original accompaniments of the 1898-1929 epoch with orchestras in Europe and North and South America. DVD, CD, and videotapes are available from Criterion Films, VAI International and BMG Classics.

José Colmeiro is Professor of Spanish and Chair of the Department of Spanish and Portuguese at Michigan State University. His major publications include *Memoria histórica e identidad cultural* (2004*), Crónica del desencanto: La narrativa de Manuel Vázquez Montalbán* (Letras de Oro prize, 1996), and *La novela policíaca española: Teoría e historia crítica* (1994). He is the editor of *Spain Today: Essays on Literature, Culture, Society* (1995) and Francisco García Pavón's *Las hermanas coloradas* (1999). He is currently working on redefinitions of identity in Hispanic cinema, particularly the representations of gay identiy and the transatlantic hispanic connections.

Ann Davies is a Lecturer in Spanish at the University of Newcastle upon Tyne. She is author of *The Metamorphoses of Don Juan's Women: Early Parity to Late Modern Pathology* (Edwin Mellen, 2004) and co-editor (with Phil Powrie and Bruce Babington) of *The Trouble with Men: Exploring Masculinities in European and Hollywood Cinema* (Wallflower Press, 2004). She was formerly Research Associate for The Carmen Project at the Centre for Research into Film and Media, University of Newcastle.

Peter Evans is Professor of Spanish at Queen Mary, University of London. He has published on various aspects of Spanish cinema. His most recent publications are the co-edited volume (with Isabel Santaolalla), *Luis Buñuel: New Readings* (BFI, 2003) and *Jamón jamón* (Paidos, 2004).

Nelly Furman is Professor of French at Cornell University. She is the author of *La Revue des Deux Mondes et le Romantisme (1831-1848),* co-editor of a volume on *Women and Language in Literature and Society*, and the editor of a special issue of *Diacritics* on Georges Bataille. She is presently working on a book length study of the figure of Carmen.

Amy Herzog is an Adjunct Lecturer in Media Studies at Queens College-City University of New York and a Ph.D. candidate in the Program in Visual and Cultural Studies at the University of Rochester. Her dissertation, 'Dreams of Difference and Songs of the Same: The Image of Time in Musical Film', explores the relations between music and image in cinema through the lens of Deleuzian theory.

Andrés Lema-Hincapié is a Ph.D. candidate in the Department of Romance Studies at Cornell University. He is currently editing a book on contemporary Spanish film with Joan Ramón Resina. He has also published on Borges, modern thinkers (Kant and Berkeley) and ancient philosophy (Parmenides and Plato). A collection of his articles on Kant's philosophy will be published by Universidad del Valle, Cali (Colombia) in 2004.

Hilaria Loyo is a Lecturer in the English and German Department at the University of Zaragoza, Spain. She has recently worked on the reception of Marlene Dietrich in the USA.

Harriet Margolis is a senior lecturer at Victoria University, New Zealand. Author of articles on women's romance novels, self-directed stereotypes, Jane Austen and cultural capital, and the cinema of Aotearoa New Zealand, she is currently coediting *Studying the Event Film: The Lord of the Rings* (Manchester University Press).

Susan McClary is Professor of Musicology at the University of California, Los Angeles. She is author of *Feminine Endings: Music, Gender, and Sexuality* (1991); *Georges Bizet: Carmen* (1992); *Conventional Wisdom: The Content of Musical Form* (2000); and *Modal Subjectivities: Self-Fashioning in the Italian Madrigal* (2004).

Chris Perriam is Professor of Modern Hispanic Studies at the University of Manchester, having moved from the University of Newcastle in August 2004. He has published *Stars and Masculinities in Spanish Cinema: From Banderas to Bardem* (OUP, 2003) and a range of articles and book chapters on Spanish cinema since 1975.

Jeremy Tambling is Professor of Comparative Literature at the University of Hong Kong. His books include work on literature, critical theory, opera, and on film, most recently *Wong Kar-wai: Happy Together* (Hong Kong University Press, 2003). His book *Allegory and the Work of Melancholy* (Rodopi, 2004) is to be followed by another study of allegory (forthcoming from Routledge).

Nicholas Till is Senior Lecturer in Music and Director of the Centre for Research in Opera and Music Theatre at the University of Sussex, and co-artistic director of the experimental music theatre company Post-Operative Productions. His books include *Mozart and the Enlightenment* (Faber, 1992). He is currently editing *the Cambridge Companion to Opera*.

Mary Wood is Reader in European Cinema at Birkbeck College University of London. Her recent publications include a chapter on Italian film noir in A. Spicer (ed.): *European Film Noir* (Manchester University Press 2004). Her book on Italian cinema will be published by Berg at the end of 2004 and she is currently working on contemporary European cinema.

Winifred Woodhull is Associate Professor of Literature and Cultural Studies at the University of California, San Diego. Her publications include *Transfigurations of the Maghreb: Feminism, Decolonization, and Literatures* (University of Minnesota Press, 1993) and articles on French, Caribbean, African, and African American literature and film.

Index